CRISIS, PURSUED BY DISASTER,
FOLLOWED CLOSELY BY CATASTROPHE

RANDOM HOUSE
New York

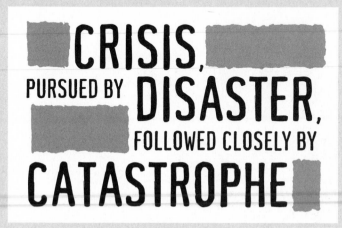

CRISIS, PURSUED BY DISASTER, FOLLOWED CLOSELY BY CATASTROPHE

A Memoir of Life on the Run

MIKE O'CONNOR

Published in the United States by Random House, an imprint of
The Random House Publishing Group, a division of Random
House, Inc., New York.

RANDOM HOUSE and colophon are registered trademarks of
Random House, Inc.

LIBRARY OF CONGRESS CATALOGING-IN-PUBLICATION DATA
O'Connor, Mike.
Crisis, pursued by disaster, followed closely by catastrophe:
a memoir of life on the run / Mike O'Connor.
p.   cm.
ISBN 978-0-375-50479-2
1. O'Connor family.   2. O'Connor, Mike.
3. Fugitives from justice—United States—Biography.
4. Communists—United States—Biography.   I. Title.
CT274.O26O28 2007
973.91092—dc22
[B]   2007001622

Printed in the United States of America on acid-free paper

www.atrandom.com

9 8 7 6 5 4 3 2 1

FIRST EDITION

Book design by Simon M. Sullivan

To Tracy. This was a long, troubled journey, going back to events and people I'd spent so long sprinting from. Whenever I glanced from the corner of my eye, Tracy was always there, sharing that harsh ride.

CONTENTS

In September 1998, a year after our mother died, I finally found the courage to look inside my father's battered, taped-together cigar box with the brand TAMPA NUGGET in embossed gold lettering on a red border. From the time Dad died, twenty-five years before her, Mom had carried most of the contents through many countries and countless home addresses. She'd left the box on her coffee table, an invitation, in her apartment in San Clemente, California, along with a couple of manila envelopes with more documents and photos. And a diary. I had been too afraid to look at any of it. Then, one day, I could.

The first thing in the box was a black-and-white snapshot of a handsome young army officer at a restaurant. He had a cleft chin, a good mustache, a daring look about him. My father, age thirty-one. On the back Mom had written "Rome."

When my parents talked about their past, they had offered no stories from before they met. It was as if their lives began when they fell in love during the Second World War. Mom was from England, working for the British equivalent of the USO. My two sisters and I breathed in her filigreed anecdotes of Roman cafés, Gypsy street musicians, and the view of the Mediterranean from a hilltop above Sorrento. But we learned almost nothing of our relatives, or of where our parents came from.

After the war, Dad became the director of a large refugee camp in Germany, where I was born. Inside one of the envelopes I found my birth certificate, issued by the military government: "Michael Fitzgerald O'Connor, Village of Gehrden, Germany, February 8, 1946, Capt. John Jeremiah O'Connor and Jessey O'Connor, parents."

I also found a certificate of identity issued to a thin young woman by the Canadian Embassy in Brussels on June 12, 1946—a temporary replacement for her British passport, which had been stolen. Height: five feet, three inches tall. Hair: brown. Eyes: hazel. Occupation: welfare worker. Her photograph was stuck to a cracked, browning sheet of paper with a purple embassy stamp in the lower left corner. She had a hairdo out of a wartime movie, and a strand of pearls. The caution in her eyes undermined her smile. My father was listed as her husband; I was listed, too. All the information was certified by the Canadian consul. Maybe it was accurate, maybe not.

A string of stamps on the back showed that shortly after Mom got the certificate of identity, she had traveled from Brussels to London to Liverpool before arriving in New York, with me and my father, I supposed. There were also stamps for trips I'd never heard of—to Canada four days after arriving in New York, down to Maine fifteen months later. Had we stayed in Canada all that time, and why?

The answers, I thought, might explain the pattern that kept repeating throughout my childhood: sudden, mysterious moves made at a moment's notice, our lives in one place deleted overnight, replaced by lives somewhere brand-new. The reasons given to my two sisters and me never made sense. The cigar box had photos of us from Texas, Mexico, and California, the places where we'd grown up, but it also had pictures of people I did not know.

The diary was bound in two-toned brown leather. Mom had told my sister Fiona that we should read it once she was gone. We'd already heard its stories, written by a woman who was clearly thrilled by the adventure of beginning a life with her American husband and their new child. But the entries stopped abruptly and forever in September 1946, three months after we'd arrived in New York. There was nothing of consequence about the next twenty-one years, nothing to explain why we'd been running. It was as if the life I'd known had not happened.

There was a batch of Dad's letters about the business deals he was trying to promote in one strange new place or another in the late sixties and early seventies. One, postmarked GUADALAJARA, came to Mom in San Jose, in 1967, just before the family fled once more to Mexico. My father had gone down first on a scouting run, and this was his report: "Crisis, pursued by disaster, followed closely by catastrophe." He was looking for a score to bring in enough money for a safe getaway, and to atone for all the agony he'd dragged his family through. Once again, his plan was not working. He ended the letter by telling Mom, "I love you and I need you and I love you and I need you." Even after the decades of hiding and running and hustling, of hoping and finding hope crushed, he still meant it. She knew that.

I pushed the cigar box aside. It held no nostalgia for me, only the old, twisting confusion leaping back from childhood. I wanted to hide the contents and hope that I'd lose them. I wanted to have a drink and go. That's what my family was good at. We got back on the road, kept moving, especially me. I'd run away from home at fourteen, in part to escape the mystery that hung over us. Later I'd run as a foreign correspondent, from country to country and war to war, looking to expose powerful people who hid the truth. Now, with bits of our past on my desk in Vienna, Austria, I got in my Jeep and drove toward the armed uprising in Kosovo, which I was covering for *The New York Times*. When I got there and had to switch to my heavily armored Land Rover, I still felt much safer than I had with my mother's memories looking up from that cracked Pandora's box, the one covered in wood-toned paper and red trimming with labels calling out that its cigars were "Good as Gold" and "2 for 15 cents." Memories of bad times past. I could not run fast enough to escape the smell of my father's cigar smoke.

YOU WANT TO believe your parents. You *need* to believe them, even more when you love them and they love you. As a small boy, I decided to believe the stories my parents told me, even though I knew they weren't true. I understood that part of our mystery was the Danger, which could crush our family if we ever stopped running and turned to look at it. I learned from the beginning that our safety came only with believing our parents' lies about our family and joining them in refusing to acknowledge the Danger. Still, the Danger was always there, and I could never hope to understand it. I could only make sure that it never got close enough to throw its shadow on me.

When I was still a child and began to doubt my parents' stories, I had pushed the questions away, turned my back to them while they kept vibrating. As a reporter for twenty-five years, I had refused to search for who my parents really were, what our truth really meant.

But for two years after Mom died, Fiona kept challenging me to investigate our mystery: "You're the journalist. It's up to you to figure all this out now." Trusting that mysteries can be solved, she only wanted what normal people want. She wanted to learn the truth about her parents, to understand them. And, in that, to understand more about herself.

With time, Fiona's reasonable questions became harder to resist. Now that our mother had passed away and was finally safe from the Danger, I began to feel that I might peek into our past. Since the cigar box was clearly only a beginning, with no answers, I would have to look into the memories of my childhood.

It turned out there were good reasons I had hidden those memories so well.

PART ONE

ONE

THE EARLIEST DATE I can tie a memory to is June 25, 1950, the first day of the Korean War. I was four. My mother had burst into terrified sobbing.

Mom and Dad and I were in our car staring through the windshield at the bridge that connected the United States and Mexico. We were on the Mexican side looking toward Laredo, Texas. My sister Mary was next to me on the backseat, in her white bassinet. She'd been born in Houston six months before. I tugged her yellow baby blanket more tautly across the top of the bassinet to keep the sun out. I was wearing my short pants, the ones with the blue stripes and shoulder straps, sitting forward with my arms on the back of the front seat. We were looking at the United States from about two blocks away, and my parents were talking nervously in hushed voices. I wondered why we were so afraid.

We'd been on a trip from our home near Houston when Dad suggested that we drive across the bridge to Mexico: Let's just take a look for a bit. And Mom said, Yes, let's do. We crossed the bridge to look at the Mexican town for a little while. It was an ugly town, I thought, dirty, with people doing strange things. They were walking in the streets with cars driving around them, and selling fruit and bread from trays they carried on their heads. Then, on the radio, a man said something about a war that made Mom and Dad talk quickly to each other, and suddenly we were all very afraid. I could tell it was bad. But I didn't know why until Mom said something to Dad about us not ever being able to go back home.

I'd heard my parents talk about war before. I knew it was when people's houses were destroyed. As Mom kept crying, I thought, *Maybe our house is gone. That must be why we're afraid.* Then Dad said something

to Mom about the border, that it would not be safe to cross—that there
would be more immigration agents there because of the war. For some
reason, we didn't want the agents to know about us. Dad said something
about Mom's papers; it sounded as though she didn't have the right ones.
I didn't know what papers were. Did I have the right ones? Did Mary? I
thought we might all use Dad's papers and we could go home and be
safe.

We can't just stay in Mexico forever, Mom said. We can't do that. We
need papers to do that, too, and money. What about the children? She
was choking on her tears, gagging but trying to control it all, her eyes
widening in the effort. She said she had to stop because people would
see. She put her head down on the seat next to Dad and almost disappeared. I'm sorry, darling, she said to him. This is so unfair. How could
we know this would happen?

The people on the street went on doing what they'd been doing, which
I thought was very strange. *Why aren't they afraid, too?* I wondered.

Dad said he didn't know what to do. That made it all worse, because
I thought he always knew what to do. Then Dad told Mom it would be
all right. He stroked her back, as she did mine when I was upset. I said,
I don't want to stay in Mexico. It's not nice here. Then I cried along with
Mom.

Finally they decided that we had to try cross the border before more
agents came—if we didn't move fast, we'd have to stay in Mexico. I
knew we were nearly trapped. I could taste my parents' panic.

Then Dad had an idea. He would walk up to the border to take a
look. I didn't know what the border was, except that we'd crossed it
back at the other end of the bridge, where men in uniforms were talking
to people in cars. Now I saw that the people in each car stopped for a
moment so the men could lean down, look inside, and say something.
Then the car kept going up a small hill into the town and another car
could come up. It had been easy crossing it when we came into Mexico.
Why would it be hard to go back to the other side, where we belonged?

Dad got out and walked across the bridge. From the backseat, standing on the floor of the car, looking past Mom, I watched to be sure nothing happened to him. Then I saw him up there, and he looked okay. My
father was a big man, and solid. He was bigger than the other men at the
border, so I wondered why he was afraid.

Mom was still scared, but she told me that nothing was wrong. No,
nothing at all, she said, except that she was not feeling well, and Dad had

gone to get her some medicine. He'd be right back and we'd have a nice ride home. She said, Isn't it so very interesting here in Mexico? The colors are so bright. It's like when your father and I were in Italy. Let's tidy up the car, shall we? Because it's better to have everything tidy when you cross a border. She told me to fold Mary's diapers. She cleaned my face with the rough washcloth, but she rubbed too hard and I knew she was still afraid. Then we saw Dad coming back, and Mom said, It's a good thing we are all tidy now because it will be better. Policemen like a family with a tidy car. When Dad got in the car and kissed Mom, I knew we were going to be safe. He said everything was fine. There weren't any extra agents yet.

On the American side of the bridge, Dad told the immigration agent that we had an emergency because Mom had gotten sick from something she ate in Mexico and we needed to get her to an American doctor right away. The man understood. He said, You have to be careful with those Mexicans because you can't trust their food and you sure can't trust the doctors. The agent didn't ask to see anyone's papers. He smiled into our car like everything was fine. I smiled back because I knew we were safe again.

We had a nice ride home and didn't talk about what happened. We never talked about it again, ever. It happened. But it didn't happen.

FROM THE TIME I was three and a half until I was eight, we lived on Muscatine Street in Jacinto City next to Houston, then beginning to boom. Jacinto City was a rickety town, a few thousand people living on flat rural lots with drainage ditches in front and vegetable gardens and chickens out back. Homes were tiny boxes on cement blocks, with doors and windows that didn't fit right and flat tar-and-gravel roofs. Everyone was poor. Even a kid could tell that, even if poor was all he'd ever seen.

But Dad didn't see it. He would say, It's a good thing that we're not poor. It's a good thing that we're just living here for a little while until we can live someplace nice. It won't be long now, not at all. Dad asked me one time, Did you see the clothesline next door? Those people have rags hanging from that line; everything they own has holes. *My clothes have holes, too,* I thought. But I learned not to notice, because it was just for a while.

No, we weren't poor, nothing like it. It was only that we had no money for the moment. And according to our parents, we were on a clear trajectory to the American dream. We're so lucky to be here, Mom would say. Your father and I brought you here because it is much nicer than in the North, in Boston, where we used to live. It's so cold there.

To hear them talk, Boston had been a quick, casual stop on the way from Germany, where Dad had been in the army and I was born, to Texas. In Houston, we'd been wise enough to arrive as the advance party for thousands of shivering Northerners who were on their way. We were among the very luckiest by coming in time for Dad to prosper by supplying what the others needed. His business, he told me, was helping people have nicer homes.

Dad was an intelligent, ambitious man with an easy charm, and he chose door-to-door sales of room additions and house repairs. There was no inventory to invest in and, in those days in Texas, no employment forms to fill out, no records of any kind that might find their way to the authorities. It was also a portable trade, dissolved in one town and re-made in the next before anyone would realize he was gone. Houston was a good place to start because it was growing fast and had a big back door for escapes: Mexico, just three hundred miles down a straight, flat, blacktopped road. Strangers did not stand out in Houston. People came from somewhere else and preferred not to get into why. Texas was a frontier where a family was not hobbled by what they'd left behind. Houston was the raw, hustling edge of America, where only the future counted. We fit in smoothly.

I was five years old when a policeman with tall boots and a big white cowboy hat came knocking on our screen door one evening. The door made a loud noise because it was loose in the frame and I'd forgotten to hook it to keep out mosquitoes and that green snake that kept popping up under the sink. The policeman smiled, but when Mom saw him she went stiff.

My father was smiling broadly, arm out in welcome, ushering the policeman in. The policeman didn't take off his hat as Mom always told me I should do when I came inside, which made me wonder about him. I also wondered why Mom and Dad were acting so pleased when I could tell there was something bad happening. The policeman said he'd heard there'd been a family from out of town living in our house for a while now and he wanted to say hello for the chief. He'd heard the woman was a foreigner but not a Mexican, so he was wondering what kind of foreigner she was, anyway. He said, Sorry, ma'am, I never meant to scare you.

We're not scared, Mom said quickly. It was the door that made me jump.

Dad laughed and said, She's not scared, of course not. After the war, with all the bombs the Germans dropped on England, my goodness, anyone would be a little jumpy. But here everything is wonderful. It was great the way England and America were such close friends, Dad went on, because no place was better than America, and especially Texas. He told the policeman that our relatives were from Texas, too, from the coast up by Port O'Connor. There must have been a hundred of his cousins named O'Connor over there, and it was a shame that his grandpa moved away years ago and his daddy had to grow up in New York. But now we were moving back home, to Texas.

The policeman said if he'd had more time he would have let me ride in his police car, which looked impressive. He showed me the big pistol on his belt but said I was still a little young to hold it. He gave me a picture of a badge, a star with six points, each point standing for something good, like telling the truth, being brave. He wanted me to join the Junior Police Club and maybe one day become a policeman. And wouldn't I feel more like a real Texan if someday Mom and Dad got me some cowboy boots like they had in the movies?

The visit couldn't have lasted more than a few minutes. It was all routine for the policeman but frightening to their marrow for my parents, and bewildering for me. Eventually, the policeman said he had to leave because there'd been trouble recently along Navigation Boulevard. "I just might have to go up there and shoot me some niggers," he told us.

Dad said he understood and it was so nice for the policeman to come by. Maybe the next time we'd have coffee and some of Mom's apple cake. As the policeman left, I tried to figure out what Dad was talking about. Mom never made apple cake.

The policeman was the first stranger I can remember in our home. Something bigger than I could understand had come into our living room. I was scared the way I'd been on the border across from Laredo. We were in danger from something. What was it? My parents had kept their faces bright and their words calm. It made me think that if there were other problems, my parents might not warn me about them either. The policeman was a stranger, so I didn't trust him, but I thought I was supposed to be able to trust my parents.

Later, I asked Mom what niggers were and why the man was going to shoot some. It sounded terrible. Mom, too, was very upset. But the only thing she said was, We don't use that word, it's better to say *colored people*. They are people with dark skin, like Sam the postman.

I thought Sam was like everybody else, except he didn't wear his hat when the sun got hot, as Mom said you had to. I liked Sam. He played with me and our squirming little taffy-colored dog, Margaret.

Dad said, Darling, in Texas people don't say *postman*, they say *mailman*. It's best to say that.

I asked them why Dad had told the man we had kinfolks in Texas, since I didn't know any. Dad explained that the policeman and other people would feel better about us if we had relatives in Texas. That turned it from a lie into one of those things that adults do for the good of others. Mom said I shouldn't talk to people about our time in Boston. It was our special secret, just as the pixies were the only ones who knew what made pixies fly.

We got me those cowboy boots, red leather with white curlicues on the sides. They impressed everybody in the kindergarten at Whittier Elementary School, especially me.

We knew our neighbors. We talked to them in our yard or theirs. Dad was naturally friendly, and Mom was, too, once she overcame her shyness. Next door were the Livingstons. Marilyn was my age, and Bubba was a bit older. His real name was Lloyd, but that didn't count. I played with them, in their yard or their house. Their mother waved at Mom and had glancing chats with her. But I could feel there was a wall around us. Our neighbors visited with one another but virtually never came inside our house. We were different from everyone else—not bad people, just different.

There was one family with whom we became close, the Blanchards, who lived around the corner. Their backyard ran into ours, and they flowed into our lives because they were a family full of love and trouble like we were, and because they, too, were lost in an alien land. They were Cajun and devoutly Catholic, and there were few of either one of those in Jacinto City. We were Catholic, too. But unlike us, the Blanchards had roots and relatives they talked about. The Blanchards came from the backwoods village of Church Point, Louisiana, a four-hour drive away, but they were nearly as out of place in Texas as we were, and had to scramble just as hard for a foothold. Edna Blanchard had spoken only Cajun French until she and her husband, Jack, moved to Texas when she was twenty-two. She was a few years older than Mom, who was forty then, and Dad, who was thirty-nine. The Blanchards had a daughter, named Joyce, fifteen years older than I was. It seemed natural for Mary and me to call Edna Blanchard "Nannan," Cajun for Godmother.

Nannan was gentle with Mom and respectful. She never called her anything but "Miz O'Connor," no matter what my mother said. "Don' ask me again, you always be Miz O'Connor t' me," she said. That ended it. Mom called her "Nannan," because Mom couldn't bear to use the first name of a woman she cared about if the woman insisted on calling her "Missus," even if the woman was the only friend she had.

Nannan visited us every day. She sat in the kitchen, helped my mother around the house a little, and listened with rapture to Mom's stories about faraway places. At first Nannan and Mom struggled to understand each other's accents and vocabulary, but somehow they met halfway.

Mom's stories barely mentioned her and Dad's life before they met, only little references without context: That she had brothers and sisters, and came from the north of England. That Dad grew up in a place where it snowed a lot in winter. Details flowed only when she talked about their wartime courtship, how Italy was so destroyed yet the people so captivating, how the twilight lit the stones at the Roman Forum. She limited her stories to the acceptable, entertaining, romantic past.

Even more, Mom needed Nannan's unwitting help in remaking the past. Nannan did more for my parents than she imagined. She helped them to live with the wonderful truth. She believed in that good truth and reflected it back, and thought it was the whole truth. For my parents, talking to her was like casting a spell into a mirror.

In our kitchen, as Nannan's hands worked her white apron from the emotion of the story, Mom told us about Sorrento, where she and Dad had gotten away together to the coast of Italy. The war was merely a backdrop. My parents were in paradise with each other. Mom said, "Oh! The palm trees and the smell of orange blossoms!" Nannan and I looked till we could see the palms. Mom stepped to the counter by the sink, picked up an orange, and broke it open. She held it up to us and said, "Can you just smell that orange in the air? Can you? That's what I remember of Sorrento."

She told us about the small fishing boats on the bay. The green, green land that slid down the hills until it touched the bluest sea in the world. At dusk, the lanterns in the fishing huts and farmhouses barely glowed until night turned completely dark, and then you could see the lanterns twinkle. Later, the moon came up, caressing the world with a warm yellow light. In Sorrento she and Dad talked about their future, she said.

About the children they'd have and the business they'd start in the United States, where they would be together forever. Still, Nannan must have felt Mom's anxieties. I did. Though neither one of us could guess what caused them.

"Your momma's deh mos' interesen woman I ever hear of," Nannan told me. "She's deh smartes', too. *Shar 'ti* Michael. We got to help you momma 'cause dey ain't no reason for her t' hurt deh way she do. Der ain't one tang she don' know 'bout, I'm tellin' you."

There were no photographs of any relatives in our house on Muscatine Street. There were no pictures of Dad in high school or a teenage Mom hiking with friends. Sam the mailman never brought birthday cards with love and kisses from grandparents who were thinking about us even though they lived too far away to visit this year. Reminders of the past were left with the past. The past was for other families. But up on the wall, in the kitchen, where Mom could look at it easily, was an oil landscape. It was painted on stiff cardboard because canvas was hard to get in Italy during the war. It was a painting of Sorrento and the bluest sea in the world.

For Nannan, Mom's stories were uplifting firsthand reports on war and Europeans and true love, from that other universe that Nannan knew must exist beyond the swamps and cotton fields of Louisiana, beyond the misery of the wrong side of Houston. And where, as Jack, her husband, would say, if it weren't for the ex-convicts, there'd be hardly any men around at all. Nannan had always known that other place existed somewhere. She just never thought she'd be talking with someone who had been there. For her part, Nannan took Mom on as a project, an act of plain Christian charity toward a woman who clearly knew little about how to manage a household. Nannan saw a challenge. She began with the basics: food, and how to shop for it. One day we set off for the nearest store, a long walk up Market Street Road. I wore my cowboy boots. As we passed the gray-green Spanish moss hanging from the pine trees, Mom slowed and stared because she wondered how plants could possibly live like that, stretched out and hanging over trees, with no roots. Nannan said that was the way the good Lord must have wanted it. She kept walking.

On days like these, Nannan wore a modified Cajun costume, her long braids pinned up on her head and her long-sleeved paisley or polka-dotted dress down to her ankles, even in the worst heat. For her, modesty was bigger than comfort. Maybe suffering was modesty's reward. Her sunbonnet covered her entire head, the floppy sides shading her cheeks. "You got t' know how t' protec' you'self in dis worl'," she said. Her eyes were blue, and in my memories she is always smiling. Mom looked like a teenager next to Nannan, who was tall and wide and sturdy. I stayed clear of the basket she swung on her arm.

As we walked, Nannan lectured Mom about being too thin. It was from Mom's worrying, or "frettin'," Nannan called it. It seemed to me that Mom was always frettin' about something she would never explain. She stared out the window at the birds in the backyard or paced our small rooms when Dad was late for supper. She jumped at small noises or, one time, at a cloud that suddenly darkened our kitchen window.

Going to the store also made Mom very tense, which made me feel that we were vulnerable to something. She never spoke much there because she dreaded the friendly local courtesy that prompted people to ask where she was from and why she had moved and how she was getting along here and if she had married a good Texan. "Oh, yes," she would say. "One of the O'Connors from Port O'Connor."

"That's real good," they'd answer.

Nannan was determined to take the mystery out of shopping. She started with tomatoes, because in her kitchen you couldn't make a salad without the best tomatoes. She showed Mom how to pinch them and what the best ones smelled like. Then it was fresh corn, then okra and greens. Mom was commenting and nodding, but I doubted the lesson would take.

We went to where the soaps stretched out on the shelves. Nannan couldn't read. She said God hadn't given her the time to learn, but he had given her so much else that she was blessed, and anyway, people who worked hard got what they needed. She walked up to a box of Tide and said, "See, I can fin' my Ti' 'cause it's got its orange circle on t' fron'." Nannan didn't need to read to shop. Tide had its orange circle. Clorox came in a brown bottle with a blue label.

Nannan put her hands on her broad hips and stood astride the aisle to give advice that sounded like commands: "Miz O'Connor, deys tangs people in t' country do to keep dey few penny. You got t' know how t' use wha' t' good Lor' give you." She explained that you could save a piece of your money if you got chicken with pinfeathers, then burned off the feathers over the range. You could spread that chicken out through the week. The drumsticks and wings with beans the first day, and the neck and gizzards with rice and gravy the last day. If all you had were collard greens and pork fat, you still had a meal, if you also had some flour and Crisco—it had to be Crisco shortening—for biscuits. Nannan said, "Mr. O'Connor ain' gonna look at you funny when you have t' fry up baloney once in a while for dinner, he jus' gonna know you doin' t' bes' dat can be did."

Mom tried to take it all in. She told me, "We are learning new things in Texas, isn't that nice?"

Nannan probably saved our lives by teaching Mom how to cook— okay, that's going too far, but she did teach Mom to make something we could eat, using the cheapest ingredients. We needed that, on and off, for many years. Mom mastered rice and gravy, struggling. If the gravy didn't lump or burn too much, it could take your mind off what it covered. There was also the regular miracle of okra in a cornmeal batter fried in bacon grease. Mom was surprised that she could get it right so often. When the miracle failed, we had hot okra pudding.

Other lessons in Texas appalled my mother. One day, as an adventure, she and I took the bus to Foley's department store in downtown Houston. At the bus station there were two water fountains, one labeled WHITE and the other COLORED. I asked Mom how colored water tasted—was it like iced tea? "There's no time for water now," she said, walking off quickly through the station with her arm straight down, pulling me along close. "Michael, don't think for a minute that what they do to colored people here is right. It is evil; I can't understand it." She was speaking quite loudly, walking quickly. People near us turned to look. She ducked her head down and pulled me to the street, away from the people. I knew to wait to ask about it. When we were home, she'd say only that we had to believe that one day colored people would be treated properly.

We believed our parents when they told us that Jacinto City was just a stop on the way to somewhere better. For Nannan, life was as good as she expected it would ever be. She'd grab a chicken, whack off its head, pluck it clean, scald it, and gut it while chattering about the dances at Church Point when she was a girl or teaching me Cajun songs. Nannan looked at her life as it was: relentlessly harsh. Life was what you got, if you were lucky. There was no point in wincing at it.

Mom did not wince so much either. She would say she was optimistic, which in her case meant that she could be anesthetized to the obvious. When the optimism pushed out the anxiety, she had a buoyancy about life that helped us all keep afloat. Nannan managed poverty with her head down and her strong legs pushing forward. Mom imagined how wonderful it would all be someday.

This gave us something the Blanchards couldn't afford. We had self-deception. We believed our dreams would come true. I don't know how our lives might have changed if my parents had looked at where we were standing instead of gazing into the sky, but they wanted to bypass the truth. The truth was that they were running from something, cut off from everyone they used to know, and getting smacked around by a bizarre place called Texas.

Maybe that truth was simply too hard to look at.

Or maybe dreams can come true only if you follow them. For a while, that philosophy seemed to pay off for us.

TWO

OTHER KIDS HAD COUSINS and uncles, and family stories told over and over, but Mom had enough imagination to fill in some of the gaps. "Come along, then, Michael, let me tell you about the gingerbread man," she'd say in the kitchen, with what might turn out to be fresh bread baking in the oven. The fairy tale never changed, and I knew it so well that I could have told it myself, but it wasn't really the story that counted, or the performance she gave in the telling. It was being together with my mother.

"Well, there was an old couple who lived in the woods. . . ." Turning toward me dramatically to open the show, she acted out the parts of the old man and woman who baked a gingerbread man in place of the child they never had. When it came time for the old woman to give her creation a currant for his nose, Mom put the tip of her finger on the tip of my nose and we laughed out loud, every time. When it was time to tell how the mean farmer and his cow chased the gingerbread man, she laughed over her shoulder. " 'Run, run as fast as you can. You'll never catch me, I'm the gingerbread man!' "

She always ended with "And would you believe, wee Michael, no one ever did catch him. And the family lived happily forever and evermore."

When I looked at my mother in those moments, I did not see the nervous, delicate woman with hands that fluttered with anxiety. I felt the tender fingers that tugged my shirt into place and saw the face looking down in approval—and still approving five minutes later, when my clothes were back in disorder. And when she called my name out over the rural lots, where I'd be chasing down a chicken or playing in a culvert, I didn't hear her British accent, so distinctive to others. I heard her caring and concern, her need to keep me in view. Because I belonged to her.

Our parents loved us and loved to be with each other and little Mary
and me in our derelict house in that busted-out town next to Houston.
The evenings, with Mom ruining supper and Dad reading his book, were
lovely. We had the radio and the newspaper comic strips, and Mary to
feed and bathe and fuss over as she walked stiff-legged in her white
shoes. And we had our plans to embroider.

Dad would go over the day with Mom and me, replay the sales calls
he'd made, looking for suggestions. "I think that couple wanted to go for
the deal," he said. "The trouble was they didn't trust me, the Boston accent. Down here, you have to *be* from down here."

Mom told him, "But look here, you're an honest man with something
people need. Look at all the homes you've improved. Surely, good will
out. They'll see it. We're all with you." That was the stuff Dad wanted to
hear. He never doubted he could do whatever he set out to do, but he
needed Mom alongside for it to work.

When I was seven years old and saw a movie with Katharine Hepburn
and Spencer Tracy, it seemed they were pretending to be my parents.
Hepburn with her bouncy elegance, the swing of her arm; Tracy with his
casual passion for what he did, his air of a man of substance. My parents
were just like that: genuine people who were going to beat their problem
because they deserved to. More than that, much more, really, there was
the dead-honest romance between Hepburn and Tracy. *My parents loved
each other that way,* I thought. Their caring romance kept telling me that
our family's compass must be true.

Dad explained his door-to-door work as helping people with their
homes, which sounded more charitable than commercial. We lived from
deal to deal, sometimes with weeks in between, so each new deal lifted
our lives. Each one was a step toward realizing Dad's many plans—to
buy a window fan for the hotbox house in Jacinto City, or a bike for me
someday, or—the big dream—a house of our own. I believed in him even
when I didn't understand what he was doing, because Dad's plans came
true. We got the fan, then a small red bike with colored plastic streamers
on the handles and training wheels.

Once, after Dad closed a very good deal, we took Nannan across the
causeway to Galveston to celebrate with ice cream. Nannan didn't like
Dad driving so fast, especially on a road with no shoulders crossing
Galveston Bay, but she pulled a flapping scarf snug over her hair and
tried to smile. "You got t' give you daddy some help when he does
good," she whispered to me.

After selling a job, Dad resold the contract to Mr. Gale, who had a lumberyard and a crew of carpenters. One time Mr. Gale came to our house for a visit. After he'd left, Mom said he'd told her that he wanted to move his family to a new neighborhood in Houston, but the people wouldn't let him because he was a Jew and they didn't let Jews buy houses there. I didn't know what Jews were, but their trouble upset my mother deeply. She said, "It's a crime the way people treat Jews. It makes me sick to think about it." She wondered what we were doing here, anyway. "It's so awful when families have to be afraid all the time when they didn't do anything wrong."

And then Mom was struck suddenly by depression. It was something that happened to her occasionally in those days, leaving me mystified, scared for her and our family, too. It happened only at home, where only we could see it. But even Dad could not stop her from crying this time. He could only pace anxiously in front of the couch, where she sat in her deep sadness. He told her to please not worry because soon it would be better. When he tried to hold her, she pulled her arms across her chest. She became smaller and smaller, a sobbing, panic-stricken, shrinking Mom. He told her, "We knew it was going to be difficult, and we were right. But it won't be difficult forever, because there's a good future here. We just need more time."

I knew she was not angry with him. They were never angry with each other. *So what is she upset about?* I wondered if there was something wrong with us, something bad, that made my mother like this. She said, "We have no home. We have no place we can go where it is safe for a family." Hearing those fears, believing they are true, will burn a child.

Then she said she had been trying to save money for a sewing machine, to make trousers for Dad, but there was always a reason she couldn't save. She wanted to make curtains, too, so we could take down the sheets from the bedroom window. When Dad worked past dark, she said, she thought something had happened and he wouldn't come at all because he had been stopped by the police. She said she couldn't eat because she was so afraid sometimes, that was why she had all the trouble with her stomach. Sometimes, she said, she thought we should move somewhere else. "But then it would be the same. This isn't fair. People should not have to do this." Then she went even darker and quieter, and said, "I don't know how much longer I can do this, I really don't."

Do what? I wondered. And what would happen to us if she couldn't? Now, of course, I understand. My mother was afraid we would be caught and our family torn apart. But I believe there was more than that, a threat that dug very deep. She was afraid that her faith in decency and justice would be proven wrong and foolish. What then?

My mother's panic sowed panic in us, but only until her mood lifted. Most of the time she acted normal, as we understood *normal*. She did fret, as Nannan called it. She often seemed preoccupied with something she would not share, and from early on I understood that she was worried about our secret, whatever it was that made us afraid. I learned to watch her for signs of danger. Years later I would do the same as a reporter, watching the eyes of the soldiers I was with to gauge how close the enemy was.

Just as Dad had promised, things got better after a while, as he began to expand from selling home improvements to contracting and managing the work. And Mom settled in to Texas a little more. One day when I was eight we sat at the kitchen table discussing the plans for our new house. Mary, who was four, said she was old enough for her own bedroom, and we all agreed. "I want to pick the color, too," she insisted. Okay. Mary was more polite than her brother, more willing to help around the house, but she always had a strong opinion about what she deserved.

Mom penciled in the family room on her sketch pad, with large windows and French doors. Dad added a deck to the master bedroom. The planning lasted for months, its own pleasure, and then Dad bought the lot and Mr. Gale's workers actually began to build the house, bit by bit, in their spare time. Each Saturday we went to see how much it had changed. Sometimes we took Nannan so she could be part of it all, too. Mary wanted banana trees in the yard because she thought they were so strange-looking. Dad found a few, and we planted them, with grass and flowers, long before the house was completed, so it would look just right when we moved in.

Our new home sat on a sloping lot on Mobile Street, a twisting road paved with shells dredged from Galveston Bay. We lived way out in the country, near the last mailbox on the rural route, but that new brown house with white trim was proof certain that we were succeeding, that dreams meant something. Not long after we moved Fiona was born. That was December 1954. Mary was almost five, and I was about to turn nine. Our lives seemed full of possibility.

NANNAN CAME TO see us when Jack could drive her out in his pickup, and I had my friends at the same parochial school. But there were practically no other houses around our new place. It was better to live where things were quiet, Dad said. To make up for the lack of neighbors, Dad got us a dog, a big collie I named Prince. Our dog Margaret had been killed by a car before we moved. Prince and I ran through the pine thickets, looking for Indians. I told myself he was probably more fun than some neighbor kid anyway. Mary loved Prince, too. He let her ride him if she was gentle. He even let her braid the long hair around his neck, just as Nannan had braided Mary's long blond hair. Mary used to squirm, but Prince didn't mind at all. The three of us would sneak up on rabbits in the tall weeds and track frogs by their footprints on the creek banks until we found the holes where they hid. On Sunday nights we'd watch *Lassie* on TV. I told Mary that Timmy, the little boy who owned Lassie, was so good that he made me mad. But Mary liked him and even copied his techniques to teach Prince to fetch and heel.

In the rainy months, Prince kept me company when I went crawdad fishing in Goodyear Creek, right behind the house. I'd dangle a string with a piece of bacon fat to entice the crawdads to grab it with a claw. I'd haul them in, then let them go after Prince inspected them.

Soon Dad's business grew to the point where he had two crews of carpenters for the jobs nearby, and in June 1955 he expanded to the Rio Grande Valley, near the southern tip of Texas. Dad told me that one key to success was to find just the right market for what he was selling. He looked for neighborhoods where working-class families had enough money to own their homes and a little extra for modest improvements. At the same time, he wanted places that hadn't been worked over by his competitors.

Dad's new territory was too far to commute, so for days at a time he stayed at an apartment in Harlingen.

Mary and I knew that Dad kept us on his mind while he was away, because he stayed on our minds. Looking back, I wonder what he did all that time when we were waiting. I can't imagine there were other women. Now, from what happened with him years later and, three decades after that, from what his siblings told me about his youth, I know he was an alcoholic, though I didn't have a hint of that then. I rarely saw him drink at home. Liquor was not part of our lives. Still, maybe he drank when he was gone and beyond my mother's influence. Maybe he was drunk for days, humiliated but doing it anyway, and staying away so he could do more.

But maybe he could stay sober, and he simply worked hard for our future and came home as often as he possibly could.

THREE

A COUPLE OF WEEKS after Dad began working in the Rio Grande Valley, about six months or so after we'd moved into our new house, a police officer saw Dad selling jobs door to door and asked to see his city license. He didn't have a license. He was arrested, taken to the police station and fingerprinted, and released. My sisters and I learned of the incident after Mom died.

Still, I can picture Dad's panic as the policeman approached him. I can see Dad responding at first with a little arrogance toward an officer from a small police department in a town on the southern edge of the country. Arrogance to mask the fear and to find self-confidence, and to make the officer wonder if Dad was perhaps too important to be bothered for something so small. Still, Dad the salesman, the man who made people like him, then believe him, would have peered down from the ledge of arrogance and filled the air with charm. It would have flowed from the military bearing he'd assume, from his bemused distance from events as the officer took him to the police station, from his easy cooperation with it all while he and the officer discussed, now equally puzzled and put upon, why they had to endure such idiocy at the whim of rules from bureaucrats who were afraid to leave their desks to walk the world. Dad would have wanted to help them both by pointing out how much more reasonable it would be for him and the officer to get back to serious matters. The police officer would have been sympathetic in their common suffering. But he followed regulations and took Dad's fingerprints for the arrest report.

All we kids knew when it happened was that we missed Dad's usual phone call to tell us he was coming home. Instead he showed up at the house looking frightened, but smiling as if life could not be one dot better. In fact, all his plans were suddenly worthless—except for the one that got us out of the country as fast as we could move.

Dad announced that he'd come with a fabulous surprise. Everything was going so well that he'd decided it was high time we went on a vacation. We'd leave immediately, for Mexico. He said there was only time to pack a few things fast and get on that road. I was nine years old, Mary five, Fiona just over six months old.

Dad had heard about a wonderful dude ranch outside Saltillo, a town in the desert in northern Mexico. As we drove south, he asked Mary and me, "Don't you think it's time to let Mom get away from the housework and let someone else fix breakfast for her?" *Well, yes,* we thought, looking at each other, *it's about time for that.* But something was wrong—our father seemed *too* happy. Mom was distracted, but Dad looked as pleased as when he'd brought home the new Pontiac convertible that Mr. Gale had given him for being such a good salesman.

"Yeah," I said, "let's let someone else cook breakfast for Mom. She deserves it." I said it, but I wondered.

In quiet conversation, acting casually, my parents considered how it might be better to cross the border at night. Mom said to us all, "Why not find a park along the way and stop there for a picnic until it's dark?"

We bought marshmallows and made a fire at a roadside rest stop. We filled in the time chatting and running around, as if stopping a couple of hours after we'd left home and waiting till dark was the natural way to start any vacation. I wanted to tell Mary about Laredo. I thought she should know that something bad could happen at the border. But I didn't know how to tell her—the whole idea was too big, deep, bewildering, and I still didn't know why we'd been so terrified at Laredo. Mary later told me that she could feel there was something to worry about, though she never asked. Like Mom and Dad, I tried to act normal, playing with Mary as if everything were fine. My parents talked about a quiet little town on the border that Dad knew, though to get to it we'd need to take a big detour. "Babe," he said to Mom, "maybe we should cross there." Mom wondered if it might be better to get to Mexico as soon as possible, even if it meant crossing at a bigger town. Neither one of them was sure, but we went to the little town.

To a nine-year-old boy in the backseat of the car, this discussion proved that something dangerous was happening. Like what happened on the border at Laredo or when the police officer came to visit us in Jacinto City, there was extraordinary fear. But Mom and Dad pretended it wasn't there. That was the safest thing to believe.

We stopped at a gas station so Dad could wash all the windows to make the car look better. Mom and Mary tidied up the inside, and Mom inspected. She and Dad decided it was best if she didn't say anything to the officers on either side of the border.

Then we began to act as if we were really on vacation. Mom turned around to talk to me about the horses I'd ride at the dude ranch. Mary wanted to hear, again, about the swimming pool. But I knew we were playing a trick on ourselves, and the border was getting closer. We went through the border town in a few blocks, and suddenly there were the lights over the guard post and the two men in uniforms talking to each other. Bugs skittered under the lights. The men waved their hands around their faces to shoo the bugs away.

My legs trembled, but I knew we had to keep going because, whatever the danger at the border, something behind us was worse.

Dad told one of the men that Mom had a cold. "From the children," he said; "you know how that is. It's all caught up in her throat and she can't say a word. Mind you, I'm not complaining about that. Let's just let her sleep while she can."

My father was a man who broadcast confidence. He always seemed to know what he was doing, and his demeanor told you to trust him. "Oh, sure," Dad told the agent, "all of us are Americans. Better than that, we're Texans." The agent took a quick look inside the car and waved his hand.

On the Mexican side, after the initial quick stop at the border, there were two small immigration posts about thirty miles apart, places where Americans driving south had to stop and pass inspection. But Dad got out of the car and gave the agents each a dollar bill and a pack of Pall Malls and a joke or two, and they didn't check us. To explain the bribes, he said, "That's the way it works in Mexico."

THE DUDE RANCH, El Morillo, had eight rooms. In front stretched a big clearing of tamped bare earth, with cactus and palm trees on the edges and the little swimming pool, half full of water. They did not have horses. They had burros.

By the third morning, Mom seemed to relax and Dad raised the idea of staying in Mexico for more than a vacation. After translating the waitress's offer of *"Scrapple teeegs?"* we were having scrambled eggs for breakfast. As though offering a prize, Dad said, "Mexico is a good place for children. Your mother and I have been talking about how much better it is for children to know about other countries. Wouldn't it be good to live in Mexico for a while? It's fun, isn't it?"

It was not the kind of fun we'd expected. El Morillo was dirty. The stableboy and I couldn't understand each other. The food was strange. All five of us were sleeping in one room, and the first night I saw my first scorpion, in the closet behind Dad's shoes. The scorpion and I froze, staring at each other, until Mom screamed and Dad brought a newspaper to kill it. When we told the lady in the office, she said it happened a lot, so we shouldn't be surprised. Then she gave us an orange-colored Black Flag pump to spray stinky poison all over—especially in the bathroom, she told us, where the mosquitoes hide. She said, "Spray real good, but don't get any on you or breathe it."

While I wondered what kind of place had scorpions in the closets, I was willing to give Mexico some more time, to treat it as an adventure. I liked the dude ranch more than Mary, who hated the smells and ugliness and wanted to go home right *now*. Mary usually did everything asked of her, but she couldn't go along with this vacation. She didn't like anything except the swimming pool, after they skimmed off the bugs that had drowned overnight. Dad said, "We'll drive to some other towns to see what it's like around here. Let's give it a chance."

Looking for another place to stay, we spent hours banging down dirt roads full of holes. Mary and I watched the dust tail kicking up behind us until the back window piled with dirt like a brown curtain. In one town on the way to Monterrey, the car suddenly started shaking because the road was paved with small stones, something else I'd never seen before. It was hard to hear inside the car with all the shaking, but Dad turned back to us and began praising cobblestone roads: cheap to make, easy to fix, last forever. As our car dropped into holes in the road, then shook and thumped back onto the cobblestones, he went on about how the Romans made stone roads to tie their empire together. He said, "The skills you children will see in Mexico have been proven for more than two thousand years. It's a good thing we are somewhere those skills are still understood.

"There's an American restaurant in Monterrey," Dad said. "Let's go there and have lunch." The restaurant was called Sanborn's. I liked it because it had an American name and inside it looked normal. There was air-conditioning, and American comic books on a rack, and everyone at the tables looked like people at home. We ordered milk shakes and hamburgers with potato salad, not Mexican food.

Dad started talking about how a lot of things in Mexico felt familiar once you got to know them. He asked the waiter about some out-of-the-way places to visit. "Somewhere the children can get to know the real heart of Mexico, the old Mexico." Mary and I were skeptical because we weren't so happy with the new Mexico.

Dad went on, "Somewhere without telephones, where people live as they used to. Maybe a village in the mountains where my wife can do her artwork. She's an excellent artist, well known in Europe." I wondered when Mom had become an artist.

The waiter told Dad about a place near Monterrey called the Villa de Santiago. We went looking for it after lunch, down a road southeast from the city. An hour later, we found a narrow street that curved to the right, up a hill, with two bell towers sticking up from behind another hill, as the waiter had said. Quickly, we came across a few houses made of what looked like hard mud.

Dad was driving, with Mom next to him and me and my sisters looking out the windows in the back. We were on the main street, which was part asphalt and part dirt. The tiny side streets were cracked dirt and loose rocks. Then Fiona said, "Dahh *ohh*." Mary and I looked where she was poking her pudgy little finger . . . at a bunch of cows where they were not supposed to be, clopping down the street and wandering between the mud houses. The people on the street didn't pay attention to them. More cows were heading our way down a side street, just nodding and walking, coming to see their cow buddies forming up all around us.

We were stuck in the middle of cows. But instead of someone herding them, as cowboys would, the cows had us trapped. People stared at us as though *we* were the ones in the wrong place. Some of the cows were staring, too—what were we doing on their street, anyway?

Dad put his head out the window and said pleasantly, "Howdy, hellooo! Howdy, there." He said "Howdy" when he was trying to be sociable in Texas. (Still, it must have been jarring for the Texans to hear a Boston accent bent around phrases like "Ya'll come back, ya hear?" or "I might could do that.") As he sang out his greeting and waved to the villagers, they only stared. Hadn't they ever heard someone say "Howdy" before?

"*Americanos, Americanos,*" Dad was saying, pointing to us and looking back at the people. One man was slapping at a cow with a stick to make her move. But she and her friends had frozen around us. It looked as if some of the men were deciding whether they should go home and come back with rifles. There was an old lady, bent over, carrying a live chicken upside down. The chicken was the only one not staring at us.

Finally, one of the men pushed the cows away to give us a stare close up. Dad said, "Howdy. *Americanos.*"

"*Americanos,*" the man replied, and then started speaking in Spanish.

"English?" Dad asked. "*¿Inglés? ¿Inglés?*"

Meanwhile, someone got the cows pushed aside just enough to let our car move again, slowly. The men walked next to us to guide us up the street. We had a parade, with people popping up all around to escort us deeper into the village, where the houses were stuck together side by side, front walls flush on the sidewalk. We couldn't tell where one house stopped and the next one began except for the changing colors, from green to yellow to blue to red. All the houses had holes where their walls were crumbling a bit, exposing adobe bricks and bits of straw. Every window had bars, with faces poking through. The walls shot up on both sides of the street, as if we were entering a deep canyon. In the cowboy movies, I thought, this would be a great place for an ambush.

Dad was grinning away as though everything was turning out perfectly. Mom said, "It's so quaint, so charming. Look, children, they are all coming out to greet us." But Mary and I were scared. She was looking straight ahead—not through the windshield but at it.

Our parade stopped where the wall turned pink, by an ancient, scarred wooden door with metal bars and straps across the front. Into a tall narrow window latticed with bars, the kids called out, "Señorita Dora, Señorita Dooora!"

Silence from the pink house for what seemed a long time. Then the wooden door squealed and slowly opened, revealing a short woman's silhouette. At first we could see only her foot on the doorjamb. But when she made her way into the sunlight, we saw that she wore a long dark dress and had short gray hair. She smiled, but I didn't think she meant it. Then she looked at us and said, "Hello." Everyone in the street became silent because they knew they'd be hearing people speak English.

Dad jumped out and said, "We're Americans, just looking around your beautiful town here. We were asking about somebody who speaks English, and these wonderful folks brought us straight to you." He was smiling big; the lady kept smiling small. Her name was Dora Mason. Dad put out his hand. She put out hers, but not too far. After a minute of chatting, Dad told us to come and meet Miss Dora Mason because she'd been nice enough to invite us to get out of the sun for a while. "How pleasant," Mom said.

"The children are tired," Dad told Miss Mason. "They only *seem* frightened. They love Mexico, don't you, kids?"

I sucked in my shoulders to make sure that I didn't rub against the strange world inside the house, where the air was dark and it smelled like nothing we knew. I didn't want to breathe too much because I didn't want any of this place inside me; it seemed shut-in and dangerous. The cracked floor tiles wiggled as we walked. The high ceiling looked like old sheets with brown stains on the edges nailed around the tops of the walls. Bugs hung from the corners. We had different bugs in Houston. I didn't know what these bugs would do.

DAD WAS TELLING Miss Mason that we all wanted to live in a charming village like this one. "How fortunate," she said, because sometimes she rented rooms in this very house. She was a religious woman, and this was a quiet, religious home. There had never been Americans here before, except for her father. He was a mining engineer who'd died long ago, she told us, her eyes down in reverence.

"Wouldn't it be good to sit down and have a cold Coca-Cola?" she asked. She went to the front door to say something to one of the kids still standing outside, and he ran off across the street. Mary was so confused she was beginning to cry, though she tried to hide it. It looked like Fiona might cry, too.

Miss Mason said she could let us have her two best rooms. "Delightful," Mom said. I knew there would be no discussion within the family, or any explanation that made sense.

We moved to Miss Mason's the next day. To the left of the front hallway was a living room full of knickknacks and a large stuffed sofa and chairs, and a table with grapevines carved along the sides and legs. A pair of glass display cabinets held dozens of ceramic figurines. It reminded me of a movie from the very old days.

Miss Mason came up, quietly and smirking, kind of slipping in between Mary and me as we carried the clothes in. "This is the room for the antiques," she said. The furniture was from when her mother and fa-

ther were alive. She said, "All those tiny things in the glass cases are special, too. They are valuable antiques. Children can only come in this
room when Miss Mason is here."

That's fine, I thought; *those chairs are so ugly they look like they
could hurt you if you tried to sit on them and there's not one ceramic
statue in those glass cases that is worth picking up.* The cases were
prominent in the small room, as if she wanted to make sure that no one
missed the chance to see any of the little girls holding a bouquet or one
of the saints looking so holy, even the ones with a crack or an arm
knocked off.

Miss Mason went to the dining room and then pointed to her two
rooms off to the side. "Children don't go there," she warned unpleas-
antly. Our two rooms were off the right side of the hallway. They were
naked except for two beds, two flimsy chairs, and two small tables on
rough concrete floors.

Mary, looking away from Miss Mason, said to me, "Why do we have
to go anywhere in this place?"

Mom told us the house was a wonderful place that would help us understand the Mexican style of living, because even if our two rooms were
a wee bit small, we could spend our time in the glorious courtyard inside
the house. People in Mexico, she said, spend time with their families at
home.

As we would learn, Miss Mason was an unhappy woman who longed
to share her unhappiness. She owned a large house left to her by her father. But her home, her life, her pleasures—all were shrinking. Most of
the building was crumbling and no longer habitable. The kitchen was in
the courtyard, with a small fire pit on a concrete table against the back
wall of the house. A clay pot bubbled on the fire, and the harsh smell of
burning mesquite and boiling beans made me step back.

Dry, leggy weeds emerged from cracks in the courtyard's stone pavers,
and plant skeletons fringed the roof overhangs and the tops of the courtyard walls. The roofline melted away from insects and rot. The courtyard also had a well, with a bucket hanging from a pulley. But because
the water from the pipes came out "only a little brown" these days, Miss
Mason said, she hardly used the well. Against the far side of the patio
was a tall, narrow room "for personal necessities," Miss Mason said.
Mary and I didn't know what that meant, so we opened the door and
found the outhouse.

As we unpacked our clothes, the kids from the day before piled up on the sidewalk to look through our bedroom window, squashing their cheeks between the bars. I was glad for those bars and the thick walls, because at least they kept us safe from whatever happened outside. A boy about my size talked to me from the sidewalk, but I couldn't tell what he was saying. He pointed to his chest and said, *"Yo Esteban."* He waited and then said, *"Yo Esteban, ¿y tú?"* and waited again. We both waited. The other kids poked him and laughed.

An older girl came up, a teenager. She examined me closely, almost squinting, and said slowly, "Cuat . . . eess . . . chur . . . nane?" She pointed at me and repeated, "Cuat . . . eess . . . chur . . . nane? Chur nane?"

I pointed to my chest and said, "Michael." A half dozen faces tried to comprehend my sounds.

Then the boy finally said, *"¡Maico! Tú Maico."* The others joined in: *"¡Maico, Maico, Maico!"* I didn't even have my name anymore.

It got dark fast when the sun went down that first night, with only a single dim streetlight down the block. You couldn't see the people sitting on chairs in front of their houses, speaking softly in a strange language, laughing and coughing in the dark.

Bringing a pair of kerosene lanterns, Miss Mason warned us to be careful to use only one or two lights at the same time. It was dangerous because the wires were too small. I thought, *Who ever heard of dangerous lights?* And I didn't want to use the pots to go to the toilet at night. Miss Mason said it was best to use them because sometimes there were lizards and other things on the ground around the outhouse. In the morning, she explained, we emptied the pots in the hole.

Mom was getting Mary and Fiona ready for bed under a small electric bulb. Mom dipped a facecloth in a bowl and then scrubbed Mary from top to bottom. It was the first day ever that we hadn't bathed; even at El Morillo we got a shower. But at Miss Mason's our shower had only a cold-water pipe. Mom said that was fine, we'd get used to the water soon enough. Sometimes we could heat it over the fire in the kitchen, then put it in the laundry tub and take a bath that way.

I could hear the mosquitoes inside our room, up by the cloth ceiling. Mom was telling Mary not to worry because tomorrow would be a good day. Mary was crying. Mom said, "Mary, you'll be happy here. It will be wonderful."

"How long do we have to stay here?" Mary asked. "Why can't we be in Texas with our friends? Why are we here, where everything is dirty?"

Mary wanted to know why she was being punished, because she hadn't done anything wrong. She was asking the same questions I was asking myself. She didn't know how to go to the bathroom in the pot, and she was terrified that she'd fall into the hole in the outhouse, which gave off a piercing, nauseating smell. "Michael," Mary said when Mom turned out the light, "Michael, will that make me sick?"

Mom answered that she couldn't smell a thing. Then she said, "Don't pay attention to it, and it will go away," and she went to the other room, with Dad and Fiona.

The feet of our beds stood in tin cans filled with stinking kerosene to keep the bugs away. "It's a good thing we have those cans," Dad had told us, trying to puff up our spirits by pointing out the countermeasures. "A lot of things come out at night." I lay there in the dark, my eyes toward the ceiling, arms and legs out, away from my body, the sheet stuck to the sweat on my chest.

Mary was crying to herself with her face in the mattress, hiding from the room and the smells. "What about the bugs on the floor?" she asked me.

"They'll fall in the kerosene and drown."

"But, Michael, bugs can jump." She pulled up her knees and made herself into a ball with her face in the mattress. I pulled my knees up, too.

Mom came back and held Mary's head in her lap. She caressed Mary's face and combed her hair with her fingertips, and sang the lullaby that Mary liked best:

> "Go to sleep, wee Mary,
> Close your little eyes.
> The lady moon is watching
> From out the darkening skies.
> The little stars are peeping
> To see if you are sleeping.
> Go to sleep, wee Mary,
> Go to sleep, good night."

Mom's voice grew sad, and it seemed as if she was also singing to make herself feel better.

FOUR

A COUPLE OF DAYS after we arrived at the Villa, Dad said he had to go to Monterrey to call the people who worked for him in Texas. There was only one telephone in the Villa, in the mayor's office, but it was broken. Dad said he was glad of that because he'd rather drive to Monterrey to find a phone than have people calling us here all the time. He said it was best to stay in the house and relax so we didn't draw too much attention. That was why he parked our car in the yard behind the wall that faced the street in the back.

He was kidding himself, of course, because everyone in the Villa knew that Americans had moved to Miss Mason's—knew, in fact, just how many bags we'd carried in from the car. We couldn't have stood out any more if we had tethered a red, white, and blue blimp in the courtyard.

A few days after we moved in, Miss Mason came and said, "Michael, will you go to the store and get us some salt for the beans?" That sounded impossible, even if Miss Mason was wearing her pleasant face. She didn't like going out in the street herself. "Michael, salt is called 'sal' in Spanish. A package is called 'un paquete.' So you only have to ask for un paquete de sal, por favor." Miss Mason said it again: "Un paquete de sal, por favor." I tried to mimic the sounds, and she helped a few times until I got it right. Then she gave me a brown coin and told me to go to the store on the corner, Doña Eva's. There was another store just across the street from us, but she didn't like the lady there, for the moment.

As I pulled back the big lock, all the kids who had been at the window, looking inside, jumped over to the front of the door, looking at me. We were all wondering what would happen next. I went out slowly, though not too slowly, because I didn't want them to think I was afraid, which I was. They started walking with me, chatting and bubbling, trying to talk to me, then talking at one another. Our little heap of kids went up to the corner, then across to the store, where they waited outside by the door. It was the smallest store I had ever seen, a tiny room in a house, with the door right on the sidewalk. There were several adults inside. I wanted to wait for them to finish and leave before I said the words I was practicing in my head. I waited. Everyone looked at me and waited right back.

"Un . . . paquete . . . de . . . sal, por . . . favor." It came out very slowly and faraway, as if someone else was speaking.

They were laughing at me! No, they were laughing because they *liked* what I said. Doña Eva looked down and handed me a small brown bag across the plank that was the counter. I gave her the coin. "Gracias," she said, and then handed me a candy. All the grown-ups were saying things I didn't understand, but I knew they meant I'd done a good job and they were glad that I'd come.

A girl from the window pointed to Doña Eva and said, "Mamá, mamá. Yo Evita." She must be the daughter, I thought. The other kids were laughing and telling me things. But the only thing I understood was when a boy named Oscar said his name and held up nine fingers.

I said, "Yo Michael," and held up nine fingers, too. The adults clapped and laughed because we had spoken to each other. I didn't know anything else to say, but I had the salt and the candy. With the heap of kids, I marched back to Miss Mason's like the brave hunter returning. They went back to the window to look inside.

I CAME TO know Miss Mason better in the next days, and I still didn't like her. She *was* giving us a place to stay, and even though I thought it was awful, I knew our parents were glad of it. I tried not to wonder why a place like Miss Mason's was something we should be glad about. Still, her character made me wince. She was overly formal, overly tight, haughty about the rest of the people in the Villa. She said she seldom went out, as if she was afraid of the people or disdainful of them.

But actually, the most pointed reason I disliked her was the way she slurped her coffee. With so much else to be upset about, I focused on the coffee drinking. She knew I hated it and did it to spite me. We were a petty child and a petty old lady. She made it with Nestlé instant coffee powder that she put in her cup first. One spoonful, using the same red plastic spoon every morning. Then she boiled milk in her little milk-boiling pan with the broken handle, so she used a cloth to bring it over to the coffee cup and spooned it in, *spoon, spoon, spoon,* and she hummed something. Finally, with ceremony, she took the scum that milk makes if it's boiled too much and plopped it in. It floated on the coffee. As she drank the thing, the scum made a noise when she got to it—which I thought she made for me to hear. And some scum always stuck to her lip.

"Why do you do it that way?" I asked her. "Doesn't it look like something on the top of a swamp?"

"Why, no, Michael. The froth on the coffee is the best part. I like to save it for last."

DAD ASKED MISS MASON if there was anyone who might lend me a burro to ride—I'd wanted a pony, like the cowboys, but a burro would be okay to start with. She said that only poor people who didn't wash rode burros. But she found a man who might rent his burro if I promised not to hurt it. *How am I going to hurt a burro?* I thought.

The owner said he didn't think anyone in the Villa had ever rented a burro to anyone, much less a foreigner. It was possible they rented burros in other villages, but it was not the custom here. But he spoke to his brothers, and they thought it would be all right to rent the burro for two hours every few days if his son, Manuel, stayed with me the whole time.

I rode in the afternoons, in the open space behind Miss Mason's house or down the street for variety. The kids from the window came with me, and I learned all their names. We still couldn't talk much, but we had a good time exploring. Afterward we'd stop at Doña Armandina's, the store right across the street from Miss Mason's. Our landlady didn't like me going there, which made the going more delicious. We'd buy a Coke to share sitting on the edge of the sidewalk, our legs splayed out in the street, pantomiming and giggling. I wasn't supposed to share Coke, according to Miss Mason, who said the kids could be sick and everyone in the house would catch it. But I didn't care.

Not long after we arrived, Dad went to Texas "for business." He said maybe he'd go to Houston and bring back some of our things so we could stay in the Villa awhile longer, since it was turning out so beautifully. Mary and I didn't think so. But the idea of living in the Villa was so far beyond our comprehension that we went on day by day without looking ahead.

One afternoon, when it was almost time to stop riding, my burro spotted another burro tied to an electricity pole and abruptly charged it, jumping like a bucking horse. I pretended to be a cowboy on a wild bronco, but then I lost control. Manuel grabbed my burro, yanking on the rope to turn the burro's head around, but couldn't stop him from throwing me and jumping on the other burro from behind.

When I got up, my left hand was hanging from my arm in a new way. It didn't hurt, but it scared me to see how funny it looked, sticking out at that angle, with a sharp bone protruding from my wrist. The kids all yelled like they were scared, too, which made it worse. Then Mom came to the door of the house and screamed. Someone went for the doctor. With Miss Mason translating, he said my arm wasn't broken—it was only a fracture, a *fractura*. But we had to go to Monterrey, to a hospital, to fix it. The doctor slowly washed around the bone, pouring a yellow liquid over the arm to kill the germs. He laid a cloth on top, and I carried my arm out to the car the doctor had borrowed. He had to stop to see two pregnant ladies on the way, because he didn't get a car very often and the ladies were in tiny villages where the buses didn't go.

I looked to Mom, who said she should stay with Mary and Fiona. How could any mother let her nine-year-old son, his arm twisted from a bleeding compound fracture, go off with a stranger? Why couldn't she have grabbed her daughters and simply gotten in the back of that car—to make sure, to be with her son? As the doctor sat me in the car and Mom stayed on the sidewalk in front of Miss Mason's, I felt utterly abandoned by the one I'd thought loved me most.

I couldn't have known that she thought that somehow I would make it on my own, but that our family could be destroyed if she were discovered in Monterrey.

The doctor visited the first woman while I stayed in the car, holding my arm. It was swelling badly, hurting more and more. It hurt most when we bounced over the holes and rocks on the dirt roads. I thought if it hurt so much with only a *fractura*, I didn't know what I'd do if it were broken.

In the second village, where the doctor brought me in and sat me on a chair on the far side of the hut, I could tell that the woman was about to have her baby. There must have been a problem, because she was screaming and thrashing, and the other women moved quickly and spoke loudly, as if something serious was just ahead.

Then a large woman with long hair tied behind her head took me back out to the car and stayed with me. Suddenly I started crying. It wasn't right for a kid to have to wait in a dirty little village he had never been to before, trying not to look at his arm, which he might never be able to use again, while wondering why his parents were doing this to him. I tried to keep looking outside the car, away from my arm, but the cloth slipped off and I saw the bone again and that made it hurt even more. I tried to imagine that it was not my arm, that I couldn't feel it. Then I thought, *What kind of boy would I be with no arm?* So I had to let it hurt again. The long-haired woman tried to be nice. She kept waving her hand to keep the flies off the bone. She brought me some water in a cup, but the cup looked dirty and Mom said we shouldn't drink water that wasn't boiled. I said, "Coca-Cola." She said, *"No hay."* Finally I had to drink the water.

When it was dark, the doctor came out and said things I didn't understand, but I could tell the baby was all right. At the hospital in Monterrey they washed me, gave me a gown, and wheeled over a gurney. "No shot," I told the new doctor. I mimed an injection and told him, "No, no." He said, *"Bueno, no."* They rolled me to a room where everybody had masks and looked down at me. I thought that Mom might come as a surprise, holding Fiona with one arm and hanging on to Mary to keep her out of the nurses' way. I watched the door, hoping, but then I knew they wouldn't come. So it was just me when the nurse came over with the big needle. I tried to see if it was sharp or dull, to see how much it might hurt. I told her, "No, no, doctor no." She said, *"Sí,"* and something I couldn't understand. I said, "Pill," pointing to my mouth with my right hand. But she gave the shot to me anyway. It sedated me, and they set my arm.

The next day the doctor from the Villa came to take me back. He had a different car, with a man driving it. I thought it must be like my burro—the doctor could use the car but somebody had to stay with it.

Mom was torn when she saw me, near tears but trying to look brave for both of us. She said, "There, you see, Michael, I knew you could do it."

I said, "Do you know how long it took to get to the hospital?" She couldn't speak for a while after that.

During the ride home, my arm had swollen, making the cast cut into my hand. Blood was pooling inside the cast. Mom rushed around the courtyard and found a pole to fasten to the bed to elevate my arm. She pushed the bed next to the window so I could look down the street and the kids could come to see me. They wanted to talk about what had happened, but all I could understand was *"burro."* I told them, *"Burro loco,"* and they laughed. One said, *"Burro,"* and I said, *"Loco,"* and we all laughed again. Then another kid said, *"Burro caliente."* That made some of them laugh even more, but I didn't know why.

A FEW DAYS AFTER I got out of the hospital, Dad returned, driving up to the door by the window. I called out in a weak, forlorn way so he could see me laid out in bed with my cast hanging over my head. He came to the window bars, and I began to tell him what had happened. "Good God!" he said, even before I got to the part about my bone sticking out. "Jesus Christ!" He said he was so damn sorry that we'd had to come to Mexico in the first place, but he couldn't help it. I skipped most of the story because he looked so miserable already. He kept saying he was sorry and there was a problem that kids wouldn't understand. That was as much of an explanation as I would ever get.

Then he said he had good news, which didn't help my morale. Every time he announced some good news, something got worse. Mom looked happy, so I worried even more. But this time I was wrong, because Dad said we were going back home. He didn't explain much about why, and we didn't ask for more. It took no time to pack and leave. And just that fast, we were on our way home.

On the road up to the border, Mary asked if we were going back because we'd learned enough about the real Mexico. Mom answered, "Yes, and wasn't it wonderful after all?" Mary said she thought the real Mexico was a dirty place where everybody looked at her. Dad turned around and told us this was all part of understanding the world, and when we got older we'd realize how much fun we'd had.

My father stretched his big arm across the back of the seat and put his hand on Mom's shoulder. In their connection with each other, in their love that was never spoken but always evident, our family began to rebuild its belief in itself. We began to turn against the obvious and the logical and look for our comfort in one another. The real reason we'd gone to Mexico was shoved away, pushed down a well. We'd had an adventure, that was all. It made me feel safe to believe that, and we sang together:

> *The stars at night are big and bright, deep in the heart of Texas.*
> *The prairie sky is wide and high, deep in the heart of Texas.*

At Reynosa, on the border, there was one small detail to take care of, Dad said. He stopped on a quiet street and leaned over to poke around in the glove compartment. "It's nothing at all," he said; "won't take a minute." He found a screwdriver and a yellow can of Ronson lighter fluid and started scraping the Mexican police sticker off the corner of the windshield. It was a round sticker the border authorities used to authorize a car to go past the border zone, deeper into Mexico.

Dad lightly explained that if the men on the American side saw our sticker, they'd ask more questions. Maybe they'd want to know about where we'd been in Mexico and what we were doing there. "Too much bother," he said. "This will get us across much faster." He scratched off most of the sticker, then squirted the lighter fluid on his handkerchief to rub away the rest.

On the American side he told them we'd crossed over to Reynosa for an hour, just to look around. "Yep, we're all Americans here, heading on home to Houston," Dad said. Mom was bent over fussing with Fiona and didn't say anything. They waved us through. Dad waved back and said, in his Boston-Texas accent, "Thank ya, now. You boys have a good day and don't get too hot out here. Sure is a hot one, ain't it?"

FIVE

WE RETURNED TO OUR REMOTE HOME on Mobile Street, which proved that trusting our parents brought success, just in time for the new school year at Our Lady of Fatima School. We'd been gone for about three weeks, which made it easier to fool ourselves and think of the dreadful episode as only an adventurous vacation, especially with school to give us something new to think about. I was about to start fourth grade and Mary first grade. She was relieved. In the Villa she'd seen us drifting toward an uncertain horizon. She'd worried that she'd never get taught by the nuns she saw in the front pew at Mass.

On the first day of school, Mom looked down at me and said, "Watch little Mary. Help her."

None of my school friends had had a summer like mine or wore a battle ribbon like the cast from my left hand up to my shoulder. I didn't tell them the truth about our trip; of course not. I didn't say we'd fled across the border into Mexico, using deceit and bribery, to wind up in a dilapidated village where my father hid our car and we slept with bugs and the stench from the outhouse. I told my friends what my parents told me: We'd had a fabulous adventure. When my friends believed it, I could believe it, too.

THREE YEARS EARLIER, on one of those Texas summer nights when the only thing that changed after the sun went down was that it got dark, because it was still too hot to move, Dad had sat me down in our house with the screen door that let in a wisp of air while it saved us from the June bugs, and told me why I had to go to Our Lady of Fatima in Galena Park, the next town. He explained that the nuns taught children to act like decent people, something I'd need as I grew up. He said, "There are certain ways civilized people behave. It's what makes us different from the savages. When a grown-up misbehaves, it's not like when a little boy misbehaves; it's much worse."

He told me that rules were important for children even if we didn't understand them. Our family didn't hide our Catholic religion, though it was another barrier between us and our neighbors. The local kids went to public school or to the nearby Baptist church. That was easier, I thought, but Dad said we had other ways.

Somehow I didn't find it strange that Dad always had an excuse for missing Mass. On Sundays he dropped us off at church and was waiting in the parking lot when Mass was over. It was a small problem, he explained, something he was correcting, nothing worth thinking about. But I could feel that there was something wrong between him and the Church. What was it?

Mom accepted Dad's strong connection to Catholicism, though she'd been raised a Protestant and was more "spiritual" than religious. She believed that people were inherently good, and that religion, or just being a good person, was a way to express our striving to make what she called "a better world for us all."

I went to Mass every day before class at Our Lady of Fatima. Mom had to drive me, but she didn't mind. Catholic school was much better, she said, because the nuns were holy women who had given their lives to the education of children. Their school had higher standards, and she liked the rule that kids had to wear shoes.

The public schools didn't have that rule. My neighbor Bubba Livingston had thick calluses on his feet from going barefoot all day. When Bubba wanted into the house, he just hosed his feet, which was a lot more fun than cleaning your shoes. But Mom said we were better than that. "Wearing shoes is like living a proper life," she told me, which was the right way to live even if it didn't make sense to children.

Our Lady of Fatima was in a poor parish that drew the few and scattered Catholics from a wide area. The classrooms reminded me of Nannan's house, where you couldn't look anywhere without seeing a saint gazing up to heaven from a field of gentle flowers, or a martyr with a small smile, the lions ready to send her to see God, or a calendar with the Sacred Heart of Jesus pierced by a sword. The images let you know there was a big power somewhere and you'd better follow the rules if you wanted to stay out of trouble.

In the first and second grades, there were two classes in each classroom, but I knew it was better than public school because we were learning how not to be barefoot savages. We sat two to each desk, pushing
with our butts for space, but not so the nuns could see. The nuns, we
knew, were beyond the inconveniences of this world. They were connected to matters we could not comprehend, though they gave us
glimpses in their stories about the saints who suffered and the martyrs
who died for the love of Jesus and to keep themselves holy.

Early on, before Dad's business took hold, it was hard to pay the tuition, but Dad insisted I go anyway. Each month I took the small manila
school envelope Mom gave me with dates stamped in red on the back
and lined up to hand it to Sister. Sometimes there were two dollars in the
envelope, so Sister could mark us paid. If Dad was having money trouble, there was only Mom's note inside and Sister didn't write anything.
That was when I tried to stand between Sister at her desk and the other
kids in line so they wouldn't see.

The nuns might once have been like ordinary people, I thought, but
along the way they'd become holy. They spoke quietly, with small, contented smiles. They were so holy that they hardly even walked but rather
glided along the floor. You never saw their feet under their black habits
unless they were striding across the play yard at recess because someone
had to be yelled at or smacked across the back of his head for his own
good. One time Sister Mary Elizabeth had to smack me so hard for my
own good that my tongue got caught in the back of my mouth and I
coughed and gagged while she watched me turn red and learn my lesson.
"Yes, Sister Mary Elizabeth, I understand when I misbehave it hurts the
suffering heart of Jesus. Thank you, Sister."

There were true miracles that no scientist could explain, the nuns
taught, and a living devil, who walked among us all, invisible. We would
enter God's paradise only when we believed what we could not understand. The lesson was: Believe those who know better than you, even if
it doesn't make sense.

For a boy without relatives, without a history, with a dark mystery
hanging over his family, Catholic ideology was comforting. It taught that
mysteries were to be accepted, not questioned.

NOT LONG AFTER we returned from Mexico and Mary started school,
she and I saw Father O'Sullivan feeding his dogs. He was a tall man with

graying hair. He had a pack of friendly wire-haired terriers that bounced around the fenced-in yard behind the church. He bred and sold them to help keep the church going.

"Ah, Mary, sweet Mary, we've all been waiting for your arrival," Father O'Sullivan said. He talked that way even when he had his hands in a giant metal bowl of dog food, breaking up the pieces of boiled gray meat, throwing in some stale bread, and swishing away the flies with his head. "Are you meeting all the new students in your class?" She was. "Aren't they all good students and lovely children?"

"Yes, Father."

Mary looked nervous, pulling on her blond pigtails. She peered up at Father O'Sullivan as if he were a saint. She had never seen him before outside the altar, where he wore his long vestments. To me, Father O'Sullivan didn't seem so holy. At one Mass he had a cold and his nose was running; he sniffed like anyone else. And now he was here with the stinky dog food up his arms, fighting the bugs, but Mary was listening to him as if he wore a halo.

Father said, "Listen to the nuns, Mary, they will teach you everything you need to know." I had heard the same admonition from Dad and Mom as well as Father O'Sullivan. I had accepted it at first, but by the time Mary started school I had my doubts. I was starting to question the nuns' wisdom, and why police and border guards were such a threat to our family, and even whether I could rely on my parents for the truth about our secret, which seemed the most dangerous thing of all.

That night I told Mary about Sister Mary Elizabeth's geography lesson. It all began when Mom remembered a funny saying about the equator when she'd been a girl in school. The teacher called it "an imaginary line" running around the center of the earth, but some kid in her class twisted it into "a menagerie lion." Everyone laughed as they pictured a lion racing around a globe.

I already knew about the equator from *With Kitchener in the Sudan,* one of the books Mom gave me about British heroes. When I told Sister Mary Elizabeth about the book and shared my funny lion story, she seemed angry and disappointed in me: "Don't ever say that 'menag' word again!" Apparently she'd never heard the word *menagerie,* and she was really angry: "What kind of words do you think you're using with the same mouth you use to pray to the Blessed Virgin?" I said I was sorry, I'd thought the word meant something like a zoo, but I would never say it again. Then Sister wondered where I'd found a book like that, because

I wasn't old enough to read it. She told me not to listen to a man with a name like a kitchen. When I got old enough, she went on, I'd learn that the equator was like a belt holding the sky together so everything didn't just float off into space and kill us all. Above the equator was heaven, where boys who read the wrong books would never go.

I told Mary the whole thing because it bothered me that Sister was so wrong about the equator. Maybe, I said unsurely, we should be careful about what the nuns taught us. It seemed possible they didn't know everything they were supposed to.

Mary was thrilled just to be at school and thought I was wrong, that I was making trouble and showing off. "Just because you're the big brother," she said, "you think you're always the smart one!" The nuns and Father O'Sullivan and Mom and Dad knew everything we needed to know, she was sure of that.

But for me at age nine, trying to align what I knew in ways that made sense, there seemed to be two distinct ideas about truth. To begin with, truth was what the grown-ups agreed was true. Everyone agreed that the nuns taught us all we needed to know, so that was true. But then there seemed to be another kind of truth, where Father O'Sullivan was a normal person who only put on special clothes for Mass. The second sort of truth included whatever it was our parents weren't telling us. That second kind of truth was probably dangerous to think about, which was why adults kept it hidden. To protect yourself, it was best to believe in the truth that everyone agreed on.

THE WORLD WAS changing around us. When we'd first moved to our new home, Nannan said it was "way, way in t' country." We had the only house on a skinny road into a pine forest. Then a company bought all the land around us and cut down the forest for a housing development called Home Owned Estates. We had new houses coming toward us. That worried me and Mary for a while, because we weren't used to people living so close. But we came to like it because it was fun to have friends around. We didn't invite them to come inside our house, just the yard. We knew that was the rule, even without Mom telling us.

The only boy my age in the new houses was Carl Thurmond, who lived in the nearest house, around a bend in the road, about a half mile away. We enjoyed being soldiers scouting for Germans in the woods. His father worked at the Sheffield Steel Mill. It helped me accept the unexplained in my life that whenever I asked Carl's dad what he did there he would only ever answer, "Shift work." Maybe dads just had secrets, I thought. Carl's family came from someplace "up in Oklahoma," as my family came from nebulous "Boston." Neither one of us could remember anything about where we came from. The difference for Carl was that he had relatives fairly nearby. "Over in Eewston" was where he said they were. When they came to visit, I watched them and Carl's family as if I were in the room but, at the same time, not there. It seemed that relatives were for others and I shouldn't get too close. I didn't want Carl and his family to notice that.

We'd still heard almost nothing about our parents' families. The shadows around our parents' pasts kept us from asking questions. We did know that Dad's two sisters were Mary and Eleanor, and that my sisters were named after them. (Fiona's first name is actually Eleanor.) I thought that showed how close my father had been to his sisters, but that was a long time ago, like something from a history book. Then one day in 1956, out of nowhere, they told us that Aunt Eleanor was coming for a visit. An aunt was going to be in our home!

Mom fussed around the house to get it ready, and we bought a new chair for the living room. We finally had something to show off to relatives. The nice house, the new Pontiac. My parents had struggled, but now it was paying off.

Even a young boy couldn't mistake that Aunt Eleanor and Dad were overjoyed to see each other. After he brought her back from the airport, they couldn't stop holding on to each other, and they laughed over almost anything, with Mom giggling. It was the first time I'd seen her really at ease with anyone other than Nannan.

Aunt Eleanor was thirty-four years old, a little taller than Mom and not quite as slim. I thought she was elegant and sophisticated. She kept a slight distance from me and my sisters, as if unsure that it was safe to share what she knew. When we asked what it was like in Boston, she explained that she lived for now in Chicago, for her work.

"What is Aunt Mary like?" I asked.

My aunt said, "Mary has two children; she stays home with them."

"What about the children, what do they do?"

"Oh, they go to school."

"What are their names?"

"Bill and Mary."

"Do they ever ask about us?"

It was less a conversation than a kid trying to ask reasonable questions about his relatives and being told politely not to ask. So I stopped, and Mary and I told Aunt Eleanor about our lives instead. We showed her Goodyear Creek behind our house, and told her about our vacation in Mexico and about the burro and my broken wrist. She was sympathetic and seemed sincerely pleased to look at our schoolwork, though Mary's was more impressive than mine.

I had the sense that Aunt Eleanor was having real conversations with Mom and Dad when we children were out of the room, their voices lowered. They were saying things that seemed private, which was disconcerting. But we didn't think it was strange, because we didn't know what a relative's visit was supposed to be like. Nor did it seem unusual that Aunt Eleanor wouldn't tell us much about Dad's family—after all, Dad wouldn't either. We just had that kind of family, I thought.

After two days, Eleanor said it was time to go back to her job, and she was gone. We all talked about her for a while after she left. Then it was like before, when we didn't have any relatives so we didn't miss them.

OUR FAMILY WAS on the upswing. We felt lighter about money. Dad spent more evenings and weekends at home, though he still went to Harlingen at times. The biggest difference was with Mom, who stopped wandering off into her worries. She wasn't as nervous; she seemed more present, more with us. She could relax even if Dad was still out working after dark. She ate normally and was proud of gaining weight.

Looking back, I see that two things had happened. First, my parents became more confident about not being caught by whatever was chasing them. We could hide and still live an acceptable life while dreaming for more. And second, most of the time Dad's business was going well.

Even school was better. My tuition envelope had cash in it every month. The school got a used Blue Bird bus, saving Mom the trip. There were more desks in the classrooms, so all the students had their own.

For a while, there were good reasons to believe we were safe, again.

SIX

HE WAS NONDESCRIPT, with a face you'd never remember, just an ordinary man sitting a few rows in front of us at the Sam Houston Coliseum. But my father caught him staring shortly after we sat down.

For my tenth birthday we'd gone to the Houston Fat Stock Show and Rodeo, just my father and me. Trying to look Texan, Dad wore cowboy boots and a white, wide-brimmed Stetson hat. Mom bought me a cowboy shirt with black and white squares and white fringe hanging down in front.

We walked into the strong smell of cattle and horses, our feet crunching over the sawdust around the livestock pens. Dad nodded toward a girl with a red sash across her chest that said FUTURE FARMERS OF AMERICA, LUFKIN. She was pulling a black-and-white calf on a rope, smiling so big I knew she'd won a prize.

We'd arrived early to stand in line to meet Roy Rogers and Dale Evans, the rodeo's big attraction. For a boy growing up in Houston in the 1950s, Roy Rogers, the King of the Cowboys, and Dale Evans, the Queen of the West, were heroes. It seemed that their life in the movies and on TV was their real life. Saccharine and homey, beloved for their showmanship and their ease with Bible verses, they reflected a time when parents and children still shared the same icons.

Dad and I went to the end of a weaving column at the rear of the auditorium, with the kids who couldn't hold back bunching up in front. Roy and Dale looked as if they'd jumped off the screen at the Grand Theater. He was tanned and crinkly. She was permed and glamorous, with a wide smile, except that I could tell she wore face powder. As kids reached the head of the line, Roy called them "buckaroos" and autographed their rodeo programs. Just before it was our turn, a man called out that Roy and Dale had to leave. They waved goodbye to the line with their big star smiles and popped behind a yellow door so quickly that it seemed they had disappeared by magic. Someone put up a sign on a tripod: ROY AND DALE ARE FEEDING TRIGGER. SEE YOU AT THE RODEO.

Dad was disappointed for me, but we talked about how great it was going to be to see all the lights flashing off the sparkles on Roy's shirt when he jumped on old Trigger—the Smartest Horse in the Movies—and galloped 'round the ring.

The show began with a stream of high school bands high-stepping with their polished horns and drums, the tassels on their white boots slapping up and down. The coliseum went dark, with spotlights on the bands: red, white, and blue. Next, the announcer introduced the Salt Grass Trail Riders. They had formed up in a field in the middle of Texas and then ridden for days, camping out at night along the trail once used to bring cattle to market in Houston. The announcer said they'd followed the path of history to ride to the opening of the fat stock show.

When the riders entered the ring, the lights went up to shine on their American and Texan flags, waving from poles stuck in pockets on their stirrups. They wore scarred leather chaps, like trail hands beat up from the ride, even the ones with shiny silver cowboy buckles the size of stop signs. The crowd let out yells that made the horses jump and twist their necks and bolt from the line. The riders made a big show of yanking their reins to get their mounts back in place.

And then, all of a sudden, Dad said we had to go. Right away.

"Not yet!" I said. "Why?"

He said, "It's nothing, Michael, just time to go, that's all."

"But we just got here. We haven't seen any bronco riding! What about Roy Rogers jumping on Trigger?" I was really upset, but Dad said I had to be quiet. So I was. When the lights had come on, he said, he'd noticed a man a few rows in front turning around and looking back at us. He pointed with his eyes toward a seat to our right. He didn't like the way the man was looking at us, and so we'd better go.

There wasn't anybody looking at us, not that I could see. The man Dad had pointed out looked like everybody else. And, like everybody else, he was watching the Salt Grass Trail Riders down in the ring. Some of the horses had reared up to walk on their back legs while their riders waved their hats over their heads and gave big cowboy yells for the people in the seats.

"We don't have time to talk about this," Dad said. "I don't know who that fellow is, but he recognized me and I don't want to talk to him now. We don't want a problem."

I thought of Laredo, and the time Mom got so scared when the policeman came by the house. And then about leaving home all of a sudden and going to Miss Mason's. Maybe the man *had* looked at us and I didn't see him. I thought, *We can't take a chance with our secret.* I said, "Yes, sir." That was all that was left to say. Whatever our trouble was, it could find us anywhere. My father was the most substantial person I knew, and if this harmless-looking man could throw him into a panic, something must be very wrong. Dad's panic was contagious.

Still, I was angry. I felt cheated. It wasn't fair that we had to leave, but fair was for some other time.

As the band played "The Yellow Rose of Texas," the people around us clapped and whooped and sang along with the Salt Grass Trail Riders. Their communal revelry echoed off the coliseum's wooden ceiling and rolled back over the stands. But Dad and I stepped sideways out of our row. We slipped up the aisle to the rear of the coliseum, where it was darkest, and down a back way. I could hear the band playing a new number as we got in our car and drove out of the lot.

ONE SATURDAY MORNING, maybe six months after the rodeo, Dad said, "Do you want to come with me on some sales calls?" Sales calls were the foundation of Dad's business, the meetings that could lead to those things he called "deals," which we needed for money and to fuel our plans. I wanted to see how they worked. Even more, I wanted to be with my father and see where he went when he left us.

We were in our new blue Buick Roadmaster convertible, with its shiny emblem on the hood and four chrome vents on either side: the best car on the road. Dad was doing well enough that Mr. Gale had bought the car for him to replace the Pontiac. The top was down as Dad lit his cigar, then leaned back into the seat. A breeze slipped over the windshield. I looked up at the sky, relaxing in the sun and in my father's world of work. He glanced over at me, his right elbow on the seat back. Then he brought me closer to his side—and told me something about the troubles from his past that he still carried.

In that moment, Dad revealed something that stuck with me; I knew it was important, though I didn't know why. It was something meant to guide my future and to justify how he earned his living. For the first time, he told me about Boston. He said, "When the Irish went to Boston, no one wanted them. Absolutely no one wanted them unless they could work like donkeys and not ask questions. People used to say the perfect Irishman had a size-fourteen neck and a size-four hat—strong and stupid."

He told me how he used to work like a donkey, too. He used to drive a truck and run a steam shovel. "But people who work like that do not have a future," he said, a lesson in his voice.

"What do you mean?" I asked. "Everyone has a future. The future is what's coming."

Dad looked at me soberly. "No, to have a real future you have to be able to control what's coming. The future will come to you, that's right, but the trick is to make sure it's a good future. Some people just wait for what's in store for them. The trick is to decide for yourself. Don't let the others decide what your life will be."

I knew he was talking about me, about how to be when I got older, but he was talking about himself, too. I thought, *He doesn't drive a truck these days. It doesn't seem like he ever could have.*

We flashed through the Washburn Tunnel, the wide lights above moving so fast that they melted together if I squinted my eyes. In a town called Pasadena, we went into a poor neighborhood with no sidewalks and houses like flat boxes, like where we used to live in Jacinto City. Now we had our own house; we had a future. I knew that Dad's work had made the difference for us.

My father drove up and down the streets, looking at the houses, not saying a word. Then he found what he wanted and parked off the street, where the grass grew down into the ditch. "This is a good place to start," he said. "Kids in the yards, people will be needing an extra room. Some people want new siding on their homes, some people need a new roof. Whatever it is, I'm not selling them anything they don't need. I'm a man who helps them get what they want."

This job was only a step along the way to more for us, he said. He was selling home improvements because he could do that well, but he had a much bigger plan: to build many new houses in a subdivision he'd name Lincoln Cedars. It was going to be in Cedar Bayou, near our home. He had partners to invest in his idea. They had started the company already. He was the construction expert. "It will grow," he said. "Just watch." They'd build about twenty homes to start, and by reinvesting the profits they'd soon have more than a hundred. It was what he and Mom had been planning for a long time now. I knew he needed me to believe in it, too, because if he and Mom and I all believed in it, he couldn't fail.

Dad put on his happy look as quickly as a hat, laid his cigar in the ashtray, and swung open the big door as if it were nothing. He looked over at me with a smile and finished his lesson. The most important thing, he said, was to believe in yourself. We walked over to the yellow house across the street so he could start what he called "canvassing."

When the lady at the house came to the screen door, I could tell she didn't like us. She looked straight through us, as if she couldn't find the person she was talking to. I felt like I must have done something wrong, so I looked down. Dad acted as if everything were perfect, as though the lady couldn't have been happier to see this tall man with curly black hair and a mustache, beaming through his eyeglasses, standing in front of her door with a small brown briefcase. Or to see me, a ten-year-old boy with freckles who'd been so excited to spend a day watching his father work. But who was suddenly so embarrassed that he could only stare down at the cracked cement step.

"Afternoon, ma'am," Dad said in his best Texas accent. To sound more authentic, he used his nickname, from his middle name, Jeremiah. "I'm Jerry O'Connor with the folks down at Lincoln Cedars Fine Homes. Maybe you and your husband have been reading about our new program in the *Chronicle*. It's going real well." The lady looked at him blankly, but Dad kept on talking. "I guess maybe you haven't had the time to read about it, with the kids to watch and all. You must be busy with the things a wife has to do these days. We're here in your neighborhood this afternoon looking to find a family that wants to make their home a little nicer. You folks have such a fine start already, but I noticed that part of the roof by the carport there needs a little work, before a small job turns into a big one. We have a special program for the first family in any neighborhood that we help. We always do a little extra on the first job because—you'll appreciate this—it helps show the neighbors the kind of work we do."

The lady frowned and shook her head, not saying a thing. She was rude to treat people like they were some nasty bugs who'd shown up on her front step. Then again, it felt as if we were doing something wrong in the first place.

Dad kept going. "Now, the reason I came to your house first is because it's the prettiest one on the whole street, so I know you folks take a whole lot of pride in it, and we specialize in roof repairs. I'd like to

show you and your husband how our program can take care of that carport for you."

Her husband was not home, she said. There was no need for Dad to
come back one evening to see them both. She had to go. I felt as if we'd
been caught stealing something, but Dad seemed as pleased as ever.
"Thank you, ma'am, glad we could stop by," he said.

We walked a few blocks, with Dad swinging his briefcase and looking
around for someone to say hello to. He saw a couple of kids in a yard
and asked them to show him which house was theirs and if their daddy
was home.

As we walked, I asked him what the *Chronicle* had said about his new
program. He replied that it hadn't said anything, really, but people liked
to hear that it had. I hadn't expected that lying was part of Dad's work,
but the offhand way he explained the lie somehow made it seem acceptable. It was just one of the things grown-ups did. Still, I'd never forget
Dad's ease with manipulating strangers and with justifying it. Maybe it
was what you did when you grew up. Maybe you did it to your family,
too.

Dad looked for whatever the houses needed, changing the truth without a bump. Sometimes we specialized in the latest rustproof gutters,
sometimes in the new asbestos siding—with the color baked right into
it—that kept a house cool on the inside every summer and looking
brand-new on the outside for a lifetime. Sometimes our finest work was
turning a garage into that extra bedroom a growing family could always
use, or screening in a front porch so an older couple could sit out in the
cool evening air with a glass of iced tea and never think about the mosquitoes that were eating up the neighbors.

The first thing, Dad said, was to get in the house. "If you're sitting on
the couch, you're on your way." We did get into a lot of houses, but after
a while the experience became painful. People were nice as long as Dad
talked about nothing, which he could do really well, but they turned cold
as soon as he suggested some construction work.

Dad pulled out pictures of past jobs, showing what the houses looked
like before the work and how beautiful they looked now. He had letters
from customers praising the work crew and how polite they'd been and
how the monthly note to the bank was so much smaller than they ever
thought it would be. But not one person wanted to take advantage of a
free technical drawing and an expert estimate.

Before he started up the Buick for us to leave, Dad looked at me with that here-comes-something-important look. There were three things he wanted me to learn from the day, he said. First, that ordinary people have ordinary jobs and work for somebody else, and we were not ordinary. Second, that the more I believed in myself, the more I could decide my future. And then he said, "You have to keep trying if you want to succeed. I just keep knocking on doors. Sometimes it's the first one, sometimes the fiftieth. I just keep knocking on doors and I know I'm going to sell a job."

I tried to understand the lessons, but I felt tawdry. It was more than Dad's lies; it was the way people had looked at us in their doorways. I was confused. I knew we were honest, my parents and my family. I knew how hard it had been to get the money to send Mary and me to Catholic school so the nuns could teach us how to follow the rules. I wondered if Dad had to pretend he was not doing something wrong so that we could have a good future. If he was pretending, I thought, it must make him feel bad, and I was sorry for him. But I also wondered what it meant for our future.

SEVEN

AFTER THE INCIDENT at the rodeo, which was never mentioned again, we once again seemed to be on the right track. As far as we children could tell, over the next two years, our family was heading straight to the kind of future our parents told us we deserved. The best thing I can say about those twenty-four months is that nothing memorable happened. Dad sold well, and my parents seemed to stop worrying so much about money. Mary and I listened to the nuns repeat their catechism, though I was becoming less convinced by what they said. Life seemed stable and comfortable.

But then a minor traffic accident started a reaction that changed our lives—and the way I viewed my parents—forever. It happened at eleven in the morning, on February 9, 1958, the day after I turned twelve. My sisters and I were riding with Mom on Federal Road in Houston when we collided with a car driven by a man named Marvin Taylor. Both Mom and Taylor said they had the green light. It's hard to know who was at fault because Mom was a nervous driver and Taylor had a bandage over one eye. After the initial impact, Mom swerved into a third car. The only one hurt in our family was Fiona, whose chin hit the dashboard hard enough to leave a small dent. Her bruise soon faded, as did our thoughts of what had happened.

Nearly forty years later, after my mother died, I learned from records in the Harris County Court archives that the driver of the third car, Joyce Josey Meglasson, was less inclined to forget the matter. She filed a lawsuit to cover medical costs for her daughter, repair bills, and compensation for suffering. The case straggled through the court system until a trial date was set for June 1958. The court records show that Mom did not appear.

In fact, we had just moved back to the Villa.

Our parents had told us we were returning to the Villa much as they had told us we were going three years before. The difference this time, they said, was that we were not coming back home.

It began in the afternoon, with Dad coming home early to Mobile Street. He usually drove to the bottom of our hill, where the driveway widened into a gravel parking area, but that day he stopped short, halfway down the slope. He jumped out of the car and crossed the grass toward us. We were watching from our family room with the big windows. He gave us a cheery wave. *He has a surprise,* I thought.

Mom joined us from the kitchen. I could tell she knew about the surprise, because she'd been on the phone with Dad. He came in and clapped his hands and said, "Guess what! We've decided to move to Mexico!"

I was frozen. I looked closely at Dad to see if he was teasing, then over at Mom to see if she'd start laughing at how they'd fooled us so we could all laugh together. But it wasn't a joke. And I wasn't laughing either.

"I don't want to go," I told them. "We are *not* going to go. What do you mean, move to Mexico?"

"Why, back to the Villa," Mom said. "We had so much fun when we were there, remember?"

Even Mary—the good little girl who helped Mom in the kitchen and did her homework just right to please the nuns—resisted. She didn't want to go either. Fiona couldn't understood the disaster yawning before us, because she was only three and a half.

I'd never been what the nuns called a "good boy." I'd resisted their rules, even their right to make the rules. The nuns, like Nannan before them, worried about the kind of man I might become. I ducked my homework and my chores at home. But I had never confronted my parents about the mysterious events in our life.

Now, first I challenged them with logic, a weak weapon in our household. Everything was working out in Houston, I told them, just like we'd always planned. There was no *reason* to leave. Dad was about to start building the Lincoln Cedars houses. It was the worst possible time to go. Besides, I said, how could we go without ever having talked about it? This wasn't *fair.* And what about our house?

Dad grew nervous, as he always did when cornered, and Mom even more so. Then I realized that nothing I said could make a difference, and we were going to leave again. We were just going to do it. Mom said,

"You see, once we're there it's going to be wonderful. Just imagine how your friends wish they could have an adventure like this."

"We're in a hurry," Dad said. "We should move fast and not worry about what we have to leave." He added that we could get everything we needed in the Villa.

How could that be? I thought. *There's nothing in the Villa.* My parents got some boxes and grocery sacks, and we filled them with clothes and kitchen equipment and other things grabbed on the fly. But it was obvious that we were leaving almost everything.

Our collie followed me and Dad back and forth as we loaded the car. "Dad, Dad, what about Prince? Where are we going to put him? We *have* to take Prince." At first Dad was surprised, as if he'd forgotten about our dog. Then he said a friend at the lumberyard was coming later to take Prince to a big ranch near Conroe, where there were two other dogs and big fields to play in. That was the best place for Prince, Dad said, because we couldn't take him with us and he'd be lonely when we were gone. Mom said nothing. She loved Prince, too. So I knew the problem was extremely serious if she agreed to leave him.

In tears, unbelieving, I felt empty, all the way empty. I knew I was letting Prince down, and I knew I couldn't do a thing about it. I'd just have to forget him. I was betraying my dog, but my parents were betraying us all.

Rushing, almost running at the end because we could feel the breath of whatever was chasing us, Dad and I jammed our things into the back of the black-and-white Chevrolet station wagon, leaving just enough room to see over. We had to keep moving quickly to push back thoughts of *why,* because I knew there was no answer to that. *Just keep moving and pretend that everything is normal.*

We did not say goodbyes, but Mom promised to write to Nannan. Prince stood alongside the car as we all got in, poking his skinny face around and wagging his tail. He wondered what we were doing, too.

We headed up the driveway, turned left on Mobile Street, left once more on Uvalde Road. I never saw our house again.

EIGHT

WE RODE SILENTLY, too much in shock for anything Mom and Dad might have said to have an effect. We slipped by the broken white lines on the asphalt, past the cow pastures and across the border, where any worry about the guard posts was smothered by the larger dread of moving to Mexico. It was very late when we reached the Villa. The streetlights were off, and it was hard to see which door was Miss Mason's. In a vain effort at a joke, Dad said, "Babe, I got us this far, but now we're lost."

Miss Mason seemed surprised to see us. *Good,* I thought, *let her be surprised, like the rest of us.* Dad confected some nonsense about how we'd all been missing her delightful hospitality and that he was interested in starting a business in Mexico. He said he'd tried to call to get her a message through the mayor's office, but the phone there was still broken. Miss Mason was a little crabby, but she was glad for our company and for the rent money.

The next day we brought our things inside—it didn't take long—and settled into our two old rooms. None of it seemed real to me. It was like a dream, or a movie, with our parents' fantasy tales for a soundtrack. When I'd seen my father lie to the policeman about our relatives in Texas, or to prospects on a sales call, I took it the way he explained it to me. It wasn't real deceit, just a social lubricant for doing what grown-ups had to do. It was hard on us children, though, when they used the same lubricant on us. When Mom took off with her isn't-this-a-wonderful-adventure spiel, it made us twist our faces to try to reconcile what she was describing with what we were seeing.

We had enough money for Dad to pay sixty dollars for two months' rent in advance, which gave us a sliver of stability. And it helped a little that we were back in the Villa, a place we knew, even if everything seemed broken and forsaken. Miss Mason had made her own home improvement, a toilet in the outhouse. She took Mom and me to the courtyard and pulled hard on the door, which still stuck. "Let me show you how it works," she said. "You just push down on this little silver thing on the back. That's all. Everything goes away."

Miss Mason had an old man called Don Jesús come to fix up our rooms and paint them. He worked very slowly. He said the painting would take a long time because he couldn't find the right brush for blue paint. Dad joked that he felt humble to have a carpenter named Jesús preparing the way for us.

The kids I knew from before came over every morning to look through the window, and this time I was allowed to go out to join them. "You're older now," Dad said. "We think you'll be all right with the kids. Just don't go past the plaza, and let's stay away from the burros." But Mary and Fiona spent most of their time just looking out the window at the street. When it got too hot or too dusty, and Mom closed the doors on the tall windows, my sisters went to the courtyard to look at the well or the chickens. Mary was especially miserable. When she started to cry about leaving all her school friends in Texas and never seeing Nannan again, Mom couldn't stop her. She could only tell my sisters that things would get better, or spin them stories about Robin Hood in the beautiful Sherwood Forest, where children didn't have toys to play with but lived happily ever after.

One day we were sitting on the bed in our parents' room. When Mary began going over her complaints, Mom changed the mood with a long story that ended with a lesson and a hint of the truth about why we were in Mexico. She said, "Now I'm going to tell you something I've never told you before. It is about the war, when the German airplanes were dropping bombs on English cities. We called it the Blitz, and it was so very unsafe for children. The cities were burning every night. Oh, my! People were simply terrified at it all, and they had every right to be frightened.

"It was so dangerous for the children that their mummies and daddies all over England decided to send them to the countryside, to farms and villages like the Villa, where they would be safe. The little children had never been away from their own homes. They wanted to stay on their own streets even though the bombs were falling all through the night.

They were afraid to go to new places and to find new friends. But their parents knew best. Sometimes we can feel afraid in a place that's the best for us. It only takes time to get used to it."

It didn't take long for the children in England to feel better, Mom said. "When the danger was over, they could go home."

Mary said, "Mom, when will we be able to go home again? It must be safe now."

Mom said, "Do you want to know what we taught the little children in England when they were in the countryside far, far from their own homes? Shall I tell you, Mary, and you, Fiona? We taught them to say the magic words *mustn't grumble*. That means we must not complain and feel sorry for ourselves. We must just carry on. And when we carry on, we will see that right around the corner something wonderful is waiting. It's like Tinker Bell, who could fly only if the children believed she could. When the children didn't grumble and believed in magic, then Tinker Bell could fly and she was saved. Wasn't she?"

Mom went on, "If the children in England could live in new places, it's nothing at all for us to live in a wonderfully interesting place like the Villa de Santiago, where we have a courtyard full of fruit trees and even our own chickens. So you see, children, when you feel like complaining, think of the children in the war and say, 'Mustn't grumble.' Those are the magic words."

Fiona tried, but she couldn't quite pronounce them. For Mary and for me, Mom's lesson wasn't much help.

WHEN DAD RETURNED to work selling home improvements, he stuck to the Rio Grande Valley. Three months after we moved, Dad went to Monterrey, about fifty minutes away by car on the bad roads, and returned with the news that Mary and I would be going to the Pan American School of Monterrey, one of the very best schools in the whole country, he said. Glowing with the luck of it, he told us, "A lot of students there go on to the top American universities. It's a private school where all the teaching is in English, and you'll be surprised at how quickly you make new friends."

He'd been fortunate, he said, to convince the school to take us, because it turned out that the records from Our Lady of Fatima had been left behind in a box in Houston. But Mr. Arpee, the director, understood how people can do that sometimes, so he took Dad's word that Mary and I had good grades. "When he sees you, he'll know in a second you're both first-class students," Dad said.

That wasn't how the nuns thought of me, I said to myself.

The next day Dad took us to the school, pumping up its reputation on the way. He wanted to convince himself that we weren't fugitives but rather bold visionaries, charging forward to new success. At first the school looked like all the other big old houses on La Purísima Plaza—"one of the city's most prestigious," as Dad pointed out. The building was brightly white. Across the top of the façade they'd painted the American and Mexican flags, and next to them, in tall black letters PAN AMERICAN SCHOOL.

Maybe this won't be so bad, I thought. We went inside, and it looked all right. Mr. Arpee moved like a very busy man, like the Mother Superior at Our Lady of Fatima, except that Mr. Arpee wore a short-sleeved white shirt and a tie. Instead of crosses or Blessed Virgins, the walls in his office had pictures of men with long rifles, standing over dead animals. *I'd better not tell Mom,* I thought.

Dad talked to Mr. Arpee about our tuition, and Mr. Arpee decided that we could start school immediately as long as we paid soon for the whole year. Dad explained that he was waiting for checks from his new bank. "Change banks, wait for service," he said in a tone that implied that any businessman, like Mr. Arpee, would understand. I'm not sure Mr. Arpee believed him any more than I did, but he let us stay.

Dad picked us up after school and asked a lady in the office how we could get there from the Villa by bus. Seeming surprised, she told us that we'd have to transfer downtown to get to the plaza across from the school. In the afternoon we'd have to transfer in reverse. Dad nodded at the lady. "Sounds easy," he said.

"What if we get lost?" I interrupted. "How will we talk to anybody to find our way?"

"Well, we'll just go out now and scout out the whole thing, like a military operation. You'll be the commanding officer, starting tomorrow." The lady seemed to agree with me, but she gave us student cards to save on the bus fare.

"This is going to be easier than you think, Michael," Dad told me back in the car. I doubted that. We found the corner of Padre Mier and General Zuazua streets, where we'd have to change buses. It was in the oldest part of town, crowded and noisy, and it looked as if there were a thousand buses to choose from. But Dad kept repeating what the lady had said: "In the morning, you get off the bus from the Villa at the Farmacia Benavides, a drugstore—just look out for the blue-and-white sign that says FARMACIA BENAVIDES. Then get on a bus that's painted purple. It goes to La Purísima Plaza. In the afternoon come back to the same corner and take a dark green bus to the Villa, only sometimes the buses are yellow and green." Dad seemed surer of this plan than the lady had been.

Back at Miss Mason's, Dad told Mom it was all worked out. When he had to go back to the States to work, she could stay in the Villa and we could get to school. Miss Mason wrote out two notes for me in Spanish, one for the morning to tell the people we were going to La Purísima Plaza, and one for the afternoon to say we wanted to go to the Villa. Both notes had the telephone number for the Pan American School because the phone in the mayor's office was still broken.

In the morning, Mom and Fiona took us down the hill to the paved road. "Now, Michael, remember, do just as your father told you." Mom seemed nervous. "You are to look after your little sister. Here's fifty centavos for this morning; now put it in your front pocket. Here's the morning note. Here's another fifty centavos and the afternoon note. You stay with your sister when you're not in class."

"Yes, ma'am, I will. It'll be okay." No matter how worried I might be, I knew that it was up to me to spare Mom from worry. By then I'd come to sense that I was the stronger one, the one responsible. The one who needed to protect her.

"Good, Michael," she said.

A dark green bus was coming, with sacks of corn and watermelons piled on the roof. Mom said, "Michael, put up your arm as we've seen people do, and stop the bus." Then she took Fiona's hand and stood back to watch. I stuck out my arm, and the bus stopped. I felt like a giant. The driver gave us a funny look: *Whatever are you doing here?* If I'd known Spanish, I still couldn't have told him. He wore a cowboy hat and huaraches, with a big knife handle of carved bone coming out of a leather scabbard on his belt. Mary started backing down the steps, so I leaned over and whispered, "It's okay. He's just a farmer driving a bus. He won't do anything." I was whispering because it was embarrassing to be so different in a bus full of people who must have been wondering the same thing as the driver.

I moved Mary by her shoulders into the crowd standing in the aisle. We were pushed into them when the bus sped up, then into the people

sitting down when it went around a bend. We both acted as if there were
nothing strange about two blond-haired American kids holding lunch
bags on a bus full of people carrying babies, chickens, and machetes. But
anyone reading our eyes would have known how panicked and bewildered we were.

A guy came toward us collecting money and handing out transfers,
which we needed for the next bus. I showed the man the two student
cards and gave him the fifty centavos for the morning tickets. He was trying to tell me something we couldn't understand. Then a man in a seat
told us something, and another man, too. The driver stopped the bus and
came back to tell us. Everything was stopped, and a small crowd was
speaking to us in Spanish, pushing their faces close to ours. Finally the
driver pulled out a coin and said, "Más, más."

"No, no," I told him.

"¿No? Bueno," the conductor said. But he didn't give me the transfers
for the purple bus. I pointed to the transfers, stapled together in a little
stack. All he had to do was tear off two for us, as he had for everyone
else. But he said, "¡No!"

It took about an hour to get downtown, with all the stops and the
traffic and confusion. We looked hard for the Farmacia Benavides sign as
the buildings got denser and taller and people crowded into the streets. I
tried to look around the people standing in front of me, to see through
the windshield. I saw the sign and pulled the cord just in time. The bus
stopped.

As we pushed through to get out, avoiding people's eyes, it felt like
everyone thought we had done something wrong just by being there. I
thought we must have, too. I just didn't know what it was.

Out on the street, I took a breath. The buses, packed tight inside and
packed close together, dominated everything. Most had no mufflers.
Their roars bounced off the building fronts as bluish exhaust smoke rose
from the street. There were people everywhere, crowding the sidewalks
and the street in between the buses, and every one of them seemed to be
staring at me and Mary. I took her hand and backed up to a building to
rest. A purple bus went by; I hadn't seen it in time. Before the next one
had a chance, I was out in the street with my arm up. We got in, and it
drove off. Okay, we did it.

I went into my pocket for the money, but I couldn't find it. I felt
around and pulled the whole pocket out: nothing. Not the notes, or the

extra peso Dad had given me, just in case, or the fifty centavos we'd need that afternoon. Up to that point, the driver hadn't looked at me. What was I going to say? When the driver spoke to me, and I looked back at him with nothing in my hand, he seemed disgusted. He stopped the bus and opened the door. "Mary," I said, "we have to get off for a minute. We'll take the next one."

I told her I'd lost the money and the notes, too. She reminded me that I was in charge. "Michael, what will we ever do now? Where is the school? Where are we?"

I walked up to a man on the corner—waiting for a bus, I supposed. My hand went out toward him; I wanted him to put something in it. He looked blankly at my hand. I suppose that he'd never seen a blue-eyed beggar wearing his best clothes for his first day at his new school, with his cowlick stuck down with Brylcreem, with the responsibility to get his sister—that little girl with her face pointing toward the ground, so no one would see her—to school and not disappoint his parents. The man said something and shook his head.

I felt ashamed. Overwhelmed, too, but quite ashamed. But I knew I had to do something. I followed my hand to other people. I can't remember how many shook their heads, but it took a long time before one man finally gave me a peso.

A purple bus came, and Mary and I stepped in among the people, weaving in the packed aisle. It was like a tunnel, with everything black around us except for what I could see straight ahead of me, down the long nose of the bus. Mary was whispering something. She was afraid, pulling at me, but I didn't care. There were other people looking at us and talking, and I didn't care about them either. If we missed La Purísima Plaza, I thought, I didn't know what we'd do. There wasn't enough left inside me if we missed the plaza.

And suddenly it was there, on the left.

The lady in the school office wanted to know why we were so late. I was breathing hard, in and out. I said, "The man on the bus saw our student cards, but he wanted more money. He didn't give me the papers we needed for the purple bus."

The lady said, "I bet I know why—he didn't think that two Americans could be students in Mexico. I'll give you a note with a stamp on it for next time."

"There's another problem, a small problem." I didn't want to show

how stupid I was, but I had to get some money to go home. "I lost the rest of the money for the bus. May I please borrow the money until tomorrow?"

She looked at these two miserable children with no future and said, with pity, "Of course."

AT NIGHT IN bed, after the streetlights went off and the people sat talking on the dark sidewalk, I lay thinking that I'd done okay, even though I'd lost the money and the notes. I began to learn something that day: that I could be smart enough to get away on my own if something bad ever happened to my parents or they were taken from me.

NINE

IF I TURNED LEFT out of Miss Mason's, the very next door was the one to Pepe Cirilo's barbershop. Usually it was full of men reading the newspaper and listening to the radio, or just sitting and talking. Every day when I arrived, people acted as if they'd been waiting for me. They helped me learn Spanish and taught me about farming and sugarcane. They talked about ordinary things, too, as though I were one of them. Pepe's drew me in, I suppose, because it was the first place where I existed apart from my family's mystery and strange ways. None of the men at the barbershop seemed to care about what made the O'Connors different.

There was no barber pole at Pepe's. Everybody in the Villa knew it was there. At busy times there might be burros and an oxcart out front. One man usually came on his bicycle, which made people wonder about him because men were supposed to walk or ride an animal.

Pepe was only twenty, much younger than most of the loiterers who sat around his shop, but he ruled the room with his sharp tongue. The men feared becoming targets but couldn't stand to miss what he might say about others. (Fortunately, as a twelve-year-old and a foreigner, I was exempt from Pepe's shots.)

In Pepe's youth, his father had told him he was too stupid to stay in school and would have to find a job. Pepe agreed because people in the Villa accepted that life wasn't fair. He started by sweeping out the Villa's other barbershop, on the far side of the plaza, and over time learned to cut hair. He had wanted to go to school instead. "That's life," he said. "*Ni modo. Así es la vida.*" You can't do anything about it. The only way you escape life is when you die. Pepe's view was precisely opposite that of my father, who insisted that your life—"your future," as he put it—

was always up to you. I found Pepe's fatalism sad but something to try to understand.

When we'd first come to the Villa, Pepe worked with hand clippers. By the time we moved back there, he'd saved enough for electric ones. Haircuts cost one peso, eight cents American. If a man had some extra money, he'd get a shave, too, though people with that much money were on the other side of the line for Pepe. There might be some good ones over there, but they'd have to prove it first.

One day he showed me his shaving technique. The man lying back in the chair had money, and you could tell from the way Pepe talked to him that he didn't like him. Flourishing his razor, Pepe treated the customer like a mannequin, flipping the hot towels on the man's face, pulling them off slowly when he flinched. Pepe told me, "I use hot water to clean them up—some people don't ever have water and soap on their face unless it's here in my chair. Then the cream and the talcum. The talcum is so they think they look nice. The cream smells like perfume, so they don't forget how nice they look."

Pepe finished the shave with alcohol and water for the razor nicks. He put a splash of alcohol in the cup of his hand and added water in varying proportions. Since he didn't like the man with money, the alcohol-water ratio skewed in favor of pain. The man went suddenly stiff, except for a shudder through his shoulders. Pepe told him, "A man like you doesn't even know what pain is. Pain is like a bird singing in a tree. A man like you hears the bird, but it means nothing. The man knows that anything that is good must hurt."

Pepe decorated his shop with pictures that reminded me of Nannan's house, one with Jesus looking heavenward and another a calendar with the Virgin of Guadalupe. Pepe told me it was good to have those pictures because you never knew how things might work out. One day you could need the help.

Gradually I came to feel comfortable in the Villa. There were still cows on the street and bugs in our bedroom, but I was used to that. From Tom Sawyer and Huck Finn, I knew that great adventures could be strung through common things. And without realizing it, I began to develop the tools of a foreign correspondent, the journalist who must absorb strange cultures. I could not figure out our life, but I began to understand how the Villa worked.

My sisters and I picked up Spanish quickly from the children on our street. Mary often stayed by the window after school and talked to them as they came by, but I went to the plaza and sometimes to the creek. I didn't tell Mom and Dad about the creek, or about the factory with machines tied by long, looping leather belts to an overhead driveshaft, which was turned by a waterwheel: power from the early industrial revolution. The workers took me into their group and showed me how they made wrought-iron benches for the plaza and small mills to grind corn for tortillas or tall ones for the sugarcane.

Though the Villa was a small place, it had the substance of centuries. People set their cooking fires and shucked their corn in the same spots as had streams of their ancestors. They were a mix of the dismally poor and the moderately impoverished, and most believed their standing would never change, no matter what they did. My family, by contrast, was just passing through. We'd be moving on and up. The people took that as a given, also. It was life. Some people were lucky, others were from the Villa.

The Villa was highly clannish, to the point where people might not trust someone born half an hour's walk away. Yet when it came to us, the *Americanos*, they were fascinated by our differences, and they took us in.

Before long, Mary, Fiona, and I found patterns in what had once seemed chaos. At first light we could hear the pigeons cooing from the tiled roofs and the chickens scratching for breakfast in the backyards. Soon it was time for the oxcarts creaking by our window, the skinny men in dirty shirts who steered their beasts by tapping their necks with sticks the size of broom handles. The carts strained under loads of sugarcane, or white bags of corn from the fields nearby, or firewood from the mountain overlooking the Villa. The men grunted words that only their animals could understand. I'd sometimes wake to the smell of the grass the oxen still chewed from breakfast, or the mud on their legs if they'd crossed a stream coming from the farm.

There were burros, too. We were friends again, though I was glad to stay off their backs. The men with the burros talked to them, too, with clicking noises and the periodic *"¡Andale, burro!"*

The fires started in the kitchens. We'd hear the echoing *clunk* from a log being split, then smell the smoke, then hear the *clap, clap, clap* when someone's mother took a ball of corn masa and slapped her hands together to make a tortilla.

We learned it was midday from the church bells. The streets emptied

as people drew away for lunch and then a siesta to escape the sun. In
the afternoon, butterflies played near Miss Mason's well and on the
bougainvilleas.

At night, lying on the thin mattress across the ropes in my bed, I
swished the mosquitoes away, but it wasn't as bad as when we'd come
the first time. It didn't feel so bad, anyway.

I wandered the Villa's few streets and discovered its past was in people's minds, not in books, where I had thought history always was. The
history of the Villa, spoken on plaza benches and at meals over clay
plates on planks in homes with low ceilings, drifted around honorable
moments in the long past. Honorable, but bloody. And told about people who endured oppression for a very long time, and then flashed violently in response.

The earliest distinction came from Simón Montemayor, a son of the
Villa who, in 1867, was in the firing squad that sent bullets from smooth-
bore rifles in a cluster into the chest of Emperor Maximilian, a foreigner
imposed on Mexico by France. The old men in the plaza pointed to my
bony sternum and said, "Right through his chest, Maico, and out the
back of his long black coat that went all the way to his boots, like this,
on a hill outside Querétaro." It was a story that gave lift to even those
who doubted it. Then, in 1913, the valiant troops of President Madero,
with their long rifles and wide-brimmed hats, homespun white shirts and
pants, and drooping bandoliers, were quartered in the Villa, officers in
the church, when they fought the mutinous soldiers supported by the
American ambassador. Then the president, Madero, honest, and a man
of his people, born in Coahuila, the next state, was executed by reac-
tionary officers with the ambassador's complicity, the son of a bitch.

Life in the Villa hadn't changed much since the nineteenth century, except for bus service to Monterrey and Don Teófilo's modern hand-crank
blacksmiths' blower and the fragile, unreliable web of electric wires
looping between houses and hung here and there with green-gray moss.
There was also the white sheet dropped every couple of months from a
mast leaned against a brace by a traveling troupe, in the opening between
the church and city hall. They sprayed the sheet with cracked, jerking images of singing charros and comedies of Cantinflas from a projector run
off a gasoline generator while we in the audience laughed, rocking on the
wooden folding chairs and batting mosquitoes.

It was as Mom had promised; we got used to the Villa. Even the bus
rides, which were more instructive than school, became familiar. As the

other passengers got to know us, we'd say hello every morning, and they helped us when our Spanish failed. We didn't grumble, as Mom had told us not to.

If I left Miss Mason's and turned right and went down the street in front of the house, Juárez Street, I could get to the plaza in less than five minutes unless I stopped to talk to someone along the way. At the plaza, I would meet up with Oscar, José, and Luisito for baseball or soccer. Sometimes the boys would ask me what it was like in Texas, that distant, intimidating place where they might swim the river one day to come home with boots instead of huaraches, and new jeans, and a few dollars from a harvest. Unless, that is, the INS got them on the other side, or the Mexican police stole their money on the way home.

PEPE HAD STRONG opinions about everyone. I remember the day he opened up on Doña Eulalia and Don Octaviano, whose daughter, Mirtala, was a friend of mine. They lived next door to us, on the other side from Pepe's. They had one of the Villa's two television sets. (The mayor had the other one.) Doña Eulalia put theirs in the living room, with the screen facing the window, so that anyone walking by could see what she had on. She told me, "Maico, it's the way we are here, so far from God that we share what we have." But Pepe saw it differently: "Some people think the only reason to have something is to show it off to people who don't have anything."

Every night people arranged their chairs in U-shaped rows on the sidewalk and into the street to look through Doña Eulalia's window bars and watch the television. Kids climbed on the tops of the bars to take turns hanging off upside down, like monkeys.

If too many people crowded around, Don Octaviano came out to yell and push the chairs about to make room for the transmission. "That damn transmission comes all the way from Monterrey," he said. "You know how far that is, so give it some damn space." He warned that anyone blocking the transmission could lose their hair—that there was a family in Allende that was bald from transmissions, the whole family. When Don Fidencio told Don Octaviano that the transmission actually came to the antenna in the tree in the courtyard, Don Octaviano called him an *idiota*.

Telling her husband to stop scaring people, Doña Eulalia went around selling homemade Popsicles. She also had one of two refrigerators in the Villa. The butcher shop had the other one, but they'd stopped using it because people complained that the meat didn't taste the same as when it hung from pegs in the open, where it got a fine glaze of dust and flies. Doña Eulalia said that everyone should buy at least one Popsicle a night because even a burro knew that the more people there are watching a television, the faster it will be used up. She'd need the money to replace it.

As it turned out, all of Don Octaviano's wealth and status could not save him from his enemies. Late one night we woke up to Doña Eulalia's moans from over the courtyard wall: *"Mi vida. Mi vida. ¿Qué te han hecho?"* Not waiting for my parents or sisters, I ran through the house and into the street to find Don Octaviano's red-and-yellow pickup parked in front of their door, not in the back as usual. The passenger door was open, and a bloody smear trailed from the bed of the truck and across the sidewalk into the house. I followed the trail into the living room, and there lay Don Octaviano. He looked okay at first, as if he'd decided to take off his shirt, lie down, and stare at the ceiling for a while. But then I noticed the three cotton balls. The cotton was turning red, and I saw he'd been shot twice in the belly and once in the face. There was so much sadness in the house that I knew he must be dead.

People stayed with the family almost till dawn, when we heard that two men had been arrested. We ran down to the mayor's office in the plaza to wait for the police to bring them in. About twenty people collected, becoming more and more angry as they drank mescal and talked revenge. Some of them began arguing about why any bastard would want to kill Don Octaviano. It turned out that there were a lot of reasons to argue.

Two police officers rolled up in a Jeep, with two men hunched over in the back. With their white homespun shirts and baggy pants, they looked like they were from the mountain above the Villa. Everyone ran toward the Jeep, but the police commanded us to stay back. One pulled out a long pistol, holding it along his right leg.

"You can't protect those bastards!" the mob shouted. "Give them to us!"

A cop said casually, "Oh, you think these are the ones who killed Don Octaviano? These are just two sons of bitches from the mountain, just two dirty peasants who will help the investigation." I thought he was lying, but he probably saved those men's lives.

To show how thorough their "investigation" would be, the officers began slapping the prisoners, then rapping them on the head with their pistols. "You pieces of shit, you're going to tell everything, right?" they threatened. The crowd calmed down. It was late, and some were too drunk to stand without weaving. It was time to go home.

The next day we went to give Doña Eulalia our condolences before the Mass. Mom tried to say something in Spanish, but it came out fractured.

When someone died in the Villa, people said he went to see the poplar trees—*"Se fue a ver los álamos"*—because poplars lined the road to the cemetery. As I joined the funeral procession, the road was so full of holes that I thought Don Octaviano's coffin would bounce out the back of the black station wagon, right in front of the family. But the driver slowed and finally turned left through the tall iron gates in the stone wall. The custodian closed the gates quickly and stood guard to keep everyone out, except for the two police officers and the doctor and the priest.

Then came the sound of sawing. Pepe explained, "They're looking for the bullet that stayed in his head, pretending they're doing an investigation. It won't hurt as much this time as it did on the mountain." He meant when Don Octaviano was shot.

People got upset about waiting outside so long, but they had to be careful not to say anything that Don Octaviano's family could hear. A man said it was stupid to build the gate so high in the wall. He was angry because the priest said the gate was designed to protect us by keeping devils inside the cemetery. "That's okay," the man said, "but the gate is twice as high as the wall. How does any priest think that he's going to keep a devil inside with that gate? Devils are not stupid—you think a devil won't just jump over the wall? He'll be in my house in five minutes and the priest will be safe, sleeping on holy ground next to the church."

That started an argument with people who insisted that the cemetery was one of the best parts about life in the Villa. At least you got buried in the shade, under the poplars. A lady said, "If you don't think that's important, go get buried in El Cercado. They don't have even one tree. How do you think you're going to rest in peace for ten thousand years with the sun blasting in your face? Don't be stupid!"

That was something to think about, and it stopped the complaints.

Once we got inside, the service was short, and everyone was glad because the tension from the crime had worn us out. Afterward, I walked around the cemetery with Ricardo the medical student, Doña Eva's son. That walk helped me understand that the Villa was a kind of family, even if the people argued and gossiped and sometimes killed one another. There were only a handful of names on the gravestones—Cavazos, Alanís, Cepeda, García, Tamez, Cirilo, and some others—and I knew them all already. The same families had been in the Villa from the time the church was built, more than two hundred years before. Ricardo said, "If you are from here, you will stay here. Even if you leave, you take the rest of us with you and we will be here when you come back. That's the way it is." He pointed to the headstones and said, "Neighbors at home, neighbors down here."

That's what made my family different, I thought. When we left somewhere, we were supposed to forget where we came from. We had no place to return to. We had only our future to hang on to, and sometimes that wasn't enough.

A MUCH BIGGER group than usual jammed Pepe's barbershop the next day, and everyone wanted to talk about Don Octaviano. The men tried to impress one another with new theories, until Don Fidencio popped out exactly the kind of observation that made people respect him. "Well, it looks like no one has told any of you about the California license plates on a car," he said. Then he sat back. His words hung in front of us, still sounding. Everything stopped.

Some people in the Villa had never been in a car. In trucks, yes, in the back, on the way to work someone else's fields. Or in buses to Monterrey, a place so removed—so full of venal power, more a dark idea than a city—that people just called it *La Capital*. In the Villa, most people didn't even have a friend with a car. To know about a car with license plates, from that place called California, made Don Fidencio the most important man in the barbershop.

Don Fidencio went back to a story we all knew, about the tragedy of the stolen water: A man from Mexico City came a few years before to look around the mountain. He had a thing like a telescope, only he pointed it flat and looked at the land, then wrote things in his book. They called him "the professor." Later, two friendly men came to look at the land records in the mayor's office. Later still, some people discovered that sections of their land had been transferred to yet another stranger, who sold it to a company that took the water from farms around the Villa and sent it in tall cement pipes to the new factories in Monterrey.

Whenever someone told this story, Pepe always reminded us that he had warned the whole Villa not to trust those two men who checked the land records. Interrupting Don Fidencio, he said, "Those bastards from the outside invited everyone in the cantina to drink beer. I knew they were betraying us, and I said it then: We should have taken them out of the cantina and hanged them in the plaza. Who comes here to buy beer for us? Who are the people from the outside we can trust?" He looked at me quickly and said, "I don't mean you, Maico, you're one of us now. It's too late for you."

Don Fidencio said, "Well, who was working as a judge when those two men were here? Wasn't it Octaviano?"

Arguments ensued. People couldn't agree on exactly when the two traitor bastards had come or exactly when Don Octaviano had been a judge. But everyone agreed that he had been a judge in city hall sometime, and that the men had been there, too, sometime. "So," Don Fidencio said, "someone had to help those men find the records. You can't find anything there without help. What I hear is that Octaviano worked with them."

Don Fidencio leaned back again, legs splayed out, as if he'd finished a chapter in his story. After a few moments, he hunched forward, and everyone went quiet. "Some people say certain things," he went on. "They say with the changes in the books, there was a family that lost its good lands and Octaviano got them. The sons of this family considered they had no future here without those lands. Two of them went to work in California, in the fields."

Don Fidencio was now tracing a history that the people of the Villa felt they lived every day: of crime, and treachery, and most of all, injustice. Pepe said that this was the way life was, but I knew he didn't think it was the way life was supposed to be. If Don Octaviano had conspired in this land fraud, then the men wanted to believe he'd paid, even if Don Octaviano lived two doors away and we all watched the television through his window. It would be proper vengeance. It would also be a warning, a thin tissue of protection for others in the Villa.

Don Fidencio went on slowly, "Two nights ago, when they killed Octaviano up there, people saw that car from California go up the mountain with two men. Now it's gone; also the men. They escaped."

Silence. But I could see that people were glad the men got away. I knew that killing Don Octaviano was wrong, a mortal sin. I thought about the night he died, about him lying on the floor, looking up, with the three tufts of reddening cotton in him. I thought about Doña Eulalia and Mirtala, my friend. Why should they hurt so much? That wasn't right. But I also knew there was no fairness for poor people in the Villa, like those who'd lost their land. And though I was only twelve years old and an outsider, it seemed me that they had a right to some kind of justice. If the only way to get it was killing Don Octaviano, then maybe they had a right to that. I felt that. Then I felt awful for feeling it, but I couldn't help myself. The Villa had seeped into me.

TEN

THE POST OFFICE in the Villa was big enough for the clerk—on a chair, between the slim counter and the shelves that climbed the back wall— and two visitors, standing. A third person could fit in there, too, if he kept half his body outside and one foot on the sidewalk.

As life in the Villa was less daunting and instead became the adventure Mom and Dad had promised, my parents changed their story. Now our move represented an entrepreneurial opportunity, an intriguing future in the export business. Over time, the nature of that opportunity would shift, from specialty ceramic tiles to slabs of a local, marblelike stone for building façades in Texas. Each brilliant idea was replaced with an even better one as Dad researched its market potential. Finally, he decided that the real payoff was in tourism, Mexico's biggest business with the United States.

Roughly six weeks after Don Octaviano's murder, Dad drove us all around the flatland on the other side of the one-and-a-half-lane high-way—through the sugarcane fields, where the government was building a large dam to store water for Monterrey's factories. He pointed out adjacent land that would be extremely valuable one day. He was going to find investors to buy a tract on the future lakeshore, to be ready for the thousands of Americans who surely would come.

"It's going to be unbelievable here," Dad told us. "I don't know how we managed to find this place at exactly the right time—it must be my keen sense of business." That was a joke on himself, because by then we all knew he had trouble translating his ideas into profits. He would say, "I deal in the big picture. Details, I leave for others."

Dad's plan was to build a hotel for large groups of Americans who wanted to be in exotic places but were reluctant to come by themselves.

Take the schoolteachers' union in Chicago as an example, he said. "Say a hundred and fifty of them get on a plane together in Chicago, fly to Monterrey, and stay here at the lake for ten days. They'll be in a foreign country with people they know. They will love it." Best of all, the plan included permanent quarters for us at the hotel, which gave us hope escaping Miss Mason's someday.

Then one day, in talking about his plan, my father said something that opened a tiny window to our past. I couldn't fully understand it at the time, though I remembered it clearly because it felt important. He said the hotel would be the place that his family in Boston could come to visit us. That was strange. We knew hardly anything about his family back in the States, except for that flash of a visit from Aunt Eleanor. Suddenly Dad was talking as if there were many other relatives, though he didn't elaborate and I didn't pry for more details.

The hotel would take a little more time, Mom told us later: "The people Dad knows in Texas don't understand what a good idea it is, so he's having just a little trouble getting them to lend him money." While he worked on the financing for this extraordinary project that would bring us wealth and stability, Dad stayed in Texas most of the time, selling construction jobs in the Rio Grande Valley. He must have worried about running across the police again. But until he could get his business going in Mexico, he had to stay with the trade he knew.

Every two weeks, Dad returned from Texas to stay with us for a few days, bringing us new stories and some cash to tide us over till the next time. We were always relieved to see him, because our money would usually be getting tight. But then, some months after we'd returned to Mexico, Dad's visits stopped. He sent a letter saying he'd come soon, then there was nothing. There had always been ups and downs in Dad's business, but this was the first time I felt that we were really in trouble.

"It's work," Mom would say to explain the delay, but she got down when Dad didn't come. I don't think she was angry at him. She was lonely. She was living in a primitive village, usually stuck in the house because she could not speak Spanish and because she worried that we'd draw attention. She felt that her life had been constricted by unjust forces beyond her control. Taken together, the circumstances of her life were just right for depression.

But with her children, my mother normally forced herself to stay optimistic: "Your father is working on some good deals, and we have the plan for the hotel. Just imagine! There will be a huge lake with boats, and all those tourists. . . ."

One morning Mom said, "There's a lot of pressure on Dad these days. We have to understand that." She was telling us this while getting Mary and me ready to go once again to the tiny post office by the plaza. We'd been going every day for a long time to pick up Dad's telegraphed money order from Texas. I knew we were almost out of money because of what had happened the day before at Doña Armandina's store, the one directly across the street from Miss Mason's. In the mornings they had fresh warm tortillas and the rolls called *"bolillos,"* and Doña Armandina ladled milk from a tall can into people's bottles. The store was filled with familiar smells, with burlap bags of coffee beans and tall sacks of rice and corn and pinto beans.

Every morning Doña Armandina would say, *"Buenos días. ¿Cómo dormistes, Maico?"* And I would say, *"Buenos días, Doña Armandina. Bien, gracias."* Then I'd tell her what Mom had sent me to get. Afterward, she took her book from under the counter and entered what I was taking and what it cost. But this morning Doña Armandina said I had to pay right then. She seemed upset when she said it, though she was trying to be nice. She said that Americans always have enough money, so we could pay what we owed.

Mom seemed blasé at the news. She said, "For the moment, we do not have the money to pay for all the food we've gotten from Doña Armandina." She'd speak with British formality when she was nervous. "There's nothing really wrong. We can simply go to Doña Eva's store on the corner and pay every day. There is nothing wrong with that. Everything is fine. Once Dad sends us the money, we will pay Doña Armandina for what's in her book."

So the next day we went back to the post office, as usual. Mom had ironed Mary's best dress so that we'd look nice for our walk through town. I was trying to do what I could, but my shoes were coming apart again. It was the left shoe at first, the side ripping off the sole. Mom had sewed it back, but then the right shoe began to fall apart, too. That morning I told her not to worry because lots of kids in the Villa didn't even wear shoes. She said that we were better than that and sent Mary for tape and glue from Doña Eulalia. She said to me, "See here, Michael, how are these shoes coming apart? Here you are all day running around the streets up and down and back again. Your father can't buy you new clothes simply to replace what you destroy." I was surprised to see her so angry. She wrapped more tape around the shoes and told me to spend more time in the house.

We walked quickly, with Mom acting as if everything were wonderful. She had on her favorite sleeveless sundress, with a white purse and a white hat with a big brim—"a proper hat for a lady," she called it. Only men wore hats in the Villa, and only Mexican cowboy hats, so everyone on the street looked at us more than usual. I had a freshly ironed shirt and was under orders to keep it tucked in this time. My shoes were clopping a little from the tape, but we ignored that.

Mom smiled at everyone. As we passed Doña Eva's store on the corner, she looked inside and said something that sounded like *"Buenos días."* Whenever we passed someone, she nodded and said it again. People smiled and replied, *"Buenos días, señora."* It seemed to me that people were starting to feel sorry for us because our money order never seemed to come.

That day the postal clerk was as polite as ever. He knew why we were there and he knew he had nothing to give us. But, as always, he turned to look in the little boxes on the wall, then picked up a stack of yellow papers on the counter and looked closely at them, too. He said it was strange that he could find nothing for Señora O'Connor. Sometimes there were problems with the telegraph lines from Texas, he said, and confusion at the main post office in Monterrey. It was so big, and so many people worked there these days, that even ordinary mail got delayed or lost.

I translated for Mom. She acted as if this were exactly what she wanted to hear, then nodded her head. *"Gracias,"* she said elegantly.

On the way back to Miss Mason's, she walked stiffly, her eyes locked straight ahead. Mary asked her something but got no answer. Mary stopped asking. We'd all been a little hungry for several days. I still got rolls from Doña Eva's store every morning, and we had some beans left and the eggs from our chickens, but we had to be careful about how much we ate since we didn't know when money would arrive. To boost everyone's morale, Mom turned abruptly and said, "Wouldn't it be lovely to have a nice meal outdoors at that little restaurant down the hill? Let's just do that, shall we?"

So instead of going home, we turned right at Doña Eva's store and went far down the hill. Mom stepped around the rocks protruding from the dirt path, head up, eyes ahead, arms swinging casually, as if there were nothing to worry about. I copied her to try to make it feel true.

The woman and her young daughter at the restaurant were astounded to see three Americans. They must have heard about us, but they'd never expected to see us sitting at a table in the dirt in front of their house. Their meal that day was rice with chicken, soup included. "Doesn't that sound good?" Mom said, sitting there like a movie star on holiday, all in white. "We'll have chicken and that rice they make with bits of tomatoes and onions—I wish I could learn to make it the way they do in Mexico. Let's have that." She checked in her purse. There wasn't enough money for three orders, so she said brightly, "We'll do with two orders—with the soup, two orders should be just right."

Mary and I were nervous about our money, and we couldn't hide it. We could tell that things were going badly, maybe worse than we'd imagined. Mom said, "Well, children, it's good that there is no telegram. It means that your father will be here in person very soon." We nodded darkly, and Mom shifted gears. "Your father and I often visited a small café much like this one in Sorrento. Just the way the sun comes through the trees, striking the table here, and then the dots of sunlight going off onto the ground there, reminds me of Sorrento." She brushed a fly from her arm without seeing it.

But it didn't feel at all like what they'd said about Sorrento. We were at one of three wobbly tables in front of a house with palm leaves for a roof. Inside, the old lady cooked the rice in a pot over a wood fire, the smoke rolling up out the door. Suddenly, a chicken ran out. The girl caught it near our table and took it back behind the house. When we heard its last squawk, Mary and I looked at each other. Mom didn't hear the chicken.

After a while, the girl brought *fideo* soup with little noodles floating in it. She was younger than I and she was nervous, too, afraid of spilling something on one of the Americans, who had strange customs and might be insulted without anyone even knowing it.

"Oh, marvelous, look at this," Mom said. She turned to the girl sweetly and nodded. Mary and I got the soup. Mom said she was barely hungry at all, she could hardly eat a thing.

The chicken and rice was mostly rice, red from the fresh tomato. The girl brought a green sauce in a bowl, a watery liquid with seeds floating on top, then put the two plates of food in the middle of the table so we could decide who got them. For days we'd had only beans, scrambled eggs, *bolillos,* and tortillas, along with milk for Fiona and boiled water for the rest of us. We were ready for those two plates. "Let's make it even better," I said as I ladled on sauce from the bowl. *Even better than that,* I thought, adding even more sauce.

I tried the food first. It turned my face into fire—my mouth burned, my eyes filled, my nose ran. The shock came first, then the pain; I couldn't catch my breath. The rice was ruined. We saved the chicken by scraping off the sauce, but there wasn't much chicken.

We tried to laugh, Mom as much as Mary and me. But then Mom lost her buoyancy. She was the one who always saw past our problems, who cast her magic light to make our lives seem better, but now we saw that light go out as we watched. She stared down at the table, as if she had finally given up. Dad was gone somewhere, and now Mom had disappeared in front of us.

For the first time, I felt that I was on my own.

Mom began to speak of Italy again, but almost sadly. Then she talked about how hard Dad had always worked for the family. "There are things we don't talk about," she said, "because children wouldn't understand them. Your father and I have worked so that we can all be together. But now sometimes I think there is so much unfairness in the world that it will be too much for us."

That was a frightening revelation for Mary and me. When life was at its worst, we needed Mom to be her strongest, her most convincing, her most deceitful. And now, at the shaky table with the ruined rice, her own fears crashed through. She seemed weak, even pathetic. It was as if she'd lost the struggle to keep believing we'd succeed.

Mary and I knew that we had sunk very low and that we were still falling. We just didn't know how much lower we'd go before we stopped. Though we spoke English and came from a rich country, we were like the poor people in the village. We had only our stories to keep us moving.

ELEVEN

WHEN DAD FINALLY CAME home, a few days later, he seemed shocked over the missing telegrams. He looked distressed, rubbing his face with frustration. Then pacing. He raised his voice and said he'd sent two, one with a money order and another to explain that he'd be delayed. He said he hadn't received the two that we'd sent him.

"It's the Mexican post office," Mom said, "that's all, dear, just those silly postal clerks. Please don't feel bad. We've been fine."

Dad said he was late because of a few small problems with his construction business. Nothing to worry about. But for me, his failure was very worrying. In our scattershot world, where the only constant was our parents, we needed to believe they were reliable. So when Dad failed for any reason, it was a blow—and in this case, his excuse felt flimsy. I wasn't angry with my father for not taking care of us; I was scared that it might happen again.

To keep our eyes on the future, Dad had brought drawings of the hotel. He said, "You've got to show people something, whether you're selling a room addition or getting money for a good idea. Don't forget, kids, you'll never go broke underestimating the public's imagination. See right here, that's what the whole thing will look like when it's done. That's the entrance, and here—this is a typical room."

We were impressed. But then Mom surprised all of us by declaring that she wanted to leave the Villa and move to Monterrey. She must have decided that we no longer had to hide quite as deeply. And she wanted a little more civilization while waiting for Dad's dream, at least a home with the toilet inside. Dad agreed immediately: "Anything you say, babe."

I was surprised because we'd come to feel at home in the Villa, just as

Mom had predicted. Mary had adjusted. Fiona blithely visited all the homes on our block and sat down to talk to anyone there. But I knew by now that none of that mattered.

I told the men in Pepe's barbershop that we were leaving. The news rippled through the village, confirming the belief that Americans were special people because we could leave in just under a year. The boys who were my closest friends wondered what life would be like for us in *La Capital*. In keeping with our parents' enthusiasm, I told them it was certain to be wonderful.

In a few days, Dad said he'd found a beautiful apartment in Monterrey, a penthouse with a panoramic view. We packed in one night. It was sad to see Miss Mason watching us load our things in boxes and to say goodbye to the people on our block and the men at Pepe's and my other friends. We left early in the morning, as the oxcarts were starting up Juárez Street, our street. Mom said we'd come back to visit because Miss Mason had helped us open a window onto this wonderful new country. But I doubted that we'd ever see the Villa again. When we left a place, it felt as if we just kept going.

On the south end of Monterrey, Avenida Hidalgo funneled traffic from the rest of Mexico—most of it trucks and buses—into the city. We drove out until there were only car repair shops and vacant lots, and then a large tractor tire hanging from a pole on the left side of the street. A sign said LLANTERIA, a shop that sold tires and fixed flats. We turned in to the open space behind the shop, where we found tall stacks of old tires and a shirtless man with a black coating on his arms and torso. His face was stuck in a truck tire, looking for the hole.

"Just you kids wait," Dad said. Mom was smiling as if she couldn't stand the excitement one more minute. In the back of the yard was a two-story cement house, painted on the bottom and naked on top. Dad pointed to the second floor and said in his best Christmas-morning voice, "Right up there, kids. There it is. The penthouse."

On top of the penthouse was a neon sign nearly two stories tall and almost as wide as the building. It had a drawing of a tire about twenty feet across and a brand name: General Popo. The Garza family owned the shop and the house and lived on the first floor. We entered through their home and up the stairs to reach our apartment, and they went through our apartment to reach a terrace on the roof. We had three small bedrooms and a living room, too, with a kitchen in the corner—much better than Miss Mason's.

Mr. Garza, who spoke a little English, came up to take us through the apartment and to share with us its glory. He flourished his arms toward the doors, with real knobs for closing, and the windows that opened with small cranks. He demonstrated, in case we didn't understand the crank concept. Finally, best of all, an indoor bathroom. But then Fiona said, "Where's the beds and the table?"

I realized what was wrong. No furniture.

Dad said, "No problem at all. Mr. Garza is working on that."

Mr. Garza said, "No prrroblem. Beds tomorrrrow."

"Oh, it's lovely, Jerry," Mom said. "And we're not sharing it with any-one—it's ours alone. For supper we'll have a delightful picnic right on our own terrace, with a view." She became even more excited on the ter-race when she spotted the road up the hill to the neighborhood where the rich kids at the Pan American School lived: Colonia del Valle. It was a marvelous valley filled with modern homes and trees and unscarred roads. From the terrace we could see the lights of the rich people's cars going over the hilltop and down to the houses with furniture.

As we sat on our cement terrace eating tuna fish sandwiches, Mom gazed at the cars and said, "Children, mark my words, we are going to live there before long." She saw my skepticism. "Don't ask me how, Michael, just mark my words."

We were still staring at the hill when a loud *bizz-bizz-bizz* erupted from the giant neon tire over our heads. Blue lights began to pulsate, making the tire seem to rotate. We all turned blue. Then yellow popped on. It was hard to see at first because we were so close, looking straight up, but the yellow lights were flashing out chunks of letters: GEN—ER—AL PO—PO. We all turned yellow, then blue again, then yellow. Fiona stuck out her arm to watch it change colors. Mom said, "This is all fascinating; what a glorious view." Mary and I didn't say anything, but we knew our fam-ily was going crazy again. Dad tipped back his beer and looked off into nowhere.

MR. GARZA CAME up in the morning. "Gud morrrning, señora," he said, bending forward with a short bow. He said the furniture wasn't exactly ready yet. Dad and I knew at once there would be trouble getting our beds. Dad looked down at me with a silent message: *Let's just keep going with this, because there's nothing else to do anyway.*

He told Mr. Garza, "Certainly, of course. These things take time." He

told Mr. Garza we'd been planning a trip to America, so not having furniture was perfectly fine. This was news to all of us, even Mom, but no
one showed surprise. We all wanted Mr. Garza to think Dad was telling
the truth.

When Mr. Garza left, Dad said, "It's all for the best, because we have
to get your Mexican tourist cards renewed anyway." According to the
law, we were supposed to get new tourist cards every six months, which
meant leaving Mexico and reentering as tourists. In reality, our parents
put off our crossings for as long as they possibly could. An expired
tourist card might be handled with a bribe, but a problem with U.S. Immigration at the border could destroy the family. Mom and Dad kept
these details to themselves, of course. Their children only knew that the
border scared us all to death.

While the INS agents often waved us through when we left the States
for Mexico, and sometimes—though less often—did the same in the
other direction, the sword always swung over our heads. We never knew
when a single question, badly answered, might end the run and do us in.
I knew that the inquisitive men at the border made a dangerous gauntlet,
though I didn't know why. I joined with my parents in pretending we had
nothing to worry about.

We put a few things in the car for the drive to McAllen, Texas, just
north of the Rio Grande, where we usually went. As we neared the border, Mom surveyed the car. It was clean, with everything neat inside. Our
clothes looked okay. When we reached the American side, the agent
looked in and said, "Everyone here American?"

"Sure thing," Dad said. Mom nodded and smiled, with Fiona on her
lap.

"Anything to declare? Did y'all buy something in Mexico?"

Dad pulled out three or four packs of Mexican cigarettes and said,
"That's all we bought. Should I pay some duty on these?" He acted as if
it were the first time in his life that he'd ever crossed back into the United
States. The agent said not to worry about a few cigarettes and waved his
hand.

We stayed overnight in McAllen. After we bought some new clothes,
Dad made the mistake of telling us to strip off the price tags so that we
wouldn't look like a carload of sneaks up for a shopping trip. He was
only trying to make a joke, knowing we all got nervous when it came
time to cross back. But it made Mom upset and she said, "Jerry, we are
not a carload of sneaks. I don't know what we are anymore, but you

shouldn't call us a carload of anything. We are a family with just a bit of trouble for the moment."

Dad was knocked back for a minute. Then he touched the side of Mom's face and said, "Dear, you're right, you're right again. We're not a carload of anything. We are a very lucky family. Especially me—I'm the luckiest, because I have you. I'm sorry."

We crossed back into Mexico with no trouble. On the Mexican side, Dad took his and Mom's Texas driver's licenses and the car's registration to a uniformed man at a table. Without looking up, the man handed Dad our tourist cards and a police sticker for the car. The tourist cards were easy to get but they only allowed us to be in Mexico as visitors, not residents or students or someone, like Dad, trying to start a business. Getting the right documents would have brought questions about who we were that my parents did not want to answer.

THOUGH THEY MIGHT have been breaking the law every day we lived in Mexico, my parents wanted the best education for their children. They wanted us to mix with people as far up the ladder as our family could strain to reach. After we moved to Monterrey, Mom and Dad got Mary and me into the city's two most prestigious private schools. While they didn't have Pan American's American teachers, they were a step up socially.

Mary's new school was Colegio Mexicano. She had a green-and-white uniform, with a vest and a white blouse, and she was proud enough to pop. Colegio Mexicano was a Catholic school for "the proper sort of girls," according to Mom. Fiona went to kindergarten there. The tuition was high, but Dad said it was just something we'd have to do.

My school—closer to the apartment, down Avenida Libertad—was another Catholic school, called Franco Mexicano, the top school for boys. The teachers were Marist brothers who, to my surprise, dressed like everybody else. But their wardrobes were deceptive; like the nuns, they seemed part of a higher life. They walked gazing over the heads of boys who rushed through the hallways between classes.

The honest fact is that I was anxious about going to a school that taught everything in Spanish, and even more intimidated by confident, neatly dressed rich boys. Maybe they'd find out I lived under the General Popo sign—what would they say then?

Mom and Dad didn't sense my concerns, which I dutifully hid from them. They only wanted us to be ready when our dreams—not just the tourist hotel but all the successes to naturally follow—came true. My school required each boy to buy a blue blazer and cream-colored trousers for special occasions. They had to come from a certain tailor and fit just so. We were going from busted-out shoes in the Villa to blazers and slacks in Monterrey. For the moment, Dad's work was thriving.

The official tailor was a soft-spoken old man with a tape measure around his neck and pins stuck into the cuffs of his shirt. The school's students, he said, were like his own sons: "I give them clothes when they are young and then when they are bigger. Then, next, their brothers come." This was just what Mom and Dad wanted to hear. They wanted us to consort with the old families, whose children were fitted by an old man who nipped at the cloth with his little piece of chalk, who'd been doing it for the same families for generations.

As soon as the old man helped me put on the sports coat, my parents started fussing with it. Mom smoothed out the shoulders while Dad tugged on the back. Then Dad found the regulation white shirts for the Franco Mexicano uniform. He fiddled with them for a minute, took one out, and asked the old man, "*¿Éste el más bueno?*" He wanted the best. After the old man smiled a yes, Dad put up two fingers and said, "*Dos* of these."

My school seemed important and orderly, especially in comparison with the ones I had known. Everything was new. The bathrooms worked. It felt scholarly, the way I imagined an important college would feel. When Dad and I went to meet the director, Dr. Mora, it was gratifying to learn that the teachers were called "*profesores.*" Finally I would have teachers who knew what they were teaching! Dad was taken, too. He walked in long strides around the school's central courtyard, hands on his hips. None of the Boston O'Connors, he said, had ever been in a school like this.

My *profesor* of physics, Brother Sergio, read to us about the *principio de Arquímedes*: what makes a boat float. I understood the idea, that a boat pushed on water and the water pushed back. But the brother confused me when he defined density as "*el cociente entre la masa y el volumen de un cuerpo*"—the relationship between the mass and volume of a body. He went on reading, casting words over us as if we understood. We silently bent over our blue notebooks with the school's insignia on the front, writing down the words. But I didn't understand what I was writing. It wasn't a language problem. I didn't understand the concept.

I raised my hand, and Brother Sergio called on me. To show respect, I stood up and kept my hands along the sides of my pants as I asked what the words meant. First, what was mass?

Brother Sergio did not like questions. He stared down on me from the platform where his desk sat. He waited. Then he said it meant exactly what he had said. He could not possibly make it more clear. "Sit down, Michael. Write it in your notebook." It was as if I had asked an impertinent question in Sister Mary Elizabeth's class at Our Lady of Fatima. Understanding didn't matter.

A few months later, though, Brother Sergio did something Sister never would have imagined. He enlisted us to solve a problem: how to smuggle a go-kart from Laredo, Texas, into Mexico as the grand prize for the school raffle. Our teacher was wonderfully animated that day. "Each student will sell his tickets, and the money is for the glory of God and the building fund. Each one will carry out his duty." Sharing a secret, he asked for a student to volunteer his family for the honor of bringing the grand prize across the border while keeping import duties out of the pockets of the criminals in uniform and the corrupt politicians. The money, he said, was "for the adoration of God and for the Franco Mexicano."

Brother Sergio was an elegantly dressed man in his late twenties; kids said he came from a very rich family. "Now," he said, "we will discuss how to use the science of physics to help God and help our school." He drew a go-kart on the blackboard and said, "*Estudiantes,* we have a weight of one hundred kilos on a length of one hundred fifty centimeters and a width of, let's say, seventy-five centimeters. *Bueno.* How do we hang this from underneath the car?"

With this joyful transformation of classwork from unbearable droning into felony fraud, we did things that were ordinarily unpardonable. We called out suggestions without asking permission to speak or even standing up. We exchanged ideas without addressing them to Brother Sergio. When the discussion moved toward the wisdom of simply using some ropes, our teacher cut in to bring us back to physics: "What are the physical properties of a rope?" He turned his head and put up his finger, as if trying to think of the answer along with the rest of us. Then he smiled and said, "A rope will get longer if you pull on it. It has the property of elasticity—it will stretch. And a rope will change its physical characteristics with heat; it will burn and be destroyed. We don't want ropes. Think, what do we want?"

As Brother Sergio paced in front of the blackboard, enthusiastic as never before, I had that horrible awakening that all children feel when supposedly moral people act in immoral ways. This was hard for a thirteen-year-old to reconcile, and I concluded that Brother Sergio was in the wrong. But as the discussion continued, it occurred to me that it was Dad who'd decided this school and its brothers were the very best.

It was in that moment, I believe, that I began to seriously question my father's judgment. Brother Sergio, under a cover of sanctimony, was involving the whole class in a criminal conspiracy. That was clearly immoral. It was becoming obvious that I could not trust school or church or government. Which left me with my parents—but what else had Dad been wrong about?

The class settled on using strands of thick wires to suspend the go-kart, sticking its wheels under a suitcase in the car's trunk, and hiding its motor under the hood, next to the engine. "Now we see how the science of physics works for us!" Brother Sergio exclaimed.

He told us all to speak with our parents to see who could go to Laredo. And he said, "Tell your fathers that, if necessary, they can bring the prize across the line first, and then consult with a priest at the Church of the Holy Spirit in Nuevo Laredo, who is a good friend of mine. He will help to be sure the prize stays under the car until after the last of the government's checkpoints beyond the border zone."

Brother Sergio's fraud was slick. The school got the go-kart without paying customs duties and cleaned up on the raffle. The laws of physics, I'd learned, were indeed powerful things.

TWELVE

I FELT AS IF nothing that I was supposed to believe in made solid sense. Nothing held out against an assault of simple logic.

I couldn't be sure whether my old foundation had turned shaky or whether something new had emerged in me that made me doubt what others saw as certain. In any case, I was at sea.

It helped for a while that, after several months, we moved yet again, from the General Popo penthouse into a nice house on Verlaine Street, a block with tall, shady trees. It was close to downtown, in Colonia Obispado, where, Dad told us, the rich people had settled when they began to move from the center of Monterrey. The neighborhood was named for the bishops' former residence on the hill overlooking us.

The house was the grandest place we'd ever lived, with two floors and nice yards, front and back. I told Mom it would be great for a collie, like Prince. Then I figured that we'd probably have to leave the new dog one day like we left Prince, so I said let's wait. Mom was still so upset about having had to abandon Prince that I was sorry to have mentioned it.

It was a good time for our parents, when their plans seemed to be working. Dad was again doing so well with his home-improvement sales that he'd hired two men to canvass for him in the Rio Grande Valley. He was optimistic once again about finding backers for the hotel on the lake near the Villa.

One day Dad went downtown to the Mercado Juárez, without Mary or me to help him translate, and brought home a cute baby parrot with a yellow stripe on his head. Mom named him Güero, or Blondie. It was our own joke, because people called us "blondies," too. Güero grew up riding on Mom's shoulder. He was always with her, except when he went out the back door to spend a little time in a tree. When he pooped on the floor, Mom acted as if nothing had happened. She kept a tissue in her pocket and—*swish!*—the poop disappeared.

The bus to school would be full by the time it got to Verlaine Street, so I'd jump on the steps and ride hanging on to the door, or climb the ladder in the back to the roof. On the one hand, the driver didn't stop for people who rode outside, he only slowed. On the other hand, if you didn't get inside, you didn't have to pay, so I could spend my bus fare on cigarettes. That was my own first serious secret—that I'd started hanging out and smoking with the guys after classes. We'd buy single cigarettes from the man who ran the candy stand on the sidewalk in front of school. When a teacher came by, we'd cup the cigarettes in our hands to pretend we weren't smoking and he'd pretend not to see the smoke lofting up through our fingers. I got cigarettes that were cheap and harsh, and fancifully named Delicados. It helped my image to be one of the rebellious boys, especially one who could handle nasty cigarettes.

There were no poor people living in our new neighborhood, a big change from the Villa. Though my father said we now had the right atmosphere for raising children, I was troubled by how our neighbors imported their own poor people. Early each morning, the maids—humble, heads down, in shabby clothes—walked up to the houses. Then a worn-out old man came through selling vegetables and fruit from a pushcart, with a boy to help him get it up the hills. He'd sing out what he had: *"¡Hay cebollas! ¡Le tenemos su papaya!"* Ladies came out and pointed to what they wanted without looking at the old man, speaking harshly to him to beat down the price. They brought their maids to stand abjectly behind them and then carry the bags back to the kitchen.

I was careful not to be too taken with our new home because I had seen success turn its back on us before. Our parents, however, were more confident than they'd been since we moved to Mexico. Perhaps they thought they had tiptoed around the worst of our troubles. Though Dad was in Texas most of the time, Mom was getting used to Monterrey and liking it. She began painting oil landscapes, panoramas of the city from the hill where the bishops' former residence commanded the city. Whenever Dad came home, he brought her canvases, sketching pencils, little tubes of color.

He also brought phonograph records—classical records for Mom, along with Broadway soundtracks like *Oklahoma!* and, for Fiona, *Peter and the Wolf.* One morning he came down the stairs singing, " 'Oh, what a beautiful morning . . .' " Then he reached out for Mom's waist and they danced slowly around the kitchen, staring at each other like prom dates.

He usually got in late at night. We wouldn't know he was home until the morning, when Mom would bounce humming into the kitchen, eager to begin the day. She'd say, "Your father's home." Then we'd see him come down the stairs and stand close to Mom while she fixed his coffee and soft-boiled eggs and toast. Fiona sat on his lap and Mary stood holding his hand, and he looked down at his three children with his big smile of affection.

Mom must have told Dad to talk to me, because he broke with routine and came out to the front of the house, where I was sitting against the tree, looking at nothing. He said, "Michael, you seem a little adrift these days." He talked about what his school was like when he was my age. "You've never seen a boring teacher until you've been stuck like a rat in a freezing New England schoolroom with a dozen other miserable kids, all watching the village idiot trying to teach us about algebra. Now that's when true desperation sets in." He laughed. "Jesus, what I wouldn't have given for a sunny classroom in Mexico, like you have! With smart brothers for teachers and a roomful of the smartest kids from the best families. That's something I never could have dreamed of, never in my wildest dreams. But we got it for you, and I'm damn glad we did, too. I can tell you, it hasn't been easy."

"I know, Dad. I know." I couldn't say anything else, because Dad had no idea. I tried to tell him that all we learned was how to memorize. I did not tell him the go-kart story, which still slashed at my respect for the school, because it called too much into question. I thought it might break his heart.

A boy wants to believe his father is a wise guide to the world. But in that conversation in the front yard, I found my father's wisdom to be unreliable. I realized there were things I could not fruitfully discuss with him. I was on my own.

In fact, school was only a part of the problem. The larger part was more dangerous and elusive: the fact that my family pretended to be something we were not. We were telling ourselves lies to feel safe, but we were not safe. I was perpetually afraid that the men at the border would ask for our papers the next time we crossed. Or maybe, I thought, men would come to the house and ask Mom something she couldn't answer, or they'd be waiting by the gate when I came out of school and they'd put me in a car and that would be the last time I saw anyone.

I didn't want to hurt my father, so I kept up my end of the deceit as best I could. I tried to pretend to believe my parents, and I lied about us to everyone else. The lies: That we were only living in Mexico for Dad to explore business prospects. That his relatives were somewhere near Port O'Connor, Texas. That while Mom obviously came from England, she was as American as anyone else. That we never heard from her family because we had simply lost contact. That my grandparents—whom I didn't know a thing about, except their first names—were the people about whom I told intricate stories. And we had not abandoned our life in Houston. Of course not; we had just decided to move.

The lies came out easily, and people believed them. But I feared that if I ever slipped up, it could be the end of my family.

Dad was saying something, his voice coming from a long way off: "Ah, you'll snap right into the groove. You and Mary have done miracles just to get as far as you have, and all of it in a new language, too. Think about it. Your mother and I are very proud of it, very proud."

"Sure," I said. "You have to keep trying. I'll keep trying, Dad."

"Well, I bet there's something else we can do for you while we're at it," he said, as if he'd been thinking about something for a while and now was a good time to bring it up. "I bet we could get you into a fine Catholic organization for young gentlemen."

I could tell right away that this was not going to be good.

Dad said he'd met an American priest, a Father Coughlan, who worked at La Purísima Church, where I took Mary to Mass once in a while—for her, not for me. He'd returned to the priest a few times for what Dad called "matters of the soul," and Father Coughlan had given Dad some things to think about, including the youth organization that the father would be pleased to tell me about as well.

His pep talk done, Dad returned to his favorite subject: what our lives would be like when we got rich.

FATHER COUGHLAN WAS an old priest who had been in what he called "the exile of the pious in a place of danger"—he meant Mexico—for a long time. He spoke slowly, as if to give you time to absorb every word he was saying and see that he was right. He liked Dad, who, he said, was doing his best to get back on the right path toward the Church. That's as far as he went about Dad, which was fine, since I didn't like to think about Dad's old, wrong path, which might have made people chase us.

Father Coughlan was glad we met. He was very worried about my immortal soul, as he knew I was. He was not at all pleased that I was attending Franco Mexicano because he'd had some bad experiences with the Marist brothers, who, he said, didn't understand the danger to the Church from politicians. These were things I wouldn't comprehend at my age, he said, but they were very bad just the same. Gazing upward, he said, "The Church is the most holy power on earth, and all the members of the Church are God's grateful servants, but some of them are very misguided, more now than ever before." Actually, he said, he was officially retired, had been for a long time, but he couldn't give up the fight to bring this country back to God.

"Father," I replied, "everyone in this country is already Catholic, everyone I know."

"That," he said, "is the great, tragic mistake everyone makes about Mexico. They believe it is a Catholic country, when only the people are Catholic and the government is not. What's the point of having a country where the One True Church only reaches the people?" Now more animated, he went on, "The government is the enemy of the Church. The people are the victims of the government. Did you know that for decades all the presidents of Mexico have secretly planned to murder foreign priests and nuns?"

"No, I didn't know that. Did they kill any?"

Father Coughlan looked disgusted, either with me for asking the question or with all the homicidal presidents. Wasn't I curious, he demanded, that he himself, a priest ordained in the Most Holy Church, was banned by the Mexican government from wearing his priestly clothes in public, so that he must dress like any common man?

He didn't wait for my answer. "I'll tell you why!" he said, so loudly that I was trying to think if he had asked me why in the first place. But there was no chance to think; he started in to tell me why anyway. "The great battle of civilization is here and now in Mexico!" he yelled. "You have to decide which side of the battle lines God will find you on, Michael. That is the why of it, Michael. The government wants to destroy the Church. We are going to prevent that."

"Does my father know about all this, Father Coughlan? Because he never told me a thing about the great battle."

"Your father is a good man with a great burden who wants to return to the path, but he doesn't understand this problem well enough. If he did, he couldn't allow you to go to those Marist brothers for their modern education."

At first I thought that Father Coughlan might be right about the presidents, and then that maybe he was trying to test my faith. But finally I thought that maybe Father Coughlan might be a little crazy. I'd seen that before in old people. When I stopped asking questions, Father Coughlan calmed down. He told me to go the next Wednesday afternoon to the meeting of the Escuderos de Colón—a youth club of the Knights of Columbus, he said, a grand Catholic organization.

The meeting was in a big room with a nicely kept pool table, a few small tables and chairs, and a snack bar against the back wall. There were about ten boys my age, supervised by an adult whom I took to be someone's father. He was resting his butt against a table in the back of the room, watching things get started.

We began with the Lord's Prayer, led by a tall kid named Juan. He spread his arms wide like an orchestra conductor's, waved them like a bird's wings, then folded his hands on his belt buckle and began, *"Padre nuestro que estás en el cielo . . ."* By then it was nearly automatic for me, and I joined in with the others. You can't be the only person not saying the words when people will sneak a look to see why one little spot in the room is quiet.

The adult came over to say he was pleased to see me, that I looked to him like a very fine Catholic boy, and that I might want to go over to the bathroom after we talked and comb my hair and fix up my clothes a little. Father Coughlan had told him about me and my good family, an American family but not Protestant. What did I think about the Escuderos? Weren't they an interesting group?

"Oh, yes," I said.

"Your father is in the construction industry?" the man asked me.

"Yes, correct. He works on the other side, in the valley."

"And your mother is here?"

"Yes, my father comes every week. I have two sisters; they go to Colegio Mexicano."

"Good. A good Catholic family."

"Yes, all of us."

Whenever a stranger asked questions about my family, it frightened me. Pointed questions might even make me stammer and betray my nervousness. I'd imagine a door closing behind me and the room getting dark with me trapped inside.

To divert the man, I asked him about Father Coughlan and the Mexican Armageddon, and went on from there: "Did you hear about the government killing priests and nuns? Father Coughlan says we have a great battle and we have to decide if we are on God's side. Did you ever see a priest they killed? I go to Franco Mexicano school. I have a friend there named José Luis Escalante. . . ."

THIRTEEN

MY FRIEND JOSÉ LUIS ESCALANTE was a "good boy." He never questioned the teaching at Franco Mexicano or smoked at the candy stand after school with the boys. As I did. But we were friends because he seemed to have less money than other kids, and he had a secret. There was something about his father; José Luis didn't talk about him. I thought he must be dead, or even have run off. His mother—pretty, withdrawn, dark clothes—was sad about something. Their home was enough off-center that for a while I felt comfortable there.

But I wanted something more extreme. For adventure. For rebellion. For the yearnings of a thirteen-year-old boy to stand on his own.

More extreme was Tony Stone. I knew him from the Pan American School. Tony lived in Colonia del Valle, Mom's dream neighborhood. His mother and stepfather wrote fabricated articles for trashy American magazines that featured tales of tragic romance and detective stories. The magazines presented the stories as true. His stepfather specialized in women's magazines and used female pseudonyms, while his mother wrote mostly for men's magazines under a string of men's names. All that seemed very sophisticated to me.

Late one afternoon, after a matinee at the Cine Reforma, it was still light outside, and Tony didn't want to go home. He was fourteen, tall, and really skinny. He moved like Jerry Lewis doing slapstick but didn't like to hear that. We both thought that his stepfather was far too harsh with him and that his mother did not care enough to stop it. I was starting to feel like Tony, more comfortable in the street than at home.

Tony's Spanish was so good that he was taken for a Mexican, even with his fair skin. As we walked aimlessly on the wide sidewalk outside the theater, Calzada Madero began to buzz with Saturday evening traffic. Tony said we should get some *tepache*. "It's great," he said. "It's like beer, but not that much." I hadn't tried beer or any other alcohol, so we took a bus to a run-down neighborhood with narrow streets and drunks lying on the sidewalks, their backs against the buildings.

Tony knew a place called Tepacheria Chulo. From the outside, it looked a little cleaner than the street or the bus station, but not exactly clean. The walls had once been a shade of blue-green. The metal tables had white enamel tops with pictures of beer bottles and the words CERVEZA CARTA BLANCA ¡EXQUISITA! A young man sat at one table in a beat-up cowboy hat and blue jeans, with a plate of crackers and a small brown clay cup. His face was down as he stared at the tabletop.

Tony knocked back his head and thrust out his chin. "*¡Quíubole!* Hey! What's going on?" he shouted like a big shot to the man behind the counter. "*Dos tepaches, 'mano. Pero de lo bueno y un montón de galletas.*" He wanted the good *tepache* and a bunch of crackers. The bartender stuck a ladle into a barrel, filled two brown clay mugs, and brought them over with a few crackers on a plate. *Tepache* turned out to be homemade fermented pineapple, with chunks of fruit and rind floating in the barrel.

The guy with the cowboy hat looked over at us amiably. In Spanish he said, "Hey, what's up, my American buddies?" He came toward us scooting sideways, like a skinny dog who's trying to show that he's not a threat. His name was Oscar, and he sat down next to Tony, pushing his hat back on his head. "You two are not tourists, right?" he asked.

"Don't be a fool, I'm pure Mexican," Tony said. "And my friend talks differently because his father is from Guanajuato. His father's name is Juan." This was Tony's way of explaining my American looks and still imperfect Spanish.

"*Ahh, claro,*" Oscar said, as if it made sense. Oscar said he was looking for work. "Maybe I'll return to selling pillows," he said. "I sell them from house to house; it's a good job. You can meet a lot of women."

Oscar said my eyes were getting red like beets and the *tepache* must be starting to hit me.

"*Ni madres,*" I replied, a tough way of disagreeing. "I can drink *tepache* from one day to the other." To prove Oscar wrong, I yelled over to the bartender for another round: "*¡Otra vuelta!*" I waved my arm in a circle, as Tony had done.

After half an hour, we were getting to like Oscar. Then he told us his secret. He stole cars. He used to be a mechanic and still works at it, but a mechanic can't get ahead without his own shop, he said. So he started stealing cars in Cadereyta and Montemorelos and driving them over back roads to a secret place in Monterrey, where he sold them for cash. He said, "You have to be brave to get ahead." The way he saw things, a car started out at a factory before going to a car agency and from there, to a rich man. Then Oscar came along and moved it again. He was just another part of the chain of distribution.

"*Claro,*" I said.

"You have to be intelligent to do it," Oscar said. "Not just anyone can do it right under the nose of the police and get away singing."

"*Claro,*" I said.

But Oscar wanted to try a legal job again—though not because stealing cars was illegal, he said. "You could say it is against the law, but it has honor. A man needs his honor, and his work must have honor, too." I nodded as if Oscar's reasoning made sense. He reminded me of my father, a good man who did things he didn't like doing to get ahead, who lied to people to sell construction jobs.

Tony wanted to know how you could sell pillows to poor people. Oscar told us about a warehouse in Colonia Nacional, where a very nasty man ran the business of pillows for poor neighborhoods. You had to get his permission to sell.

"But most of those houses don't even have a bed," Tony said. "How do you sell a pillow to a family with no beds?"

"That's the trick of it," Oscar said with a smile, pointing at Tony with a finger that had grease in the lines and cracks and then shaking his head slowly, enjoying his own joke. "You tell them pillows come first, then they'll have one when they get a bed. People will never get beds, but at least they will have pillows to dream on for the beds that will never come. A dream is something nobody can take from you.

"I tell them, 'Look, ma'am, tonight you will move that pile of old clothes where your husband puts his head and you will give him the best gift in this life. What man can ask for more than the tranquillity of a good dream?' "

AFTER A FEW months of our doing well, the gaps between Dad's visits grew wider. Mary and I didn't find this suspicious. We figured that he was having problems getting the money to build the hotel. Still, Mom was having trouble eating again. Finally she had us take her to the main post office to use the telephone to call him. Mom told Dad that the checks must be getting lost in the mail again. Then I heard her say, "But really, I'm nearly desperate now. We've simply got to have some cash soon or I don't know what I'll do for food."

That was a shock to hear, for Dad as well as for me. He sent another check, registered mail, special delivery. A man in a blue hat rode his bicycle to our house, blew on his post office whistle from the sidewalk, and gave the letter to Mom. But when we took the check to the bank, they said we had to wait two weeks for it to clear. Then they told us that Dad's bank in Texas wouldn't cash it.

Now what could we do? Using adolescent logic, I decided the very smartest thing would be to steal something and sell it. I knew the pawnbrokers' street downtown, the windows with tools and musical instruments that people said were stolen goods. No, that wouldn't work. What would I say to Mom if I got caught?

Maybe I could sell pillows door-to-door like Oscar. I thought it would be wise to learn how to support myself—who knew when I might be on my own? And, it would be an adventure. I tried to remember what Oscar had told us about the pillow company's location, somewhere in Colonia Nacional, near the central bus station.

After I walked around for a while, a man showed me a tiny street off Avenida Colón. At the end of the block, hanging from the second floor of a building buckling with age, an old sign read SOLICITAMOS VENDE-DORES. Salesmen wanted.

Then I realized it was easy to be brave about something you planned on doing later.

At the top of a stairway that had shaken partly loose from the wall, there was a room full of pillows and dust, and an old man slouching on a chair, watching me approach. *Here's where it's important to look good,* I thought, like there was not a thing to worry about. "Hola, señor," I said as if I was visiting a neighbor. "¿Qué paso? ¿Cómo está?"

"Who are you?" he said, looking as mean as Oscar had said. I'd seen men like him many times in Mexico, the angry, hard men at the bottom. I'd seen them on the street in rags, hauling things on their backs around Mercado Juárez, or loading trucks, or selling old faucets and cracked radios from blankets on the sidewalk. This man was like them, only harder, because he could sit and look down on the others in the street.

I said, "My name is Miguel. Oscar, the one who fixes cars, told me this is the place to come to sell pillows. I mean, that you can get pillows to sell to the ladies in the houses."

"You are American. What do you want?"

I said, "My father lives in Guanajuato."

"How old are you? Where do you come from?"

"Oscar told me this is a good job. I am a good worker. Señor, are you Juan? Oscar said Juan was the boss."

"I am the boss," Juan said. "This grand business is mine. Don't say 'señor' to me, like you say to some great man sitting on his horse. This business is for people who must work. Do you have to work? This is not a place for little games with pretty boys. Your mama, did she wash you well in the morning?"

I said, "I have to work, too." It wasn't in the plan to tell him that. I wasn't about to tell Juan about my father and the bad check, but I had to make him know that I was serious.

"If you want to play selling my pillows, I'll give you a chance. First, you only have to give me money. You will give me six pesos for a pillow. You will buy three of them—one hard, one soft, one special."

"How much do I sell them for?"

He laughed. "How much? How much? You sell them for what you can, *bruto*. Try to sell them for twenty pesos, or a hundred pesos."

I wished Oscar was there. He would know how to do this thing. "Is Oscar around these days?" I asked.

"Oscar?" the boss said offhandedly. "Oscar the car thief? Oh, they killed him."

He wants to make me cry, I thought. *I won't be sad for him. I won't ask who killed Oscar.* Then I did cry, a little, but he didn't see it. I wiped my face quickly with my shirt to make it look like the tears were just sweat.

I went home, stole eighteen pesos from the envelope in Mom's chest of drawers, and bought three pillows from Juan. "The hard one is a little harder than the soft one, but you can't tell without the labels," he said. "You have the route on Calle Ramírez, Colonia Independencia. Don't leave Calle Ramírez. It's a shit street. It's yours this morning. By the afternoon you'll be at home with your mother."

On the bus to Colonia Independencia, I asked the driver about a stop near Calle Ramírez. He looked at me, estimating how stupid I might be, and said, "There are new streets every day and the old ones get filled with houses. Pull the rope when you want to get off." A boy said he thought the stop was after the giant hole being dug by a tall yellow machine. I got off there with my great bag of pillows hanging down my back, wondering what I was doing. I told myself to act happy, like Dad did, as if I were bringing people the one thing in this whole world they'd been waiting for.

I found my first couple in a shack near the corner. I smiled up to the couple and told them about good dreams and that they needed a pillow now, so when they got a bed they'd be ready. They were curious, but they weren't buying: *"No, 'jito. No tenemos pa' almohadas."*

"Señora," I told her, "you can have a soft one or a hard one, and it only costs ten pesos. It's a good pillow; it will help your husband rest after work." She answered that her husband had spent three months resting and that was why they had no money for a pillow. We all laughed, including a neighbor who heard through the wall made of sticks. Then the husband said he wanted to try one, because he'd seen them on beds in store windows.

Here was a problem I hadn't thought about. He was getting down on the floor, where they slept on a mat in the corner. He wanted to put the pillow there. I knew the mat was dirty and his head was, too, and the pillow was white. Ni modo, I thought to myself in Spanish. *There's nothing you can do about it. You can't come into a family's home with a bag of pillows and say they can't even test them.*

Then the lady wanted to try it, jabbing the man in his side to get him off the mat. She didn't want me to see them there together. She said, "You know, the old woman up there at the corner has money." She made a half circle with her thumb and her index finger, to show she was talking about a big coin, a lot of money. "Take your sack up there," she said. "Tell her if she buys one from you, she can lend it to me one afternoon."

By then the shack was filling up with kids, and adults were poking through to see the strange-looking visitor. The kids showed me where to find the woman, named Laura, the one people called La Vieja, the old lady of the neighborhood. When I found her she was bent over in her shack, peering at the people coming into her backyard. "Here come your pillows!" a kid said, dancing, as if the old woman had been wondering where her pillows had been.

La Vieja started mumbling something about a lost chicken, pointing with her stick to an empty corner by the fence. "It's supposed to be out here in the yard," she said, "but maybe it ran off or somebody from the outside took it." Then she looked inside my sack and said, "Yes, those are pillows. Are they mine?"

"No," a kid said. "You have to buy them."

I knew that I was supposed to mention the nice dreams a nice pillow brought, but it seemed wrong to talk about an old lady sleeping. It was too private to say in front of everyone.

La Vieja said, "So you want me to buy these things, is that it?"

"*Sí, señora,*" I said, glad to get into my sales pitch. "They are very good pillows—one is soft, one is normal, and one is special. The lady down there said you would like them, and her husband said the soft one is good." I told her that one pillow cost ten pesos.

Then something wonderful happened. La Vieja told the children that since her back hurt these days, maybe a pillow would be good. She said she wanted the special one. While I was standing wondering what to do now, she went inside her shack and came back with a tiny square of paper. She unfolded it. It was a torn ten-peso bill. I gave her the pillow marked ESPECIAL, and the kids all clapped—some of the adults, too.

Right away the old woman went back inside and lay down on her mat along the wall. Her hand slipped out to the ground first to let her down easily. She rested her head on a soiled, bunched-up sack, the way she always did, and laid the pillow across her stomach, just so. "I think this is the right one," she said as she cuddled the pillow and closed her eyes. She looked like she was remembering something nice from long ago.

Still, I didn't feel good selling pillows—I was nervous, and I felt guilty because the people didn't really need what I was selling. But I told myself that I was selling dreams, and as long as I didn't lie, it was all right.

After a while the kids grew tired of coming along with me, except for one boy about eight years old, who kept watching, trying to grasp what I was doing. We went up the street to visit every home—one by one, just like Dad did. *Sometimes it's the first one, sometimes the fiftieth. . . .* But after La Vieja, I couldn't get anyone to listen for more than a minute before turning me down. There were lots of ways of saying no: "*No, crea-tura*"; "*No, mi'jo*"; "*'Horita no tenemos.*" Dad didn't feel the nos the way I did. They bounced off him, but they demoralized me.

I got tired from the tension of peddling and of thinking about why I was doing it. I told the curious boy, named Jesús, that I'd come back the next day. When I got home, I snuck the ten pesos into my mother's purse, hoping she would think that she'd found some money she'd misplaced.

Though my family was desperate, it took me several days to get back the courage to return to Calle Ramírez. As soon as I stepped off the bus, Jesús came over to ask where I'd been. He'd found a lot of people who wanted pillows, and they were all disappointed that I hadn't come.

Over the next two weeks, Jesús and I went all over his neighborhood and then up the hill to the shacks in the fields. We wound up selling sixteen pillows. Jesús made a lot of the sales before I got there, so all I had to do was come by and talk with the people for a few minutes to be polite. We agreed that Jesús should get a peso for each pillow sold, which was enough for him to buy the wood he needed to make a shoeshine box, plus the waxes, and some money for his mother. I didn't tell him that I was also giving money to my mother, because our family's troubles felt demeaning to me.

THREE SATURDAYS AFTER I first went to sell pillows, Dad was already sitting in the kitchen when I came down for breakfast. I was mad at him, but I only said how glad I was that he was home. That was true, too.

"God, it's good to be here," he said. "Your mother's been frantic." He was really upset.

Feeling sullen, I said, "Dad, why did you stay away so long this time? We were worried that something happened to you." But I didn't say what I was thinking: *What happened to the money you were supposed to send us, because we damn well needed it and we damn well counted on you to send it.*

"I had no idea there was this trouble," he said. "None at all. Now that I'm here, I see how bad it's been for your mother. My letters are getting lost, or someone in the post office is stealing them. That's a well-known problem, you know that." He said there had been trouble with two jobs in Falfurrias, north of the valley, and he'd had to stay up there. While he was at it, he'd sold more jobs. He'd thought his checks had gotten to us.

By then I'd learned that we could never be sure what happened with Dad. You could either believe his story or, like me, doubt it and berate yourself for not trusting him. If he was lying to us, I had no idea what he might have been doing. Was it connected to our secret?

Mom came in and put her hand on his shoulder. She was so relieved that he was back. She just wanted to touch him, to reassure herself that he was really there. I could tell that Dad was happy, too, as he looked at

Mom in that special way of his. She ran her hand through his hair and said, "It's time for another trim. I'll just get my scissors after you've had your coffee."

Dad began an explanation about why the bank wouldn't cash the check he sent: A man in Weslaco had lost his job just as he was to pay for his contract with Dad, and Dad had had to wait until the man borrowed the money from his brother-in-law. And then what happened was . . .

I stopped hearing it. The truth that mattered to me was simple: There had been no money, and no Dad, for a long time.

But Mom believed every word of it, as always, and wanted me to believe him, too.

It could *be true,* I thought. The world was complicated, and lots of things that didn't make sense were true. That was what you learned when you grew up a little.

Still, there were too many things that didn't add up, at home and at school and everywhere else. I felt I was now old enough to find a life that made sense to me, a world I could have for my own.

Soon enough, that notion proved more dangerous than bold.

FOURTEEN

WHILE THE ESCUDEROS DE COLÓN lost their appeal when I realized that they were more about religion than about pool, they gave ideal cover for hanging out with my friend and drinking buddy Tony Stone. As I neared my fourteenth birthday, I spent most of my free time with Tony at the Plaza Zaragoza, the city's main square. Now and then we dropped by Tepacheria Chulo before going home, but usually we'd just sit around on the outdoor benches, talking to whomever we felt like, relishing our freedom.

Plaza Zaragoza was a rectangle of several square blocks, with a canopy of trees, a covered bandstand, and a fountain in the center. Its cathedral had two grand towers, one for bells and the other for a clock. Inside, it intimidated with scenes of Jesus on the cross, slashed and bleeding in agony, or of people dying in the dirt with vicious wounds before they floated up toward the clouds.

The plaza was the tourists' first stop in Monterrey. We chatted with them as a way to reconnect with the United States. Before long I was working as a paid tourist guide, at first helping families and couples who were thrilled to have an American show them around the church and other attractions. That was easy money because I simply repeated what I found in tourist magazines. I soon progressed to helping single men, who generally want one thing: local girls. So I learned about hookers.

One day, as I sat in the plaza by myself waiting for something to happen, I met Harry, a pipeline worker from somewhere in Texas. He was a kind of tough-looking fellow, lanky and blond. I guessed he was somewhere in his mid-thirties. He said he'd thought about visiting some border towns, but then "I flat out figured I'd get me a look at a big ol' Mezican city and some of them city girls, too."

Harry was on a bench getting his boots shined, with his jeans hiked up to keep the wax off them. I told him I was a guide, and he liked the idea of having an American kid show him around. He said excitedly, "Say, whur they have them fightin' cocks at? Whur everythin' gets all tore up and you can bet money, too?"

"I don't know," I said; then, trying to sound like a smart guide, "but I know where the bullfights are. The bulls get killed. There's blood all over the place and the people all yell, '¡Olé! ¡Olé!' "

But Harry wanted cockfights, so I ran over to ask Jorge the taxi driver. When he told me the cocks fought only on the weekends and there were no bullfights that day, I suggested that we take Harry to the slaughterhouse instead: "This tourist seems to like to see things get cut up."

Jorge said, "Don't be a fool, my little gringo. If we don't take him to the bulls or the roosters, he'll be very content with the girls."

By then I was used to taking male tourists by taxi to the red-light districts known collectively as Las Zonas: La Coyotera, Acapulco, and El Dengue. Each was many square blocks of cheap whorehouses and bars, all filthy and dangerous, with hookers at the bottom of their careers. Everything was much better in the houses like Casa Carmen, in a respectable neighborhood a few blocks from La Purísima Church.

I told Harry, "Sir, I can show you the slaughterhouse. There are a whole lot of cows getting killed there. Sometimes they use an ax to do it. The cockfights aren't until this weekend; the same for the bulls. Or, sir, we can go to see the girls."

Harry said, "Yew don' gotta call me 'sir,' Harry's good enough. An' I don' wanna go to no goddamn stinkin' slaughterhouse, neither."

"Yes, sir. I mean yes, Mr. Harry. We can go right over here to see the cathedral, and I can tell you what the paintings mean; some people like that. You can see Jesus on a cross with a crown of thorns. And they have the big cut in his side where the soldiers stabbed him with a spear. Or we can go see the girls. Carmen's house is open by now, and later on the Zones will be active. You can play pool and bet, like you wanted to."

He said, "Tell yew what, we'll jest hold off on that church for the next time. Right now, let's trickle on down to that Carmela's house and look around there for a while."

At Carmen's they gave me all the Coca-Cola I wanted, or Sidral, an apple-flavored soda. The cook often let me have some beans and rice or tacos. Though no one gave me money except my tourists.

It was clean and quiet at Carmen's. There were always police around, the patrolmen down the street in their uniforms, sometimes the *comandantes* drinking tequila or—if they were important enough—whiskey at the bar. The other thing that impressed me about Carmen's was that they had spittoons, to keep men from spitting on the floor. It seemed to me that for some reason men liked to spit a lot in a bar. They'd wait all day without spitting if they weren't around enough people, then start spitting like crazy as soon as they were with their friends.

Harry acted right at home at Carmen's. He got a beer, then pulled up his jeans, tugged on his cowboy belt, and waved to a girl at the bar. Then he went right over, stuck out his hand, and tried to speak with her.

Señora Lola, the owner or the manager, I didn't know which, was there with her hair that unusual shade of red. She was probably in her fifties, and no longer shapely, but she kept her head straight when she walked, her arms out like those of a ballet dancer. She spoke slowly, watching you listen; she commanded your interest. The girls all seemed to like her. They saw her as the wise if stern head of their family, and that was the way she acted with them.

"*Hola, güerito. ¿Qué tal? ¿Quién me trais ahora?*" she said. Hello, little blondie, how's everything? Who did you bring me today? *Another tourist?*

"Yes, he wants to go to the roosters. Maybe on the weekend. Where's the best place to go?"

"Roosters!" She gasped. "Rooster fights! What a disgrace. What lack of manners to take a visitor to where two chickens are killing each other. And all those dirty men drinking their beer and screaming like Indians from the streets. Give your pretty tourist to me until the weekend and he will return to the north with his legs shaking. He will thank you for that.

"We understand our clients," Señora Lola went on. "If he is an ordinary man with money to spend, like your tourist, even with his blue jeans, we will receive him in the same manner as our rich clients. We know the rich man requires more understanding than the others. Who works the most? The rich ones. Who has more to worry about than the others? The rich ones. Then who deserves most to relax and not think about anything, even if it's once a week?" She was telling me that Harry would be treated properly no matter how rough he looked.

"*Sí*, Señora Lola, there's never trouble here," I said.

"You are right, Miguel," she declared, agreeing that I was right in agreeing with her. "This is because the *comandantes* are my friends and I teach my girls how to make men comfortable. Are you comfortable, Miguelito?"

"Yes, señora."

"Well, one of these days when you're already a man, we will make you feel comfortable with one of my girls."

Both eager and scared, I said, "I'm almost a man these days. Do you hear it in my voice? Listen. Do you think that's close enough?"

"One of these days," she repeated, then returned to business. "Tell your tourists that we are very discreet. *Muy discretitas*. That's our way, even in how we dress. *No hay que enseñar hasta el apellido*. You don't have to show everything. Men with class prefer women with class, usually."

Señora Lola was probably trying to make it up to me for saying that I was not yet a man when she told me to dance with Viki, a small girl who looked like the youngest one there. Viki said, "Sure, *gringito*, let's dance, the music is good." She stood up and swayed back and forth, waving me to her. I got up most of the way, then sat down again, cursing myself. Dance? I couldn't do it; I never did it. Everyone watched to see what the gringo kid would do. "Come on, come here," Viki said sweetly. If she had asked once more, I thought, I might have found my courage, but she quit asking and I quit trying.

When Harry came back, I looked to see if his legs were already shaking. No, it didn't seem like it. He said, "Little pardner, yew want a beer? Ah'm gettin' one."

"No, I don't drink beer. I got me a Coke right here."

"Well, ah'll tell yew wha', this here was better 'n any bullfight, or cockfight, too. This is a fine place. Whadda yew doin' tommarah? Ah mean, after school?"

"Nothing that I know of. I can meet you."

"Yeah, let's do tha' then. 'Cause, like the man said, thur's more pretty gals than one."

That was how we got to El Dengue, which was named after a disease like malaria. It was one of the nasty districts, out by the railroad tracks on the edge of Monterrey, full of whorehouses smelling of vomit. After Jorge brought us to a bar at the edge of the Zone in his taxi, Harry wanted him to stay awhile longer, even invited him for a beer. Harry was looking down the alleys, quickly left and right. Then looking behind us, his head craned and twisted in a circle. "Ah'd feel one whole lot better,"

Harry said, "havin' a way ta get the fuck outta here if things go bad real quick." But that didn't work because Jorge said his car cost him too much to leave it parked in El Dengue, and his wife wouldn't wash his clothes if they smelled from the mud on the streets there.

As we sat down in the bar, a man at the next table said, "Tell your friend from the other side not to be afraid. Tell him he's in the heart of the Dengue and no one will bother him, not the thieves or the cops."

I translated for Harry. I also told him that we'd better be careful with that guy and his friends. But Harry was starting to relax. "Pool?" he said to the men, hooking up arm and pantomiming a shot. "Pool?" The ugliest guy at the table said yes. Another guy started singing a song about the bliss of complete drunkenness. A third man was telling everyone that the only problem with being drunk was that you didn't know at the time how much fun you were having, and then you forgot.

Harry strutted around the bar. He pulled down his shirt in the front, yanked on the bottoms of his pant legs to bring them down over his big cowboy boots, getting ready to show off his pool game.

"Just look at the damn boots this gringo's wearing," the ugly guy said. When he added that Harry must be one of the Texas Rangers, I began to get nervous. It was not good to be called a Texas Ranger in El Dengue unless you had about twenty real Texas Rangers with you.

"Right," the drunken singer said, standing for a better look at Harry's boots. "One of the Rangers that goes around fucking over poor Mexicans on the other side. What's he doing here?"

Harry looked to me for information. "Whad'a they sayin'? What's the deal?"

"Oh, nothing, Harry. They like your fancy boots. Just smile. It's the custom here for the visitor to invite people to have a beer."

Harry grudgingly invited them, but it wasn't enough. The ugly one wanted to know why Americans like Harry "could come to Mexico with no trouble and fuck the Mexican women, but a poor Mexican can't even go to the United States to pick tomatoes without permission from some blue-eyed son of a bitch at the border."

I told the man, "That is a situation of a great injustice against ordinary people like you and me. For me, personally, I am studying to become a lawyer to help poor people fight the rich who abuse us." He thought that was a good idea. He shook my hand and left us alone. But I told Harry it was time to get going.

No matter how often I'd taken people to El Dengue, seeing the main street made me feel awful. There were three layers of a dark tragedy that only visitors could escape. In the sky, birds swooped to look for a piece of garbage, gliding through the flat, yellow smoke from cooking fires that waited for a wind someday. Below them, women hung out in front of their open rooms, pacing, fighting, screaming, or drinking. At the bottom layer were the women's small children, playing or crawling in the street, and the torn-up dogs and cats. Pools of sewage flowed everywhere, so vile that they repelled even the mosquitoes, which preferred the stagnant rainwater. Often men would pee in a puddle to make it smell like sewage—to fight the mosquitoes, they'd laugh.

When Harry left the bar and got his first look at the main street, he saw no higher than the women, nor any lower, either. His mouth was open but not moving until he managed to say, "Lookee here. Lookee *here*!" He set off down the street, nodding and waving and calling everyone "darlin' " and "honey."

They called back: *"Oye, chulo."* Come on, baby. Both Harry and the girls thought they'd found gold. He looked down at me, pleased. "Ah like 'em raunchy, yew know."

In almost every tiny room we passed there was some makeshift chapel—a picture of Mary, a plastic rose, a candle, a rosary. And family photos of mothers and children. No fathers. Aside from a bed, there might be a chair or a stool, or a broken beer crate. The closet was a nail on the wall with a blouse hanging from it.

We reached the El Local bar, a place where everyone called the bartender Perico, or Parrot. It was his nose. Perico was a fat man who wore loose shirts and slept on a mat behind the bar. On the shelf above the bar he'd put up half a dozen Christmas tree lights, a picture of the Virgin Mary, and a photo of his mother in a dark dress. "Don't forget," he liked to say, "your mother is one who loves you when all the others steal your tortillas."

Perico got a beer for Harry, who'd hardly taken a gulp before a truly ugly woman ran in from the street and couldn't stop until her nose was half an inch from Harry's. Her old blue dress was falling off her skinny shoulders. *"Hola,* Meester Texas," she said, laughing.

To a young observer, it seemed that all the women in places like El Dengue fell into one of two groups. Most were so sad or drunk that they sat around waiting—to die, I thought. The other group was constantly moving, jumping, vibrating, always looking for something. When there were no men around to be looked for, they'd cackle at one another's sto-

ries or start a fight. Looks did not determine which group a woman belonged to. Harry was attacked by Lucy, one of the ugly, jumpy ones, and
that was fine with him.

"Hello, my big frien', my big macho man, my big gringo," Lucy said.
"Where have you beeen? What we gonna do?"

Harry liked this game. "Tell her ah ain' got no money," he said.

Lucy acted incredulous. "No money? All the Americans have money,
especially the pretty ones." She waved her shoulders, stuck out her lips,
wagged her butt a few times, and went into Harry's front pocket as if
checking for money. Instead, she grabbed his penis and started rubbing.

A couple of regulars came by, ignoring Harry and Lucy. They waved a
big hello to Perico and shook hands with the men at a table littered with
empty brown beer bottles. You could tell from their lunch bags that they
were on the way to their jobs at a factory. Some girls showed up from the
street, followed by a trio of musicians. Soon people were grabbing girls
by the waist and pushing them around the floor in the dance they did in
cheap whorehouses. The working men danced with the tops of their
lunch bags stuck up under their belts. They were going to be sure they
still had their lunches when the dance ended.

I just sat there, mad at myself for not having danced with Viki, when
a man at the next table hissed at me and said, "That skinny girl's going
to eat up that gringo." That meant she was going to do him wrong, take
his money or worse. Lucy was up at the bar with Harry, twisting on his
nipples through his shirt. Harry was giggling with his eyes closed and his
head back so far that it looked like he was trying to gargle.

"I doubt it," I told the man. "That's why I'm here." I tried to look
hard, hoping he wouldn't guess that my plan in case of trouble was to act
mean as hell—and, if that didn't work, to take off like a rabbit through
the side door.

But it all went fine. The workers left for their factory. The musicians
moved on, and most of the girls, too. Harry and Lucy went off to a
room, which left me with Perico and his newspaper and my friend Esmeralda, a fat girl named after her green eyes. She was sitting on a Coke
box, her vast belly stretching the fabric at her waist, working on her em-
broidery. She tugged on the needle, pulling green thread through a white
cloth stretched across a wooden ring. She said, "This is going to be a
bowl of fruit."

Esmeralda was from a village north of Monterrey, though she
wouldn't say which one. "It's the truck drivers," she'd explained. "I see

them in my work, and later they go on the highway near my village. What happens if one stops at the gas station and says he knows me from here?"

Which made me worry: *What if someone I know sees* me *around here?*

To kill time while I waited for Harry, I asked Esmeralda about her village, where she returned every few months to visit her three daughters and her mother. She said, "All my three girls are in school. All three! I have wonderful stories for them about my work in the factory of cardboard boxes."

"What factory?" I said. "You don't work in a factory, do you?"

"Not in my true life," she said. "In my true life I am here, but in my head I have my factory. My little girls always want to know about the women at the factory and about the times I go shopping with them on the big streets of the city. My little girls ask about the men who clean the streets with their brooms and their little barrels with wheels.

"I always tell my mother about Mass," she went on. "The priest in his long dress, right to the floor, that moves when he walks and pulls your eyes. Then the father lifts that big gold thing with the Host in it and they swing the other gold thing that has religious smoke coming out with the smell. We don't have such elegance in my village. My mother has never seen it."

I asked her if she went to the cathedral on Sunday.

"No, never—what shame! But it doesn't matter, I go in my head. I tell my mother, and she sees it, too. You can say I am lying to *mi'amá*, but also you could say I am giving her a gift. Two things together." Esmeralda rubbed her thick index fingers together to make one thing of two things.

Then she asked me, "Did you know that the soccer team at my factory of cardboard boxes is doing very well this year in the Industrial League? If they win the championship, we will have a morning without work and a party with a cake." There was no soccer team, of course. It was just another story, another gift for Esmeralda's girls, to go along with the embroidered bowl of fruit that her family would hang on the wall, thinking of her whenever they saw it. "A good idea, no?" she asked.

Very good, I told her, though it was pathetic. But I wasn't thinking about Esmeralda's family anymore. I was thinking about other people who lied to themselves and their families to make something terrible feel not quite so bad. My parents did that to me, I felt certain. By being here, I was lying to them, too.

"Miguelito, how do you see why I invent my stories for my little girls and my mother? Isn't it the best thing? It hurts me in the heart to lie to my mother. It's the worst thing for a daughter to do, but it's correct."

"Yes, Esmeralda, a person must sacrifice themself for their mother."

As the months passed, the people at Casa Carmen and Las Zonas had become my friends. They let me live in their world for a little while, like the men at Pepe's barbershop, and treated me as they would anyone else. They didn't understand what I was doing there, but they didn't mind. They liked me, and they knew I liked them. It was a lesson I would use many years later as a journalist—that people are pleased when someone is sincerely interested in who they are.

MY TOUR GUIDE days came to an end one spring day at Plaza Zaragoza. Two licensed tour guides in cheap suits with cheap smiles told me that if I didn't stop, they would report me to the police. Then they knocked me off the bench, throwing me hard onto the sidewalk, face-first. They laughed at what they could do to a kid.

Once I got past the pain and injustice of their assault, I started to grasp their threat—and how my family might be at risk. How could I be so irresponsible as to even think about working across from city hall, where the police were always leaning against the building and the parked cars, pretending to be on guard? I lay on the sidewalk for a minute, berating myself. What if the licensed guides had already reported me?

Jorge the taxi driver ran over and said, "Don't worry about those guys. It's only that they are jealous because you speak English better." He said we could still find a way to work together, and the other drivers would support me. But I knew that life in the plaza was over. I went back to the Escuderos de Colón and tried to pay more attention in school, to be the boy my father wanted me to be.

FIFTEEN

WHILE I FOUND FRIENDSHIP and a sense of belonging in Casa Carmen and Las Zonas, it wasn't like that at school or with the Escuderos. It wasn't their fault, but each day with those boys left me angrier and more envious about the normalcy of their families. When I visited one of their homes, the house itself would be similar to ours on Verlaine Street. But we rented rather than owned, and I always sensed that we were only a sales slump away from going back to Miss Mason's. I stopped going to those homes.

I couldn't blame the other boys. It was my problem, mine and my family's. Our problem was only sharper whenever I was with another family. The other boys belonged to a self-perpetuating elite, held together by family and financial ties. They all had a past they knew about and a future they could count on, too. For the other boys, what they were doing today was only part of a whole long river of events. They came from somewhere, they would be doing normal things in the future. They could look backward and they could look ahead, without losing their balance.

By contrast, for my family, time was only *now*. We were only on a dot called "today." What had happened before was gone, just gone; don't try to recall it. And who knew where we'd be later on? So we would retell one another our principal family story, the myth we needed, that success was about to blossom.

Those rich kids had something we didn't know about, and it was not money. That made it painful to be around them. You can't keep yourself from comparing no matter how much you try.

. . .

AT SCHOOL WE had military classes twice a week. We called it "march-ing" because that was about all we did. We lined up in the center court-yard and marched out to the soccer field in the back. *"¡De frente! ¡Marchen! Uno, dos, uno, dos."* Our instructor was an army lieutenant named Mariano López Ocampo. He told us, "If the country calls in the hour of glory, then it is for each one of you to respond to the victory that will follow." Then he said if there was ever a war, we would automati-cally become army cadets. That didn't sound good.

I couldn't forget Father Coughlan's warning of the great looming bat-tle between the government and the Church, and how the Escuderos had to defend God. But I couldn't put it all together. If Father Coughlan's war came, would the boys in the Escuderos be defending God against the cadets from school, who would be defending the government? Some of them were the same boys.

According to Lieutenant López, learning how to move in a group was the first step toward becoming soldiers. "It may seem to some," he said, "that you are only marching and not learning to fight. But if the flag is in danger, then you will know the answer. Who will protect Mexico's lakes and mountains and our own sisters from the foreign invader if we don't march in a straight file today?"

I didn't have an answer to that.

On the Fifth of May, the whole school had a *reunión conmemorativa* to celebrate Mexico's victory over the French in the Battle of Puebla. The brothers told us to wear our school uniforms—the blue blazers and cream-colored slacks—to show our solemn respect for the traditions of the fatherland.

It looked good to see us all dressed the same. It made me feel part of the school and of something even bigger. We were all excited. Some of the boys were acting silly, yanking on people's shirt collars and address-ing one another as waiters: "Young man! Bring me another punch, with lots of ice. Quick, don't be a peasant!"

As we formed in groups according to classroom on the courtyard under the harsh sun, we immediately began sweating into our sports coats. The national colors—red, green, white—were everywhere: in the flower arrangements on a stage, in the streams of cloth bunting, in flags. A recording of the national anthem played for the second or third time: *"Mexicanos, al grito de guerra. . . ."* We all sang along, marching up and down, bumping into the fool in front, who'd stopped for no reason, getting smacked by the idiot behind, who hadn't seen that we'd stopped. I hoped that we wouldn't have to go off to the army too soon, because we weren't too good at marching. I thought we'd probably all be killed before we even reached the foreign invaders.

Finally we got back to where we'd begun, standing straight as broomsticks with sweat dripping off our noses. "Don't move in the ranks!" a brother screamed from the edge of the courtyard. One of the men onstage began a speech about how we were all sons of the fatherland, ready to pay the ultimate price for liberty. But *he* didn't look ready to pay, not with that big belly bulging from his suit; he must have been talking about us. More than one hundred years ago, he said, there had been *una intervención de un país vecino,* an intervention by a neighbor country, that resulted in much sadness and the theft of the Mexican national patrimony. It was an intervention of cowards, he said, with traitors and massacres. The fat man's voice got louder and higher, and he flapped his arms to signal when we should be most upset.

I stood there like a good soldier and a good student, pretending to be a good Catholic at this school where we got the best possible education, wondering about what neighbor country the man was talking about. Then it became clear. He said: "The invaders from the north were victorious militarily, but they were humiliated by six young Mexican heroes who died instead of surrendering to the Yankees, just as you boys of Franco Mexicano are ready to do."

I couldn't believe what I was hearing. He was talking about the Americans! The enemy was *us.*

After that, none of what I'd heard made sense. Were we supposed to be brave cadets in the war to protect the flag and our sisters? Or were we going to be brave Catholic soldiers defending the Holy Church from the government? And what if the Americans came back? Whose side would I be on then? No one, especially me, thought I was anything but an American.

A new military tune came over the loudspeakers, and someone toward the back of the stage read a passage about Chapultepec Castle and the military school where the six students had died instead of surrendering to the invaders. He read out a name. On cue, everyone but me yelled, "*¡Murió por la patria!*" He died for the fatherland! Then another name, and they all yelled again, my classmates, the men on the stage, and the brothers together.

They must be the names of the boy heroes, I thought. My head was locked straight forward, but my eyes scanned to see if the others were looking at me. Maybe they saw me as an invader who'd come back early, an advance guard.

By the time the fourth boy hero's name was called out, I knew what I had to do. *"¡Murió por la patria!"* I yelled, just like everyone else.

I may have yelled it the loudest, because I felt the most alone.

SIXTEEN

IN THE SUMMER OF 1960, as school let out, I could not put my world in order. All that my parents thought worthy—my school, the pious Catholic youth group Escuderos de Colón, the loud ranting of Father Coughlan about an imminent religious war—seemed to glisten with slippery morality or to be ridiculous or inscrutable. I had no place to go. I couldn't even hang out at Plaza Zaragoza anymore, afraid that the official guides might think I was back in business and turn me in.

Everyone else at home was thriving. Mary loved her school and had made some close friends there. Fiona was finishing kindergarten. The two of them went off in their uniforms to the bus stop every morning, proud and happy to be there. I could never tell exactly how well Dad's business was going in the Rio Grande Valley, but it seemed to be doing well enough, judging by his mood, the frequency of his stays with us, and the flow of money. Mom, meanwhile, was engrossed in a new plan of her own. She was creating designs to be applied by poor Mexicans to curtains, tablecloths, and napkins, which would then be distributed through a network Dad would arrange in the United States.

I was the misfit, the one who was "adrift," as Dad said. And that was the summer when I drifted all the way to Los Angeles for an adventure, and to escape the hidden danger and contradictions of life with my parents.

IT WAS A trip that started with Tony Stone and me dreaming out loud the question "Wouldn't it be great to go to . . . ?" We thought about Mexico City and other places, but L.A. was the farthest place we had a contact: Tony's uncle Bill.

We didn't tell our parents because we knew they would say no. Our idea was to hitchhike fifteen hundred miles to L.A., pay a surprise visit to Uncle Bill, and then perhaps go to Houston to see my old house and Nannan. I thought of the big kiss I'd give her when I saw her. We'd be back in time for school to start in September.

We were each supposed to bring ten dollars: a figure reached with contempt for common sense. Uncle Bill lived in Hollywood, so we assumed that he had a lot of money and a big house, and that he'd probably get us summer jobs making movies. We'd have stories for our friends about how we helped make a film then showing in Monterrey. But I was already having doubts, because I'd been able to pull together only a little over two dollars.

Our house was quiet when Tony came by to pick me up. Even Güero had his little head stuck up under his wing, asleep on his perch in the kitchen. I snuck out the back door, because the one in front squeaked.

Tony, nervous yet eager, said, "Let's get going before everyone gets up."

Feeling uneasy, I told Tony that I didn't have enough money and maybe we should wait a week.

"Wait?" Tony said angrily. "We can't do that now, we're all set." Blustering, he said that the night before he'd had a fight with his mother and his stepfather. "I ran out of the house and told them I wasn't coming back. Now we *got* to go."

We left my house and saw the bus that went to Franco Mexicano and continued toward Saltillo. Tony stopped it and got on, and I followed, our momentum and aimlessness carrying me forward.

We got off at the fork in the road between Saltillo to the west and Laredo to the north, undecided about what to do next—two miles from my bedroom and we were stumped. The quickest way to L.A. was through Laredo, but we decided to go to Saltillo and then cross the border at Villa Acuña—it was much farther, but it was the smallest and sleepiest border town we knew of—and to do it late at night: a lesson I'd learned from my parents.

We had agreed on a story for anyone who wondered why two kids were hitchhiking by themselves: We were brothers, our parents divorced. Our father, who lived in Monterrey, had drunk away all his money, and we were on our way to California to live with our mother. We couldn't go to the police for help, because they'd take us back to our father, who had our papers. A tale that only the willing could believe. But people didn't question it. In Mexico, the truth is often strange. And besides, who would think that two nice American boys would be such liars?

About three hours from home, standing on the roadside in Saltillo, I was finally beginning to feel optimistic when Tony confessed that all he had was two quarters he'd stolen from his mother's purse, giving us less than three dollars total. Once again I wavered about going back, especially since I'd forgotten to leave a note for Mom and Dad telling them not to worry, we'd just gone up to L.A. for a while.

"Maybe you wanted to make them worry," Tony said. "I want my mother to worry. I don't think she ever does."

For a moment I thought that he was right, that maybe it would make me feel I'd get more help with figuring things out if my parents were more concerned. But then I imagined Mom going up to my bed looking for me, then calling for me out in the backyard, asking Dad and my sisters if they'd seen me, and then . . . But imagining their panic and sadness was so hard that I blocked it from my mind. We'd come this far, I told myself. The damage was done.

Feigning courage, I said, "Let's keep going. We're already in a pile of trouble." Then, in Spanish, *"Que valga la pena."* Let's make it worthwhile.

A big red truck stopped. It had yellow and green running lights on its front fenders. A fat driver was alone up in the cab. *"Hola, chavos. ¿'Onde van?"*

"Villa Acuña."

"Get in," the driver said. "That's my route."

His name was Carlos. He had a white T-shirt, patched pants, and huaraches. He was short—his head not far above the steering wheel—with a smile he tried to make look sincere. His truck was empty, which made it bounce like a beach ball on the buckled road. He said he was going to pick up a load of auto parts and take it to Villa Acuña. We told him our story and got in.

On the other side of Monclova, the road emptied of all vehicles and practically disappeared. It had wrinkles and waves, and whole sections of asphalt were cracked off and gone. We were in the desert amid gullies and ravines, the mountains around Saltillo way behind us. I was used to heat, but the sun here was so strong that it seemed to have burned the color out of everything, even the rocks. There was nothing alive but gray cactus and us.

Probably four hours later, with Tony and me smashed by the heat, the

exhaust fumes, and the ride, Carlos slowed and said to look up at what
he'd found. A truck sat off the left side of the road, pointing toward
Saltillo, with broken parts hanging underneath. Two young men were
under there, too, lying in the shade.

"Now the fiesta is ready," Carlos said. From their clothes and their
stringy builds, we could tell the two men were used to rough labor,
badly paid. They rubbed their bellies and yawned and came over to
look at us. Carlos popped open his door, swung down, and extended
his arms wide. "I have a surprise for everyone!" he told us all. "My
Mexican friends, you are going to learn to relax like the Americans do.
And my two American friends, you are going to learn to work like
Mexicans."

Carlos spoke to us as if giving a lesson in class, leaving the four of us
confused at first: "You can see there a truck with a small mechanical imperfection." We all looked at the broken truck. "And here you can see a
truck with no imperfection." We looked at our truck. "The truck over
there is full of boxes containing old automobile parts. A man in Saltillo
is waiting for these very valuable parts. We have something that is out of
balance here. The parts are in the truck that is broken; the truck that is
working has no parts. You, *mis gringitos,* will correct this imbalance.
You will take the boxes from there and you will put them here."

"No, we will not," I said, indignant. "You didn't say anything about
this when you picked us up. Forget it. *Adiós.* We will walk to Acuña
from here."

Tony told Carlos to fuck his mother, making the other two guys laugh.
We jumped from the truck, still shaky from the jangling ride, and fell on
the ground. As we stalked off into the desert, Tony yelled back that we
were going to find the police, which made the men laugh, loudly and sincerely.

Carlos came running up with a long club he must have pulled from behind his driver's seat. "Come on, my little friends, give me a hand. I
drove you all the way from Saltillo, and you see, you are very close to
Acuña now. One more ride is all you need. When we finish, perhaps I can
take you myself. Come on." His voice was mellow, but he was swinging
that club ominously.

Tony and I didn't have to look at each other to know what we were
thinking. " *'Ta bien,* " I told Carlos. "Okay. Just give us some water before we start."

Carlos said, "With pleasure, anything you want." Then he and the other two crossed the cracked road to lie in the shade of some cactus plants. Two of the three would sleep as the other watched us.

Even the smallest boxes were heavy, and slippery, too, from the oil dripping out of them. We moved slowly, pushing and sliding each box over the top of the others to the edge of the broken truck's bed. Then we took turns hauling boxes on our backs to the good truck, and together we shoved them into place. Soon we were covered in sweat and staggering from the exertion.

About halfway through the job, Carlos approached us with a nasty smile and said, "You know what, my American friends, I think I'm going to kill you—why not?" I was terrified, because there was nothing to stop them from killing us and hiding our bodies. How could we convince this maniac that people would miss us and know where to look if we didn't turn up?

"Carlos," I said slowly, trying to hide my quivering, "what we said before is not true. Our parents are not getting a divorce. We tell people that so they'll feel sorry for us and do not ask us questions."

"Aha!" Carlos said. "Then what is the truth about my strange little Americans?"

"The real, real truth is that we are going to a boarding school in El Paso," I lied, with the earnestness of a boy trying to stay alive. Then I said our parents were waiting for us in Del Rio. Carlos acted as though he didn't believe me, but I could tell he wasn't sure. He was thinking, squinting, turning his head slightly but staring at me. He looked over at the others, who only looked back, because they weren't sure either. He was measuring the risks. Though I was probably lying, how much of a chance could he take that I was telling the truth? He let it drop and walked away silently.

After we'd worked for another couple of hours, it was nearly dark, and the men started a small fire behind each of the trucks so we could see to finish the job. The dead mesquite branches crackled and smelled strong. The firelight made Carlos look like a ghost. At times I thought they might not kill us, at times I was sure they would, but they'd wait until the work was done. If we slowed, Carlos yelled at us and showed us the club. *He wants to get to the killing,* I thought.

I said to him, "So, Carlos, when our parents call the police and the American government, the Texas Rangers will come down this road looking for us. You know, that's their job. They have a headquarters in El Paso that is responsible for this area."

"What a big liar!" he screamed at me, leaning forward from the waist. Then he laughed. "Now you will tell me that your father has a plane to see us from the sky."

But my threat floated in the air. After Tony and I finished the work and sat and drank some water, we waited a minute more. No one said a word. Showing more confidence than we felt, we stood and walked down the road. Stiff and stumbling in pain, we did not talk or look back. We weren't sure they'd let us go without at least robbing us. Because they couldn't have known how little we had. We walked past the circle of light from the fires and kept going into the dark, up the road and over the hill, afraid of breaking the spell that had allowed us to escape. In a ravine hidden from the road, we lay down to sleep, cheeks on the sand, saying nothing, because the only thing in our minds was safety, and then sleep.

When Tony woke me, stars were out from one end of the sky to the other. "*Vamos,*" he said. Everything still hurt. We walked stiffly down the road as fast as we could, listening for trucks. A few hours later, we were nearing the border and came across a small cement-block house on the left side of the road, with a police car in front. Inside, a light flickered from a lantern.

When we went in, we surprised a pair of immigration agents like the ones Dad always gave some cigarettes and a few dollars to. One of the men was too drunk to stand up. He must have thought that we were somehow important, because he saluted us and said, "*¡A sus órdenes!*" At your orders! Then he lay his forehead back on the table. The other one was naked on a cot, with a woman covered by a sheet. The lantern sputtered on the table next to them. If we'd been thinking, we would have stayed away from uniforms. Instead, we went to sleep on the floor.

In the morning, the agents were drinking their warm beer. Their breath stank, and their puffy eyes squinted in the early sunlight. One of them agreed to let us ride with him to the border. Close to the Rio Grande, the road hooked to the left, out of sight of the crossing, so the Americans didn't see when we left the police car, near a roadside soda pop stand.

I'd seen my father's strategy for easy border crossings. His trick was to divert the agent's attention from what he was supposed to be doing, make him think of something else. I collected the few coins we had to buy a pack of Delicados, the cheapest Mexican cigarettes. Up a slight rise and across the bridge, we arrived at the American side of the river. The immigration agent said, "Hello, fellas. What are you doin'?"

I showed the agent the Delicados and—feigning naïveté, just like Dad—asked if I needed to pay import taxes or anything.

"No, son," the agent said. "You don't need to pay on them cigarettes. But you're not old enough to be smoking."

"No, sir. These here are for my dad. I promised to bring him some when we were eating breakfast this morning at the hotel."

The agent said, "Okay, go ahead."

We kept on walking into Del Rio until we found a big street and asked a man about the road to El Paso. "You're on it now," he said. "Just head north, thataway."

The people looked Mexican, but the town was U.S. It felt familiar, and we relaxed a little. There were a few tall buildings downtown, but within blocks it was all small houses and front yards, and then even the houses stopped.

All we could see was the two lanes of asphalt wiggling off into the distance, where the road disappeared into the desert. There wasn't a patch of shade wider than a cactus plant. I told Tony that the next time we ran away, we ought to bring a bag of sandwiches.

We put our thumbs out, not thinking of how filthy and battered the last twenty-four hours had left us. Some cars passed, likely folks from Del Rio who weren't going to take a chance on two shabby strangers. The sun got higher by the minute. Finally a blue car rolled up beside us, a man driving and a woman next to him with wide eyes and a panicked look. She rolled down the window fast and said, "Is there a accident? Your momma and poppa all right?"

I said, "Ahh, no, ma'am, there's no accident. We're just looking to get a ride."

"Well," she said, "you two look such a state and all, we just thought there was a accident. You sure?"

"Yes, ma'am, we don't have a car, that's why we're here. Are you going up this road? Can we have a ride?"

The man said, "Fellas, where you going?" He was a dark-haired, country sort of man, about the same age as the woman, late twenties. I had the feeling he was stopping because she was worried.

"We need to go see our mother," Tony told him.

Then the lady said to the man, "Well, for goodness' sakes, we can carry them up the road a ways, at least. Get on in, boys."

We jumped into the backseat and found a baby in a bassinet between us. But all I cared about was the cool air streaming over me from the air-conditioning. I put my head back and retreated into myself. I felt the drops of sweat dry on my face and scalp; I could feel the hairs grow stiff with the residue of salt and dust. The car was moving and I was inside it. I began to feel safe.

The lady was named Marsha. Her husband was Tyler, and the baby was Debbie. After a few moments of reserve, they began shooting questions at us: What in the world had happened that left our clothes all kinda tore up and greasy? And why was it, if we didn't mind them asking, why was it that our momma and daddy would let us be out here hitching rides?

The lady reached back between us to rock the baby. "How far you boys need to go to see your mother?"

I said, "Oh, it's on the other side of the next town."

"You mean past Sanderson?"

"Uh-huh."

"Well, we're going home to El Paso."

Tony looked up with a start: "That's on the way to Los Angeles, isn't it?"

The man laughed and said, "Well, now, how far you boys going?"

"Oh, just to Los Angeles," Tony said. Then the car got quiet suddenly. No one said anything for a while.

When the silence was too much, we began taking turns telling our story, about our parents divorcing and our father drinking up the money and our having to get to L.A. with no papers. Marsha thought it was terrible that a family should break up. "It's not the Christian way," she said. "Let's pray your daddy follows the right road."

"Yes, ma'am, we do," Tony said. Marsha said she was going to have Tyler stop at the first place he could so we could have a good meal. She suspected we didn't have much money in our pockets.

In Sanderson they bought hamburgers and French fries with real American ketchup, like I remembered from Houston. Marsha said that as soon as we got to El Paso she knew just the store to buy two new shirts. And maybe we would stay in her house a day because there was all that space in the living room, if we didn't mind sleeping on a blanket on the floor.

"No, ma'am," I said. "That would be real nice."

Marsha got so excited by her own Christian charity that she went into her purse, pulled out a ten-dollar bill, and gave it to Tony. "For later on. I can't do less than that. Isn't that the least we can do, Tyler?" He said it was.

We were flying along the blacktop with bright faces, sitting back and looking out at the cactus and sand go by, watching the clouds get darker and lower over the desert ahead. Marsha and Tyler were being so nice that I was feeling worse and worse about lying to them. The guilt began pushing up inside me, and after a while I couldn't keep up the deception and the truth came out. I said, "Well, you know, ah, we really live in Monterrey."

"How's that?" Tyler asked.

"We're going out to Los Angeles to see Tony's uncle. Tony and me are not really brothers, either, so it's just his uncle. His name is Bill, and he lives in Hollywood. We might get a job in the movies, or we could go to see my friends in Houston."

Tony must have thought he wasn't hearing me right. He kept staring past Tyler's head and out into the desert. Marsha asked, "Well, what about your momma in Los Angeles, waiting on you to get there?"

"Our momma's in Monterrey. Well, we have two different mommas. One for Tony and one for me. It's like we're brothers and all, only we're not related."

The car was quiet again. Still, I was feeling better about being honest. A sticky fog of lying had left the car, and now we could all be closer.

"Uh-*huh*," Tyler said after a while. "So your poppa doesn't drink?"

Trying to help, Tony said *his* poppa drank, but then he looked like he wished he hadn't said anything.

"Well, sir, we have two poppas, too," I said.

Marsha reached back and picked up Debbie from the bassinet. She swung the baby away from us and held her close. "So where are your mommas and why ya'll going to Los Angeles?"

I started telling them about the problem we'd had with fat Carlos, the truck driver. They had trouble understanding how anyone could be so cruel, but I went on. All of a sudden, I could not help telling Tyler and Marsha all the things I hadn't been able to tell other grown-ups. I just had to tell someone, and it came spilling out. I told them all about the Franco Mexicano school, where the brothers didn't seem to teach that much. Marsha interrupted me and asked, with distaste, "Is that one of those Catholic schools, then? Are you a Catholic?"

I said I was and kept on going. About how Father Coughlan said there was a great war coming, and if it did come I'd be a cadet in the Mexican army. I told her how you can sell pillows to people without beds, and that there were a lot of places in Monterrey where American tourists liked to go and some of the girls in those places weren't as bad as folks thought, they were only working to save up to buy a little store in their village, and they gave money to their mothers whenever they could.

When I stopped talking, the car was dead silent again. Everyone looked outside. Until Tyler asked, "Well, Tony, what does your daddy do down there in Monterrey?"

"He writes magazine articles" was all Tony could say. But I picked it up and said that they probably wouldn't know if they'd read any of the articles, because Mr. Stone used a woman's name and pretended to be the lady in the story. And that Tony's mother wrote articles, too, about flying saucers and crime, but she usually used a man's name, so she was famous but not as a woman.

I felt as if there were only inconsistencies in my life, except when there were contradictions. I was reviewing them all, for the first time out loud, trying to put them together, and sharing them with strangers who looked normal. Grasping at this couple who had rescued us and who seemed decent and wise.

We'd driven long enough to reach the dark clouds. The raindrops plunked the car's roof as the tires sang through the water on the road.

Tyler looked over at Marsha, holding Debbie. I could tell that my barrage of honesty had killed any affection they'd felt for us.

Trying to make it casual, Tyler said, "I've been thinking about it, and it's probably best we stop to see some of my relatives before we get to El Paso. What I'll do is, we got a town coming up soon, and I'll let you fellas off there so it'll be easier to catch your next ride. How's that sound?" Tony and I didn't say anything; we didn't have to. We looked at the road out ahead. I felt rejected by the people I'd turned to. But I had finally realized what Tony knew all along: telling the truth can be stupid. A good lie is much better.

In the next town, through the sharp rain, we saw a hamburger stand on the right side of the road with a big orange-and-black A&W root beer sign. No one said anything when we saw it, but we all knew that was where Tony and I would be getting out.

SEVENTEEN

I SUFFERED NO MORE SPASMS of honesty for the rest of our trip. It took us three days to get from southwest Texas to Los Angeles. And because we lied so well, nearly everyone who picked us up gave us at least one meal and some pocket money. Still, it wasn't an easy time. We slept sitting up in cars, in a ditch, and once, in Scottsdale, in the rain, behind a billboard. At the end of the trip our faces were raw and peeling from the sun and our lips were so cracked and swollen that we could barely understand each other speaking.

The last ride took us right into Hollywood. Tony tried calling his uncle Bill for several hours before finally getting an answer. I listened hopefully as he eagerly said, "Hi, Uncle Bill, it's me—Tony from Mexico. I came to visit you." As he heard the response, his face became sadder and sadder. It seemed that while Uncle Bill would pick us up, he would not be able to help us in the way that we'd hoped.

Uncle Bill's part of Hollywood was not the plush lawns and mansions we had imagined. It was narrow streets, fading apartment buildings, and brown palm trees. Uncle Bill didn't have a big job in the movies after all. He didn't have any kind of job, though he thought he had one "lined up." Even worse, since he had not paid rent for a while and he'd just had a fight with his roommate, he had three days to move out of the apartment. Now that we'd shown up, he said he might have to move sooner.

Uncle Bill was a short, stocky, jumpy guy in his late thirties, with a loud shirt. There was an unpleasant scar coming through his receding hair. "Korean War," he said, pointing to the scar. He spent a lot of time pacing, but it was a small apartment, and after three long steps he had to turn around, which made him frustrated as well as nervous.

He told us we could stay one night. He could give us a few dollars if he sold a set of golf clubs, but he didn't know of any jobs for us, so we should probably try another town. Did we have some other place in mind?

Our clothes were filthy and torn. We hadn't washed in four days. We'd kept going with lies and hope to reach Hollywood, and we'd found despair. I said, "Well, we were thinking about going to Houston after Hollywood, so we could go there."

Uncle Bill wanted us to call home before anything else. I was lucky, because we didn't have a telephone at our house, but Tony had to call his mother. Uncle Bill talked to her first for a bit, telling her that we were okay and he would do what he could for us, but it wasn't much and he was sorry. He told her we were going to Houston, and then he listened for a long time. He said he'd get us to San Diego in the morning because from there it was a straight shot to Houston. That was the best he could do, he said. He was sorry.

Then Tony spoke to his mother for just a minute, because Uncle Bill kept saying that long-distance phone calls were damn expensive. That was fine with Tony, who kept saying he was sorry, too.

Early on the morning we left Monterrey, Tony's mother had seen that he was missing and remembered the fight they'd had the night before— and that Tony had said he was going to Laredo. She called my mother, and soon it was clear that we had both run away. My family was panicked. Fiona and Mary were frantic wondering why I'd left and whether I would do something that got me hurt. My parents, putting on a façade that even young Fiona saw through, acted as if all was under control.

While Dad searched along the roads leading from Monterrey, Tony's stepfather drove to Laredo, hoping to see us on the road—and, if not, to alert U.S. officials at the Laredo border crossing. Nobody guessed that we'd slipped through at Del Rio, 150 miles northwest of Laredo, the smallest town on the Texas border. With no word from any authorities, the two families gave up their hunt and waited for us to contact them.

The day after we arrived in Los Angeles, Uncle Bill drove us toward San Diego. He didn't have a job or a home, but he had a Porsche convertible with a glossy gray finish and red leather seats. We were flying past Disneyland and then alongside the Pacific Ocean. It really was deep blue, not like the brown gulf water off Galveston, Texas. As we flashed past the surf and seagulls, we felt that we'd made it to Hollywood after all.

Since Tony and I wanted the top down, even if the sun and wind tore up our blistered faces, Uncle Bill stopped at a drugstore for a white cream for us to smear on. It made us look like Indians with war paint. Whenever we raced by another car, we screamed, "Geronimo!" and threw up our arms, just to make people look.

As we got close to San Diego, Uncle Bill swooped into a gas station and yelled over to the attendant, "Say, where's the road to Houston from here?" The guy said he thought it was the same highway as the one to Yuma, go down a few miles and we'd see it. A few minutes later, Uncle Bill said he was pretty sure he'd gotten us to the right place. That road off to the left must be the one to Yuma, he said. It was time to get out. He gave a few bills to Tony and said, "You guys know that if there was any way I could do more, I would do it. Tell your Mom that."

We thanked him, and he was gone, with his arm up, waving from his Porsche, but his eyes straight ahead. We were on our own.

We hadn't gotten far down the road when a policeman came up on a motorcycle. He looked like he was from the movies, too. He had tall black boots, polished, with a pen stuck down in the boot on his right leg. His motorcycle was shining, with chrome pipes in the front. I noticed his very pretty brown uniform was clean everywhere and pressed. Tony and I had already decided that our story had worked well enough to get us to Los Angeles, so we were going to keep it. The only change was that we were leaving L.A. to get to our mother in Houston. The policeman didn't worry us.

"Hello, gentlemen. What are you two doing on the freeway? You know it's dangerous out here."

That confused Tony. "What's a freeway?" he asked.

I whispered, "It's the highway, remember? Uncle Bill called it a freeway."

"Oh, the freeway!" Tony said. "Yes, we're going to get a ride."

"Well, gentlemen, you can't hitch a ride on the freeway. That's illegal. Didn't you know that? Where are you going?"

I told him casually, "Oh, just to Houston." Then I thought that might have been a mistake. I could have said we were going to someplace nearby if I had known the name of someplace nearby. But when I said "Houston," the situation changed. The policeman wanted to know why. We told him our new story. He said to wait while he checked something on the radio. Then he told us we'd have to wait awhile because another policeman was coming to drive us to a special San Diego motel where kids could stay a few days for free. That sounded good to us.

When the police car arrived, the second officer said he'd take us to the motel, just hop on in. Ten minutes later, we arrived at a large, sand-colored building with tall palm trees and grass. We'd been daydreaming out loud in the backseat about a comfortable motel with a pool out front, but this turned out to be the police station.

A stern policeman in civilian clothes came up and said he was the "juvie officer," a new phrase for us. He said he needed our folks' phone numbers so they could come down and get us. We let him have our story, then some other stories that he didn't believe either. By the time we got to the truth, about our parents living in Monterrey, he said, "I'm ready to give up on you two. You're going somewheres else till I get this all figured out. Let's see you put your hands behind your backs and I'll just slip these cuffs on till we get down to the Hall."

I asked Tony, "Do you think the Hall is the same as the motel?"

"No, Mike, there is no motel."

We arrived at San Diego County's Juvenile Hall five days after we'd begun our journey. We gladly followed the order to shower. They gave us tennis shoes, blue jeans, and white T-shirts. A man said we might as well throw our old clothes away because they looked so bad. But we pleaded to save them, since we'd need them in a day or two when we left. I asked if I could keep my belt to use with the jeans, but the man said, "We don't use belts here; just hang on to your pants." He said it would go just fine for us if we smartened up and went along with the rules. Most of all, we had to stop lying to adults who just wanted to help us.

"Now," he said, "here's a little secret for you. What you don't want to be, what you want to spend all your time not being, is one of our knuckleheads."

"Okay, sir. What's a knucklehead?" Tony asked.

"That's a knucklehead right there!" he said. "When you take up my time asking me what a knucklehead is, you're doing it. So don't."

He said that Juvenile Hall protected the public from delinquent minors. I told him that I'd never hurt anyone in the public, but it was getting to where every time I turned around somebody in the public was doing something to me.

They took us to our "room," which was actually a cell with cement walls and a small window made of hard, scratched plastic, with bars behind it. The door was thick metal. There were two bunk beds, each one with a blanket and a white sheet folded over the top very straight and neat. I took the top bunk and fell asleep until the next morning.

We learned the next day that the police had tried to reach Uncle Bill, but he wasn't at the apartment and they wouldn't call Tony's parents in Mexico. The man in charge said he'd never heard such wild crap from a couple of kids, and he wasn't going to follow our line of bullshit and call all the way down to Monterrey just to find out we'd been lying our little asses off about that, too.

We didn't care that much anyway. I told Tony this was a pretty good jail, a lot better than the way most people lived in Mexico, and a lot cleaner, too. They had magazines and a small library. They let us watch TV in the rec room, and the food was good. We decided that we'd stay long enough to rest up and for our faces to heal and then we'd work on getting on to Houston. But it did start to feel strange when a kid told me that no one had belts so we wouldn't hang ourselves. "Some guys would do it right off the top bunk," he said offhandedly.

That was very tough for me to absorb, and I tried not to think about it. Still, it told me there was more in Juvenile Hall than TV and good food. This was a hard place, with hard people, some of them desperate.

They finally reached Uncle Bill after a couple of days, and he had Tony's parents call. They gave permission for Uncle Bill, as a relative, to pick Tony up and send him home. That day or the next, he was gone.

The juvenile authorities were surprised that we hadn't been lying about everything, but they were still angry at me because my parents were not cooperating with the law. They said Dad had called—informed by Tony's parents. But he told the men at the Hall that he wouldn't come to get me. I didn't believe them. I was certain my father would not abandon me like that.

Later I'd learn from my sisters that Dad was panicking even after my family found out where I was. Mary and Fiona thought that was strange, because at least in Juvenile Hall I was safe. Mom seemed hurt, or at least Mary thought so. Not angry with me, hurt that something unfair was happening.

THE INMATES AT juvie were called "wards," and the men in charge of them were called "coaches." One morning, about a week after I got there, I met with a coach in charge of my case to prepare for my hearing, where they'd decide what to do with me. He was a younger man, with a blond crew cut. A college student, he said, about to get a degree in physical education. I thought it was a silly thing to study in college. He was confused by my case and upset with me. He said, "You won't get out of here until your dad shapes up. That's a straight promise."

In his little office, the coach pulled out my file, looked it up and down, then turned the page before glaring at me. "You sure you didn't lie to us when you said you don't have any relatives? Everybody's got somebody, an aunt or a cousin, even if they don't live close by."

"No, sir. Just my dad's relatives somewhere in Boston. That's it."

"What about your mother's folks?"

"No, sir. She's got folks in England somewhere, but that's all I know."

He didn't believe me. As I had learned from Tyler and Marsha, the truth was not always helpful. In juvie it was the same deal, except that my lies wouldn't help me either.

Coach wanted to know why my folks didn't come to get me, or at least send a relative. I was feeling sad about this myself, and I said, "Why don't you ask them?" *Or why don't you let me ask them?* I thought. Because the coaches wouldn't let me speak to my parents by phone, no matter how much I said it wasn't fair.

He said, "Your dad told me he won't come—he said to send you home on a bus. Is he scared of the law or something? I mean, why can't he get up here to get you?"

"No, sir, he's not afraid of the law. I guess he's just pretty busy right now." That was what I wanted to be true. Sometimes I believed it. But then there was my doubt—and my anger. Was it something about our secret, like the time at the border in Laredo, and when we ran from the rodeo? If that was it, I'd never know for sure. I had learned that much. But what kind of trouble would keep my parents from picking me up from Juvenile Hall? And why couldn't they fix the problem so we could be normal?

Coach checked everything I had told the others: our home address, Dad's work in the valley. I told him, "Sometimes he works in Weslaco, sometimes Brownsville or McAllen. Then he might go all the way up to Falfurrias. I don't know where he's staying right now." I told him where we used to live on Muscatine Street, then Mobile Street. I told him about Nannan and her husband, Jack, but Coach couldn't find a telephone number for them, and I told him about the Villa.

He said, "That ain't near enough for us to go on. How do we call a place with no working phone?"

"But that's all there is, Coach. That's us."

Coach kept getting more upset. "Don't hunch up your shoulders telling me that's all there is. If you came from the United States, you got to have somebody in the United States."

"Nope," I said. "I don't know anyone else."

"Well, we're not going to put you on any bus to Mexico. The law don't allow that. We got to release you to a close relative, not a bus driver."

Still foolish, I asked, "Why don't you give me some money and let me go and I'll get home on my own? I got here on my own." That made him mad.

"Don't make me mad," he said, a growing resentment in his voice. "I'd love to get you out of here, but now you're going to get a hearing." He told me he was sure I'd get "intake," and if I didn't start remembering relatives or if Dad didn't start cooperating, I would wind up with "commitment," which meant they could keep me until I was eighteen. Neither one sounded good.

A few days later, Coach took me to the hearing room, where we sat on the two plain chairs in front of a metal desk. The man behind it looked like a coach, too; crew cut, short-sleeved white shirt, too busy to pay much attention. There was an American flag on the varnished plywood wall. Coach said that I wouldn't cooperate and neither would my family, and we were trying the patience of the whole system.

I asked, "Am I on trial or something? Are you going to do something else to me? Just let me go, and I promise I won't hitchhike on the freeway." It seemed like a good solution to me, but it only aggravated them because I seemed unrepentant.

The man behind the desk said they hadn't charged me with a crime, but they were thinking about it. "So just sit right there and keep it zipped. You're a danger to yourself, and we're going to keep you."

I said, "Well, you people are a danger to people being treated the right way." That made him mad, too.

"Raymond," the man said, "we have to hold you until we can turn you over to your parents. I know your case very well. That's how it's going to end."

"If you know my case so well, how come you don't know my name is Michael?" I answered back.

"It doesn't make any difference what your name is, that's the law." Then he gave me "intake," which meant I could be assigned a job. I worked in the kitchen for approximately the next month, all the while trusting that my father would come for me if he could. *It must be our secret that's keeping him away,* I thought, and that suspicion made me furious—with my parents, with the damn mystery that controlled our lives. I blamed them for having gotten us into whatever trouble made us do the things we did. My anger made me what the coaches called "a behavioral problem." Twice I attacked other kids. I leapt on one for not moving fast enough in line and the other for looking at me funny on the ball field. I viciously punched and kicked them both, but it was more fury than real fighting. There were a few bruises and loose teeth, nothing more serious, but I scared myself. I was doing things I had never done before. I couldn't control myself.

As I look back at it, violence had been in my life in the Villa and had sat there in the background ever since, like an ugly buzz off a high-tension line. It was more than the murder of Don Octaviano, or the tour guides' assault on me. It was the violence of a society where people felt abused by others who could not be touched. It was the poor people slammed together and covered with exhaust on Monterrey's buses; it was fat Carlos forcing us to work for him. In those ways, rage and violence were always present in Mexico. And I, locked up, angry and confused about my family, felt the violence emerge in assaults on boys who had done nothing to me.

The only explanation I would hear from my father later was that he and my mother had been doing the best they could and were glad I was off the road. Besides, Dad said, he thought the experience would be the best punishment he could imagine for my running away.

Still, overall, juvie was not so bad. There were the classes to get through—basic English, arithmetic—and time for sports. Some of the coaches seemed aloof or dim-witted, many actually wanted to help the wards.

My job was to clean off five tables after every meal, take the dishes to the kitchen, and wash all the big pots for Mr. Johnson, the cook. He was a tall, wide black man with white hair who treated me paternally, though his defenses were up against feeling too much for any of the damaged kids who passed through his kitchen. Usually he let me have a cigarette break between the tables and the washing. Since I was under sixteen, I couldn't have my own cigarettes, but the coaches usually let me sit at the table and get a hit from the older guys. We called them "toke smokes." I told the coach in the dining hall they'd be smarter to let me have a smoke once in a while because it was easier to stay locked up that way without jumping another kid. The coach said he thought so, too.

With intake status came a roommate. One afternoon I was reading in bed when I heard someone say, "Jackson." I looked down from my bunk, and there he was, standing in the doorway looking at me as if I were in his room by mistake. "They said you were from Mexico, but you don't look Mexican."

"No," I said. "I live in Mexico, but I'm American."

I couldn't tell if Jackson was really mean or only wanted to look mean. He was a black kid about my age, shorter than I was, but he already had well-defined muscles and a swagger.

Usually, Jackson said, they put the white kids together if they could, "so there must be something wrong with you." He told me he was in for stealing a big Pontiac that he drove around for a day until they got him. He said they called him a "troubled youth" but said that was backwards. "I'm not troubled. I *give* people trouble, and fuck 'em."

Jackson spent most of his time in our cell asleep. I spent a lot of time pacing, which bothered him. "You the movin'est son of a bitch ever. Are you better off here or back there doing whatever you was doing?" Which told me that juvie was better than Jackson's foster home.

Jackson—he wouldn't say if it was his first name or his last—had been in foster homes and juvie most of his life, and he could barely read. But as we lay in our bunks after lights out, I told him stories from books I'd read—about Hannibal and his elephants, and Wolfe on the Plains of Abraham, and Huck Finn. I tried to tell him about taking tourists around Monterrey, but he said he'd never heard of a white pimp so I must be making it up. He still wanted to hear about it, though.

Jackson repaid me by teaching me all the words to Chuck Berry's "Maybellene," which was already a classic. We sang it over and over, with Jackson slapping the bunk frame to keep time and me rapping on the plastic window. We howled, " 'Maybellene, why can't you be true?' " until a night coach pounded on the cell door for us to shut up. Then Jackson taught me Fats Domino's popular "Blueberry Hill," singing it in his deepest voice, almost whispering because of the coach. He wiggled and pranced around the cell like a nightclub act. I jumped in. It was the first time I ever danced.

• • •

ABOUT SIX WEEKS after I got there, one morning before sunrise, the overnight coach woke me and led me to the empty dining hall, where he said I was going home. At first I didn't believe him—was I dreaming? It was too early for breakfast, but a coach in the kitchen made me toast and hot chocolate. "Time to go," he said, "or you'll miss that bus." They gave me the paper bag with the clothes I'd come in with and told me to stand in the corner of an office and get changed. Then a coach drove me to the Greyhound station. The county had paid for my ticket to Brownsville, Texas, where my family would meet me.

The coach said, "Your dad's got to pay back this ticket and the per diem, all of it. That's the law. You tell him that."

"What's a per diem?" I asked.

"That's the money the county charges for every day we have a kid in juvie." The coach didn't know why they had suddenly decided to let me go, except they were getting tired of my being there and didn't see any future in it. And they thought there was something wrong with my dad.

Just before I stepped up into the bus, the coach gave me a twenty-dollar bill. "You gotta sign here for the money, to make sure you got it," he said. Then he gave the ticket to the bus driver and told him, "Make sure he goes all the way." The driver answered that he just had the bus up to Phoenix.

"Well," the coach said, "can you tell the next guy?"

Clear as that, Dad had won, I thought. They—the police, the coaches, the justice system—had just turned me loose, hoping that one unnamed bus driver would tell the next one to keep an eye on me. It made me think that whatever reasons there were for my family not coming to get me, Dad was strong and he had been correct in his judgment. Just as he had wanted, I was on my way to them.

EIGHTEEN

WHEN I GOT to the Brownsville bus station, my whole family was waiting. I didn't know if I was a terrible kid for leaving or a brave adventurer for returning safely, and my sisters weren't sure either. Fiona looked at me from behind Mom's skirt, peeking around, not wanting to get too close until she knew how much trouble I was in. Mary kept back, too, watching, smiling, but cautious. No one seemed to know what to do until Mom ran over with a big hug, holding me close and rocking me back and forth. "Oh, Michael, oh, Michael," she said. "Thank God we have you back." Dad came up more slowly, with a hard look at first, but then he couldn't hide his relief either.

My own emotions were clashing. It was good to be wrapped again in my family's love, but I assumed that I'd been trapped in juvie because of the family's mysteries. I'd made it back, but to what?

It wasn't until we were alone that night that Dad and I had the conversation I'd been dreading, when I had to explain why I had run away. Dad set the agenda. He said he knew I could see how much my immature behavior had hurt my mother and sisters, so he didn't have to belabor the point. By having stayed locked up, I'd been punished enough. In other words, the account books were balanced and we could forget the whole mess. I felt so guilty that I couldn't challenge him, couldn't show how bitter I was that he'd deserted me. I mumbled something about how it had worked out differently than Tony and I had planned and that I wouldn't do it again. That was it, and I was glad.

Tony had already been sent off to a boarding school in Torreón, on the other side of Saltillo. My parents, and his, thought it was best if he and I didn't communicate. That seemed like an overreaction to me, but I agreed and kept my word.

What I wouldn't know until recently was that my brush with the police in California had brought us once again too close to the attention of American authorities. San Diego County had finally given in when they realized my father wasn't going to come and pick me up, but they hadn't closed my case. The juvenile court judge was suspicious, plus they wanted Dad to pay for my stay and the bus fare, and the twenty-dollar bill the coach had given me for meals on the ride to Brownsville. Without understanding the consequences, I had given them our address in Monterrey and the name Weslaco Lumber, a company where Dad did business in the valley. That was enough for the judge to write Dad to demand an explanation and, in the next few months, for other juvenile authorities to send us letters demanding payment. Those letters were enough to make our parents feel vulnerable again.

And when that happened, we always ran.

Four months after I returned, near Christmas, Dad came back from a short stay in Texas and said, unexpectedly, that it was time we finally moved to California. I was fourteen, Mary ten, and Fiona had just turned six.

Though there had been vague talk of living in California for several years, moving there had never seemed likely. True, Mom and Dad were becoming more concerned that Mary and Fiona were losing the United States as their reference point, especially when my sisters spoke Spanish with each other. And, after nearly three years, Dad had not been able to start a business in Mexico.

But the main reason we were going, according to Dad, was that we'd always wanted to go there, though that was news to me. Besides, there were so many good business opportunities in California. "It's going to be a little difficult at first," Mom told us, "but nothing we haven't done before."

Mary wasn't satisfied. "If it's going to be difficult, why do we have to do it?"

"Well, we just explained that, Mary, didn't we?" Mom said. "Just you wait until we all get to California, you'll see. It's going to be wonderful for us all. We're making a clean break of it."

Mom told us that going to California had been her dream for years, ever since what happened in a bomb shelter in England during World War II. "Well, children," she said as if she were beginning a fairy tale, "during the war everything was rationed. We had ration coupons for even a tiny bit of butter. Then one day in that bomb shelter, someone passed around little packets of raisins. That was a godsend to us all—just the relief that there was occasionally something good, something from America. Something from that magic place, California." On each packet was the picture of a young woman, the Sun-Maid raisin logo. "Oh, she was lovely, and so happy. Not like any of us in that smelly bomb shelter, with the explosions going all the night long. This girl had long curls and a red bonnet, with her huge basket filled to the brim with lovely green grapes. I promised myself then and there that one day I would go to California."

UNLIKE THE OTHER runs, this one gave us a little time to prepare. We could tell the kids in our schools, though we couldn't quite tell them everything. Dad said it was best to say that we were returning to Texas. Actually, though I didn't buy the reasons we were moving, I was glad to be leaving Franco Mexicano and all its contradictions. I was also glad to return to the States, where I'd fit in better. But it was hard for Mary and Fiona to say goodbye at Colegio Mexicano, especially for Mary. Her friends there gave her a party in the classroom, including gifts of holy cards with hints on how to live a good life and to help her remember the saints. She thought the cards were good to have.

Dad went to Texas again and returned a few days later with a trailer painted silver, with corrugated metal sides and two small wheels that wobbled, but "not that much," he said. "We'll get it straightened up in Harlingen." By that point he was in a hurry. We loaded the trailer full and started off the next morning. Mary began crying, and Fiona joined her. Mom was jumpy. When the lady from across the street came out to see what we were doing, Dad waved at her, as if we were off to a picnic. The last one in was Güero. He came along on Mom's hand, and she put him on the front seat between her and Dad.

Close to the border crossing at Reynosa, Mom told us about parrot fever, a disease parrots catch from one another. Bringing a parrot into the United States meant several weeks of quarantine, but because Güero hadn't been with other parrots, she was sure he wasn't sick. She said, "We're not going to bother with all the checking they'll want to do, so this is how we'll handle it. We'll just get him drunk until he goes to sleep, and we'll hide him."

That sounded smart to me, maybe even entertaining. "Mom, do you think he'll sing when he gets drunk?" I asked.

We pulled off the main street in Reynosa to scrape the tourist stickers from the car window. Güero had never been in the car this long. He was getting cranky. Mom bought a bottle of tequila and splashed some on a piece of bread but couldn't get him to eat it. "Come on, Güero," she cooed. "Come on. Take a wee bite." She laid him on his back in her left hand and stroked his little parrot throat, which he usually enjoyed. But Güero twisted his face away from the bread. Mom persisted: "Come on, then, Güero, have just a taste. You may learn to like it." Nothing. He shut his beak tight.

Mom looked at Dad, and we looked at them both and at Güero lying there stubbornly on Mom's palm. "All right," Mom said resignedly. "All right, then. There's nothing else for it." She got one of the cloths we'd packed to make us tidy for the border, doused it with tequila, and laid it across Güero's face. He didn't like that either, but she held him until he stopped squirming. And *plop*, she put him into the straw bag next to her, his little claws sticking straight up, his head drooped over to one side.

I was shocked. "Mom, you killed Güero!"

"Not at all," she said. "He's breathing fine—he's only drunk. Let's go, then." She waved the cloth out the window to whisk away the tequila smell, then laid it across Güero to cover him.

DAD'S PLACE IN Harlingen, we discovered, was a single room. There was a sink and a hot plate and a kitchen table, a desk and a couch, but the furniture was small and crammed together. *Strange,* I thought. This was where our father spent so much of his time instead of with us. This was his other life, and there wasn't much to it. I wasn't so jealous anymore. It looked nearly pitiful.

Dad kept moving around, opening the blinds, pulling out a chair for Mom. We could see how bad he felt that this was all he had. But Mom complimented the curtains and said it was just the right size, less bother to clean.

Nobody was sure how long we'd stay in Harlingen, so we rented a house. A few days after we'd arrived, when Dad was out working and we were hanging our clothes in the one closet, I asked my mother the questions that were bothering me. Why hadn't we stayed in Monterrey until it was time to go to California? Why did we have to leave so quickly just to stop in Harlingen? Then Mary wanted to know, too.

At first Mom answered calmly. We'd come to Harlingen, she said, to get a little more money. "Your father and I know things," she said, "and there was a good reason to leave when we did. It was time to leave Monterrey behind us. It will be so nice for us all in California, and we'll start a new life, all of us together."

But Mom's face told us more than her calm words. She was looking over at the cupboard, which was open and empty. Our cardboard boxes of belongings were heaped around us. Mom walked toward the kitchen and leaned against the wall, staring at nothing. She told someone we couldn't see, "I'm going 'round the *bend*." She said it quietly, and then much louder: *"Right 'round the bend!"* She slipped down the wall into a lump of Mom on the floor. She went away right in front of us. I thought she had died—on the floor, with the boxes. All I could do was blink my eyes. When they opened again, she was still in the lump. Who knew what to do when your mother just died in front of you, with your father away working, and it was up to you to take care of your sisters? What would we tell Dad?

At last Mom moved her head. She shook a little bit, sat up for a minute. Then she stood, wiped her hands on the white apron, and came back to finish putting the clothes away. "I think it's the heat that got to me," she said. "Come along, children, let's get this done now."

Later I told Mary that we had to be careful about questions. She said she knew.

WE'D PLANNED TO get brakes for the trailer when the money came in, but a few weeks after arriving in Harlingen, we again had to leave all of a sudden. Dad came home early one day, saying it was time to go: "Let's get packed up, and we'll set off early. It's always best to get going early." So we did. Mary was in charge of the map and showed us the road going north, a line straight as a ruler. When we got to the road, it cut through orange and grapefruit orchards and then fields with cattle. The air went from smelling of oranges to smelling of grass and cow patties.

Just past Kingsville, Dad pulled over so that the car and trailer were almost off the blacktop. He turned around to the three of us sitting in the backseat, me on the left, Fiona in the middle, then Mary. His right arm lay on the seat back, his elbow bent. He looked excited, as if he had a grand surprise to share. He said, "Here's where you three are going to decide something big for all of us. Not many kids can do that, but you three are old enough now."

Yeah, I thought, *I'm old enough for that.*

Dad said, "See the sign up there? It's going to help you decide what we do now." It was a yellow sign at the top of a short hill, where our northbound road ended at another road going east and west. Two black arrows curved up from the bottom of the sign and pointed in opposite directions to the names of two towns. To the right was Corpus Christi, to the left, San Antonio. I still didn't understand, because we were supposed to be going to California.

Dad told us that we had only enough money for one more tank of gasoline and a couple nights in a motel. We were going to decide right there which town we'd go to for a while so he could make some money for California. "Where do you kids want to go?" he said.

What a great deal, I marveled. *We can pick our next home.* I began lobbying Mary. "How about San Antonio, because that's where the Alamo is?" But she wasn't sure, and didn't say anything at first.

Fiona said, "What's the Alamo?"

I reminded Mary about the Davy Crockett movie we'd seen, and that he had been at the Alamo. "It's a big place where kids can have a real good time," I told her. "And what's in Corpus Christi?"

Mary caught my enthusiasm and said, "Yes, San Antonio is good, Dad. What about San Antonio?"

"Great," he said. "San Antonio, Texas, coming right up."

NINETEEN

In San Antonio we stayed in a motel on the highway outside of town and deferred our adventure to California. Dad went out and got a job selling in the building business. Almost immediately there was more money. In a few weeks there was enough to buy a better car, a used Ford station wagon, red and white.

We rented an apartment near Brackenridge Park, a middle-class neighborhood. Fiona did not go to school, but Mary enrolled in St. Peter's School, and I went to Central Catholic High, another "very fine Marist institution for young Catholic gentlemen," Dad said. He told me it was time I started thinking about the kind of man I was to become. He said the world was open to me, though I wondered about that, considering how we lived. He said a fine education made for a successful and contented man, that and what one learned at home, and he was sure I was getting the best of both of those.

As the next step toward our move to California, Dad traded a roof repair to a man in return for a homemade trailer to replace our dilapidated one. He said that a top-of-the-line trailer—solid, with safety lights on the corners and first-class electric brakes—laid the foundation for a successful trip. He and I eagerly visited the work in the man's front yard and watched the trailer going up, from frame to roof panels. At the end, Dad had it painted a creamy shade of white. To make the best impression, he had the Ford station wagon painted to match.

We estimated that getting to California would take four days—maybe three with Mom driving, too. She planned to make sandwiches each morning in the motel, and we would stick them in the ice chest to eat on the way. Before long, even Mary was eager.

At the end of the school year, six months after we arrived, our preparations were complete. For the first time we felt as if we were in charge of our future, that we were moving because it made sense, not to flee something chasing us. Mary planned our route to San Jose, our new home, with Mom and Dad overseeing to make sure we kept to the small roads—they had less traffic and would be easier for towing the trailer. Reading the map's legend, Mary said we'd be going on secondary roads. Dad objected that our family did nothing secondary, and we shouldn't think of the roads that way either. We were using the small roads because that was the only logical way a family could hope to see the real West.

It was a struggle to get every single toy and book and colored block into the red toy chest that we'd had since Houston, but Mary and Fiona kept fighting to get it right, pulling things out, then jamming them back in a different way. Fiona sat on top of the box and bounced away until it closed. "See, Mom, all done."

We finally had the trailer loaded up—extra loaded, really. That bothered Dad, because we had to tie one box and Mary's bike to the back of the trailer. "Makes us look like refugees," he said, "and we're not."

Of course we were not. We were just a family running fast from our chronic disasters and telling ourselves it would all be better somewhere else. But when we got the loaded trailer on the main road, where we could pick up speed, there was a problem. As soon as Dad got up to thirty-five miles an hour or so, the trailer started bobbing, then swinging, then veering from one side of the lane to the other. Mom kept reaching over with a handkerchief to wipe Dad's face and his neck. "Don't worry about a thing, darling," she'd say softly. "There's no rush. We've got the rest of our lives together."

The real excitement was when a truck came up. It began with Mary or Fiona turning to see behind us and saying, "Truck's coming."

Sounding nervous, Dad said, "Yes, I see it." Mom looked around to tell us with her eyes that everything was simply wonderful. Dad touched the brakes, which made the trailer bounce, which shook the station wagon, which led to Dad exclaiming "Damnation!" and left poor Güero screaming and flapping as he slid off the front seat onto the floor.

"There's nothing wrong that we can't get fixed easily enough," Dad said, with all of us wanting to believe him. "Probably some small adjustment somewhere."

Right, I thought, *that must be right. He wouldn't get us out here in the*

West Texas hills with some big problem he can't fix. ~~With all his evident~~
failures, Dad was still the person we counted on. We wanted to—we
did—believe he was reliable.

PAST SANDERSON, WHERE Tyler and Marsha had dropped me and Tony
Stone at the A&W stand, Dad said, "I have to take a break. We'll find a
place here for the night."

Whew! Everyone was glad to hear that. We had our choice of motels,
a pink one with a wagon wheel propped up out front or one with an In-
dian carved from a tree trunk. The second one had more space in the
back to park the trailer. "This is fine," Dad said, and he went to check in.
As we drove to our room, crunching over the gravel driveway, I saw a
piece of paper taped to the office window: TELEPHONE IN HERE. It made
me think how lonely our family was. There was no one for us to phone.
No one anywhere who even cared where we were.

The next day, at a gas station in Alpine, they said a guy up by the
restaurant knew about trailers. Dad brought him over, telling him that
the problem was the silliest damn thing and he was sure glad to have
found a real mechanic who could fix it right up in a twinkle. The mechanic walked around the trailer, stood back, and said, "Yeah, there it is.
That there tar's wrong. That 'n right there on the back wheel. Wrong size
from the others."

Pleased, Mom explained to us that we simply had the wrong tar, nothing to worry about. She asked Dad, "Does the trailer have tar on it?"

"No, dear, this gentleman is saying we have the wrong tire in the
back."

"Ooh."

But the man could not get the tire off, even with a big wrench that he
pulled hard enough to contort his face and turn it red. He went from
squatting to standing. He stood on the tire wrench. He jumped on it.
When some men came out of the restaurant to watch, one of them said
to Dad, "Y'all got a trailer, huh?"

Dad said, "Yep." Exasperated, his face was turning red, too.

The man said, "Puuurty."

A long pipe for more leverage didn't loosen the nuts; neither did a
blowtorch. I felt as if the situation was out of control because our father
had gotten us to the emptiest part of Texas and then let an idiot take
over.

The mechanic said he had to go home to dinner. He'd think about it overnight; maybe we'd have to cut off the wheel with an acetylene torch.

"Well, we're in luck today," Dad told us. "We have a place to sleep right here in the station wagon, comfy as can be. This is what a good plan can do for you." Because there was no way to be sure what the repairs would cost or how long it would take us to get to California, the smartest thing to do was to start saving money by camping out.

The mechanic came in the morning and said he was wondering if maybe the fellow who made the trailer might have somehow put on three regular wheels and one wheel with bolts that went in the opposite direction. Dad dismissed the hypothesis, saying that the trailer was designed and built by a professional and that Dad himself had supervised the whole job. But there was nothing else to try—and bingo, the tire came off!

"Well, that tar's not the only problem, if you ask me," the mechanic said. "That suspension is all crossed up under there. Top of that, you got too much weight." He said the weight problem would be helped if we added a trailer dolly between the station wagon and the trailer—a dolly that, lucky for us, one of the other men was just then assembling. The dolly was several hues of green and ugly, but Dad said fine, because we were not about to leave anything behind. We'd just go slow and camp.

The men warned us to be extra careful because we were heading out across the desert with too much of a load, and with five people, the car was going to feel it. They told us to get an extra ice chest, suntan lotion to keep from blistering when the sun came through the windows, bug spray for sleeping out at night or when we stopped, something for the chiggers, a tarp and poles and rope and stakes to make a sunshade off the side of the car when we took a break, at least one kerosene lantern, a camp stove, a flashlight and extra batteries, some big bottles for drinking water, and water bags for the radiator. Water bags, we learned, were canvas sacks that seeped, so we hung them by their rope handles outside the car, much as people did in covered wagon days. We got six bags that read JIMBO'S TRADING POST in red and hung three from the front bumper and three off the rear.

Dad's vision of his handsome cream-colored unit of car and trailer, rolling across the plains to victory in California, was getting tarnished.

Leaving Alpine, we were all ready for a smooth ride. Mom and Dad decided that it was indeed much better—"Oh, ever so much," Mom said. But it wasn't. We were still bouncing, and we still meandered across the two-lane road when Dad hit thirty-five miles an hour. So he stayed at twenty-five and said, "This is perfectly agreeable." He stuck his elbow out the window as if we were on a Sunday spin for ice cream. He could do that until there was a hill or a curve or a bumpy road, or until a car— or worse, a truck—came toward us from either direction, when he had to seize the wheel in a two-handed death grip. Every two hours, he had to stop for a breather.

At the end of the third day, Mary said El Paso was forty miles ahead, with nothing else before we got there. While there was still light, we pulled way off the road, down a small trail and behind some sand dunes, as far as we could without the car getting stuck in the sand. The next morning, our fourth day, we'd finally be leaving Texas. It had taken Tony and me less than a day to get from Del Rio to El Paso, but I thought it was best not to mention that.

Dad would not admit that we were camping in the desert because we were almost out of money and we didn't know how long it would take to reach California, not to mention how long it would take him to get more money after we got there. "You're missing the point," Dad told me after the sun went down and it was black everywhere except for the red end of his cigarette. We had planned on having the lantern going, but it came without a wick. He said, "The point is that we are not crossing the whole damn country like a batch of Okies running from the dust bowl. You children will learn more about the country on this trip than in a year of study in any school. This is the most educational way to travel. It's the perfect way to be reintroduced to this country after all your successes in Mexico."

An hour after the June sun came up on the desert, forty miles east of El Paso, it got too hot to touch the car you were riding in. Mom stuck towels against the windows to soften the glare, but the heat shot right through. "I know," Mom said. "Let's play noughts and crosses," which is what she called tic-tac-toe. As Fiona handed her the tablet so she could draw the lines for the game, a huge truck came up behind us, its engine roaring, the chains hanging off its cab banging and jangling. The whole road felt as if it were vibrating. The truck and its trailer filled the lane next to us, blocking out the light. Up so high and so close I couldn't see him anymore, the driver changed gears. His air brakes rasped. It felt as if the truck had reached over with a big greasy hand and started shaking our car. Everything in the world stopped except for the shaking and the noise.

Dad's arms were nearly straight out as he fought the steering wheel, forcing it a little one way and then the other, feeling the car about to slide away from him. When the truck passed, its wake was even worse, a goodbye punch. But Mom simply finished drawing the lines for noughts and crosses and handed the tablet back to Fiona. "Here you are, dear."

Old Güero was doing worst of all. Fiona reasoned that a jungle bird should be able to stand the heat. But that desert was hot enough to kill a parrot. He lay back in Mom's palm, a little green ball of misery with a yellow top. His tongue stuck out, and he tried stretching his wings to cool down, but mostly he lay still. "This is quite alarming," Mom said from time to time. And, "Oh, dear. Look at Güero!"

"Jesus!" Dad said. "This is just what I need right now, a dying parrot. Maybe he'll take me with him."

Mom blew on Güero's chest, lifting his green feathers and the tiny gray feathers underneath until we could see his pale skin. Then she took a piece of ice from the chest and rubbed him all over. He came out of it a bit, but we could see he was suffering. "I mean, really, we have to do something here for poor Güero," she told Dad.

"Right you are," he said.

A few miles later a gas station with a little white café advertised COOL INSIDE. "Here we are," Dad said. We went into the back, as close as we could to the fan. But when Mom held Güero up to the cool air, the waitress rushed over and said, "You can't have no pets in this place."

"He's not a pet, he's a highly valuable tropical specimen," Dad told her. "We've just brought him from Latin America."

"Ain't that a parrot?" she said.

"Not at all," Dad said. "Only this week there are scientists in Chicago trying to name it."

That didn't work. She said, "Sir, we can't have no pets in here. If they's dogs or alligators or a parrot. I can't have that. Next thing you know people'll have their mules lined up with them at the counter for coffee in the morning."

"Come, babe," Dad snapped, angry that he couldn't even get a parrot cooled down. "These people are barbarians. Whatever happened to Texas hospitality?"

Mary said, "Dad, this isn't Texas. This is New Mexico."

Mom went back to rubbing ice on Güero's belly and saying, "There, there, wee Güero. Hang on. It's going to be all right soon."

The road went up the short hills and down through a brown-and-gray land with parched yellow, light green, and gray bushes in patches and a few cactus plants. It was all gulches and cracked ground. Dead, dry mountains popped out on the horizon. It was beautiful, but it was empty and it made us feel even more alone. When we stopped for a breather, all we could see was a string of a two-lane blacktop trailing back in the sand from where we'd come and running up ahead. The only other human markers were telephone poles. At the edges of the road, the asphalt dribbled into the sand, and from there on it was all desert.

As long as we took turns icing him, Güero did okay. He was worst in the middle of the day, but we could get him through that. Sometimes it seemed that in the whole world there were just the six of us, five people and a parrot, poking forward slowly enough to keep the trailer on the road, too slow to get far before it was time to stop again. Fiona listened to the *clickety-clickety* sounds we made crossing the road's patches. If the sounds came too close together, she'd say, "Daaaad, are we going a little too fast again?"

He would remind her that speed is a function of both time and distance, and that the cracks must be closer together on this particular stretch of the road.

Late one afternoon, after days of failure and cold meals, Dad got the camp stove to work. The first thing he did was boil water to make Mom a cup of tea. With ceremony, he moved a short camp chair to the shaded side of the car, brought a suitcase for a footrest, and presented her with the tea. They kissed.

The sun had dropped low enough that we could sit on the sand without being burned. Relaxing together, just a bit, Mom and Dad talked as a married couple. "Thank you for hanging on," Dad said softly, seeing only her.

"I'm not hanging on alone," she said. "You're with me."

We had given up estimating how far we'd drive the next day, because it only led to disappointment. But that evening Mom and Dad held hands and he told her, "We're going to make it, and we'll do just fine."

ON PERHAPS THE sixth day, a gas station man said, "You got a real unnatural kind of sound coming from the front of the hood." Dad told us he'd been hearing it for a while, but it was nothing.

Mom said, "Since we're here, dear, do you think it would be wise to have this man look at it?" Mary thought that was a good idea.

The man said it was a bad water pump. "Look there, where it's leaking bad. It's shot." He said it looked like we'd been running real hot; all the oil and grease on the engine was burned right off. "Musta smelled a lot, too."

"Yes, well, yes. I can see that now," Dad said. "Let's just put on another pump."

"Ain't got one right now. What we can do for you is have it on the Greyhound from Las Cruces, or elst Deming, if that don't work. Day or two."

Dad got upset. "What? A day or two?"

The man said, "Don't take but thirty minutes to put it on."

Dad went over to Mom and told her that we'd be staying there a couple of days, but he wanted to drive out a little ways to wait. I knew that he didn't like the idea of us camping next to the gas station. But Mom said, "Why, it's so lovely here, let's simply stop now." She was really saying that she was afraid the engine would explode if we went one more mile, and we'd be trapped in the desert.

Three days later, we got a radiator hose and the water pump, and we gave back the two plastic folding chairs the man's wife had lent us. She told us about how she'd come out West from Oklahoma with her folks years before and she knew how hard the trip could be, because their old car had trouble like we were having and she thought they'd never make it either. When Dad tried to show a distinction between the Okie migrants of the 1930s and us by implying that we were leaving a success story behind so we could do even better in California, she smiled over at Mom and said, "Oh, yeah, we was moving to California, too. Only we got stuck right here. But the Lord will protect his flock, and now we got a home and a business."

THERE WAS NOTHING to go back to, so we kept going ahead. We learned how the engine smelled when it was too hot to continue. We learned to tune our ears to the tiny sounds that meant trouble in the engine, brakes, suspension, fan belts, trailer hitch, or transmission. When the tires changed pitch, conversation stopped and we swiveled our heads until we could be sure it was only a different road surface.

We came to hate the smell of engine oil, gear lube, human sweat, and melting road tar at the lean-to car repair shops and wrecking yards where we stopped to hear some stranger in overalls tell Dad how much of all the money we had in the world it would take to get us back on the road. We learned to be sure to save something from the water bags for a sponge bath in the desert when it got dark enough. We watched out for chiggers that burrowed under the elastic of our underwear, because the infections there swelled up and burned when we sweated.

I can't be certain how long it took us to get to California. For my sisters and me, it was like a trip to the dentist when he pulls all your wisdom teeth: all red pain with orange flashes. My best guess is that it lasted for two weeks. I remember the night I went to sleep in Arizona and woke up in California, at a dark truck stop in Needles. A blinking sign announced TIME: 2:15 A.M. And then TEMP: 101.

1945 Dad, in a photo from the cigar box Mom left for us to find. On the back, she had simply written "Rome," which is where the wartime romance that had started on a troopship became a love affair that lasted all their lives.

1945 Dad was a tank officer in the fighting in Europe.

1946 Mom and me, near the misery of the refugee camp Dad ran in Germany, where about four thousand Polish former slave workers were being encouraged or forced to return to Soviet-occupied Poland.

1946 Our Gehrden home: a pleasant scene that masks postwar traumas. The two girls on the left are ethnic German refugees who lived near us after their families were expelled from the area in Eastern Europe occupied by the Soviet army. Next to them is Mom, wearing a wedding ring. She always claimed she'd been married in Rome, though that was not legally possible. In the center is the Bauer family: ten-year-old Peter; his mother, Isolde; his father, Curt. The first floor of their home had been requisitioned by the allied military government for my family's use. Gerhard Lücke, a local friend, stands next to Dad and me.

1946 The travel document Dad was issued in Germany permitting him to travel home. Mom could not get a similar permit. This meant they had to smuggle her, and me, through Germany and Holland.

UNRRA ZONE HEADQUARTERS
— SPENGE —
BAOR.

Date 6 June 1946

MOVEMENT ORDER NO. 2819

The undermentioned personnel:

NAME .... Mr. J.J.O'CONNER.

GRADE .... Director

NATIONALITY .... U.S.A.

TEAM or HQ .... U.N.R.R.A.

is / are authorized to proceed

from .... U.N.R.R.A. H.Q. Spenge

on .... 6 June 1946

to .... Brussels

PURPOSE of JOURNEY .... Reporting to Home Station.

and on completion of duties to return to .... --------

Means of transport .... Road

Has been supplied with food up to .... ----

U.N.R.R.A. HQ.

Zone Director
British Occupied Zone.

No. 392
Series 2

Date June 12th 1946.

CERTIFICATE OF IDENTITY
CERTIFICAT D'IDENTITÉ

issued by the
délivré par le

DEPARTMENT OF EXTERNAL AFFAIRS
MINISTÈRE DES AFFAIRES EXTÉRIEURES
OTTAWA, CANADA

Signature of holder
Signature du titulaire

DESCRIPTION
SIGNALEMENT

Age .... 33 years
Âge

Height .... 5ft 5ins.
Taille

Hair .... Brown
Cheveux

Eyes .... Hazel
Yeux

Distinguishing marks .... Scar on
Signes particuliers .... forehead.

Remarks .... This Certificate has
Observations .... been issued to bearer
because of theft of her passport
No.38911, issued by United
Kingdom Passport Office,
London, on June 4th 1944.

Valid until .... December 15th 1946.
Valable jusqu'

For travel to .... BELGIUM, UNITED KINGDOM,
Pour aller à .... UNITED STATES and CANADA.

(no extension can be granted without prior reference to the Department of External Affairs, Ottawa.

aucune prolongation ne peut être accordée sans référence préalable au Ministère des affaires extérieures, Ottawa.)

The present certificate is issued for the sole purpose of providing the holder with identity papers in lieu of a national passport. For the purposes of protection and relief the holder is deemed to be a British subject and a Canadian national. Upon revocation or expiration of this certificate, or upon receipt of a national passport, it ceases to be valid and must be surrendered to the issuing authorities.

Le présent certificat est délivré à seule fin de munir son titulaire de papiers d'identité tenant lieu de passeport national. Aux fins de protection et d'assistance, le titulaire est réputé sujet britannique et ressortissant du Canada. A l'expiration ou sur révocation de ce certificat, ou sur délivrance d'un passeport national, il perd toute validité et doit être rendu aux autorités qui l'ont émis.

Surname .... O'CONNOR
Nom de famille

Given names .... Jessie.
Prénoms

Address .... Altanta Hotel, BRUSSELS.
Adresse

Date of birth .... February 1st 1913.
Date de naissance

Place of birth .... BURNLEY, Lancs., England.
Lieu de naissance

Nationality of origin .... British.
Nationalité d'origine

1946 Mom's travel document, issued by the Canadian Embassy in Belgium after we had snuck through Germany and Holland. Fiona and I found this in the cigar box, also. It gave us the most documented picture of our parents' early travels. In addition, on the back, it showed mysterious travels that I had never heard about. Though the June document clearly says it is good only until December 15, 1946, they used it successfully for more than a year.

1950 This family picture in Houston is another successful deceit. Though we were quite poor at this point, the picture was sent to Mom's family in England to show how well we were doing.

1950 Nannan in her Cajun sunbonnet and Mary in hers.

1951 Me and Mom in our Muscatine Street backyard, with the neighbor's vegetable garden behind us—a more accurate scene than the 1950 picture above, in a place where country people got along by raising vegetables and chickens for their own table. The doll on the ground is Mary's Raggedy Andy.

1954 or 1955 Mom is holding Fiona, who was born in December and appears to be brand-new to a few weeks old here. Mary and I are with them in the large yard of our new house on Mobile Street, an isolated location Nannan called "way, way in t' country." Looking back, it seems as if it was a place chosen to help us hide, but at the time, we were all very proud of having our own home. We'd gotten Prince, the collie, after Margaret was killed by a car. When we fled this home for Mexico, we had to leave Prince standing in the driveway, watching us depart.

1955 Fiona in the sunroom of our home, where the family read books together.

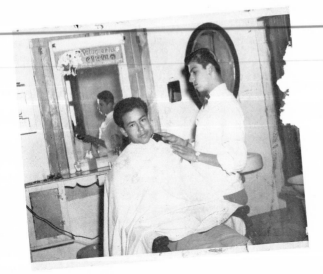

1958 Pepe Cirilo's sparse barbershop in Villa de Santiago, the village we fled to. Haircuts were eight cents, U.S., and Pepe had just gone from hand clippers to electric. Though at first the shop and village were bizarrely foreign to me, Pepe and his customers took me in, helped me understand the ways of the Villa, and accepted my family.

1960 Fiona and Mary in the living room of our place on Verlaine Street. We thought our lives had finally straightened out, and we were living in the grandest home we'd ever had. Mary and Fiona were in an upper-class Catholic school and doing well with their instruction in Spanish. Shortly, though, we were running again.

1962 Mom and Mary in our apartment in San Jose. It was a brand-new place that even had a dishwasher and a built-in stove. We were lulled into believing that this time we really could settle down.

Undated, probably 1940s My grandmother, whom everyone called Ma, was a woman whose values were influenced first by strong Catholic teaching on a rural Canadian farm, and then by life in the Boston Irish immigrant world. She expected her children to follow the same rules she had learned. In the family she ran, there were no alternatives to that.

The first clues to understanding our secret were
documents and photographs my mother carried in
this taped-together cigar box.

TWENTY

WHY DID IT TAKE ME until I was fifteen to begin to really give up on my parents? Sometime before that the average fool might have yelled out: *That's it!* I wasn't a fool, but I wanted to believe that our parents were smart and wise in the big matters and forgivably human in the rest of their mistakes. That's what I wanted to believe, so I did.

In our world, we thought that our parents were the only adults we could trust. Before leaving Monterrey, I'd worried about the secret that held so much power over us, but I thought our parents could still protect us. They'd always stood for what was strong and sure and *right*—until the debacle of our trip to California, which proved that they could be pathetically wrong. True, our other trips had been underlain with fear and moments of great vulnerability—as at a border—but they lasted only hours. The road to California was potholed with endless fiascos that crushed my faith in our parents. We were a tiny band of nomads who had to count on their leaders, and the leaders had failed us. They were just and good, and certainly bold. They had conquered many obstacles. But they had failed, and they couldn't cover it up anymore. I finally began to see it.

If they'd only told me the truth about us, I might have accepted it and trusted them.

As it was, I began to blame them for everything that was wrong about us: our perpetual fear; the deceit that tried to smother the fear; our life's uncertainty, which could catapult us from any home with little warning; my own social isolation and my never expecting to fit in anyplace we lived. I blamed them for our extreme financial precariousness, which had slapped us in the face on the road to California and had begun to seem perpetual.

. . .

WITH ALL OF that, the vision that appeared as we descended the Diablo Range of mountains into the Santa Clara Valley was so entrancing that it briefly overwhelmed my disillusionment, even if it felt as if we'd walked from San Antonio and dragged the trailer behind us on a rope. The hills were low and green, with doilies of orange poppies and huge patches of mustard flowers that ran around the fruit trees and scattered in every direction. There were orchards everywhere and farmers in straw hats and kids in kiddie cowboy shirts hawking fruit from little roadside stands.

"Oh my, just look!" Mom kept saying, and we did. Five faces smeared with tension and exhaustion gawked out from the windows of a road-stained station wagon, with a parrot trying to keep his balance on the front seat and six water bags hanging off the bumpers.

"Well, kids, we did it," Dad kept saying, because he couldn't believe it either. He looked around at us in the back with a smile that was bigger than the bug-smeared windshield.

After a few nights at the Oasis Motel just south of San Jose, we rented an apartment in a blue-and-cream-colored, four-unit building on Concord Avenue, a new street full of families also set on making their futures in California. We thought the apartment was as modern as you could get. It had a cottage-cheese plaster ceiling and a fan in the bathroom wall. Beyond our backyard stretched a plum orchard so vast that you couldn't see beyond it.

Dad quickly got a job selling room additions. For a time, the truth of how we'd lived before was painted over by our hope that we'd finally reached the right place. Success, as Dad kept saying, was in the air. But the torturous trip from San Antonio was too much to forget. It was too much to leave unexplained, as Dad and Mom had always done. It made me feel stupid and betrayed for all the times I'd put my doubt aside and believed them.

The rift between us opened when it came time to choose our schools in San Jose. Dad said that Bellarmine College Preparatory, a Jesuit high school, was the right place for a young gentleman—and I said I wasn't going. I was sick of the mindless dogma of Catholic schools, and I wanted to find friends from the neighborhood who went to the local school. It was the first time I'd challenged my parents on anything important. I said the choice was mine, and I wanted to go to a public school.

The nearest public high school was Del Mar. I found so much new there that it took a day to realize I was the only one who bounced to attention beside my desk—hands down by the seams of my pants, eyes straight—when a teacher called on me. Compared with the other schools I'd known, Del Mar felt like a blast of freedom.

Mary and Fiona got their new uniforms and merged easily with the students at St. Leo's Catholic School, near our apartment. Their rebellion would come later.

ALMOST A YEAR after we'd arrived in San Jose, at the start of the next cherry season, Dad's sales slowed and we were short of money yet again. In the summer after my sophomore year of school, I worked for the season in the plum orchard behind our apartment and gave the money to Mom, keeping a little for my contraband beer and cigarettes. I knew that my mother was glad but embarrassed to accept it, so she took it nonchalantly. No one needed to say that we shouldn't humiliate Dad by telling him. By the time school started up again, the initial happiness I'd felt as a result of the fact that I wasn't attending a Jesuit school had passed. I had begun to feel like a misfit. For instance, I couldn't share the communal heartbreak over the Del Mar Dons, who could not win a football game. When I tentatively confided small bits of my past to a few teachers and students, they seemed to think I was making it up.

Dad could tell I was drifting again. He brought home a set of the Great Books of Western Civilization: fifty-four volumes, brand-new, in their own genuine wood-veneer bookcase, with a unique guide. They filled three or four boxes, which he set on the kitchen table with a big smile, looking as if he were hauling in a load of treasure chests. "These are the world's greatest thinkers from the beginning until now," he told me with a sincere sense of wonder. "A young man who can absorb what's here will be ready for his next step."

Soon he was testing me on my readings: "Can you tell me what befell Candide among the Bulgars?"

I answered, blandly, that Candide slept in ditches and was nearly beaten to death after getting drafted into the army. The king saved him, and then he was almost killed in a war that killed almost everyone else.

Dad pounced on the lesson to all this: "He kept going, my lad, because he had faith in the future."

"But he was an idiot," I said.

"No, he was an optimist. He knew how to rise above."

Dad was fascinated by Saint Thomas Aquinas. Over breakfast he prodded, "Have you read him enough to see the trouble with ethics? Doing what is right and moral is easy in a simple world. But before you know it, things get more complicated than you ever imagined. That's when doing what is moral may be a matter of dispute. For people who don't lead a simple life . . . Well, we have to work at it more than others do."

I resisted the books at first, because Dad had wanted me to read them. But then I became fascinated. I came to the conviction that there was no point in going to school, where, once again, I didn't think I was learning much. My parents would not even discuss my quitting school, so I simply stopped going to many classes. The school administrators and my parents reached the unofficial agreement that it was better to have me go to at least some classes than be expelled.

Whenever I cut school I'd go to the library, either the main city library or the one nearby at San Jose City College, both of which had an intimidating number of books. I was less interested in literature and more in facts, in history and political science and sociology above all. The fiction I read had to seem real. It had to be believable, more so because there was something in my own life—our secret—which was covered in lies. Charles Dickens seemed real, Victor Hugo did not. After the Great Books, I went through Gibbon's *The History of the Decline and Fall of the Roman Empire,* then worked my way toward the twentieth century. I was trying to understand how things worked and why events happened the way they did; I was trying to organize what I saw in a way that made sense. As I had in the Villa and the red-light districts and the hillsides where I sold pillows, I was struggling to understand the outside world because I could not understand what was wrong with my family. The books were interesting in themselves; I would have read them anyway. But I felt as if I was making an investment in my future by absorbing facts, storing them, adding to what I had read before, so that when I finally moved away from my family, I could be informed enough to make a life on my own, and to be safe.

The summer of 1963, our third in San Jose, was as bad for my father's business as the one before. At the age of seventeen, I went back to the orchards, and I blamed Dad for it every day. I kept giving most of my money to Mom on the sly, so he wouldn't know and be ashamed.

Santa Clara County had more fruit trees than houses. It was easy to find a job in the harvest season, as long as you got to the orchard by seven in the morning. I only had to look down the farm roads for a clot of banged-up cars, or out in the orchards for the pickers hopping among the pear, apricot, and cherry trees or stooping under the plum trees. Plums were picked off the ground, where the ripe ones fell.

You just had to show up and tell the man in charge you were ready. He would be the one standing in the shade next to a truck or a tall farm trailer. He might be a Mexican guy, more likely the Anglo son of the owner, but never a black man. He gave out buckets and a ladder, and the pickers got going. Pay was determined by how much you picked, which drove the children to pick alongside their parents. Pickers had to move quickly to make money. Farmers needed to get the crop in fast; one day it was ready, a few days later too ripe.

After a few weeks of picking I went just north of San Jose to the Fox Brothers orchards, a more substantial outfit than I was used to. I told the man in charge that I was eighteen. When he surprised me by asking for my Social Security number, I made one up. He paused, then said it needed to be longer.

"How much longer?" I asked.

"It's got to be nine numbers long. You only give me seven."

"Okay, here's two more." They hired me, but at the end of the week, they shorted me half my pay.

The one good thing about plums—which we called "prunes"—was that the ripe ones fell to the ground, so you worked under the tree, in some shade. But it was tough to scramble over the broken clods of dirt and squat or kneel to scoop up prunes quickly with both hands. It wore you out more than running up and down a ladder.

It took me longer than it should have to notice that I was almost the only picker I'd seen who wasn't Latino or black. Most of them were men or families following the harvest until they ended the season in Washington State, with apples. There was a fellowship of those on the wrong side of acceptable. None of us had real skills or we would've been working another job. Under the fruit trees we were the same, and we didn't ask to be lied to by inquiring about one another's personal histories. At the lunch break I'd collapse on the dirt with Mexican families, talking back and forth in Spanish about the simple times in rural Mexico. They shared tortillas and jalapeño peppers with me, making me nostalgic for the Villa.

As the sun rose higher over the fields, the pickers' world got smaller and smaller, as if you were in your own glass tube. You tried to reach a trance state where you shut out everything but what you were doing. The world ended at the reach of your arm.

I have never worked as hard for such prolonged periods of time as I did that summer. From the time you started picking, the sweat ran down your face and arms, turning the dirt on your hands to mud. Grab the three-legged ladder. Plant it next to the cherry tree and run up to the top. Fill that bucket fast. If you wanted to make any money, you hunched up your shoulders, moved as fast as you could, and didn't waste time whining about aches. My mother had trained me well that we "mustn't grumble." That helped keep me moving.

Still, the anger mounted. I hated the man in charge. He was a different man in different orchards, but I hated him equally, whoever he was. I hated the people who would eat the fruit I was picking. I hated my own sweat and the warm drinking water they gave us, which tasted like a plastic hose. Most of all, I hated my father because I had to hide from him what I was doing so that I could make up for what he wasn't doing, at twenty-nine cents for a full lug box of picked 'cots, with the man in charge glaring while I dumped the box into the trailer, slowly, to show there were no goddamn green 'cots mixed in with the ripe ones. I had to be sure to get home and shower before Dad returned from work, which was almost always past dark. (I learned that baths are only for people who are not dirty.) I tried to hide the anger, but at times it bubbled so loudly my father must have wondered what was wrong with his son now. What was wrong was that his son was piling up even more reasons to think he was an irresponsible father.

But then, in the fall of that year, I had to wonder if I'd been uncharitable, because Dad's work began to click. On November 29, 1963, we bought a house at 1208 Mariposa Avenue. It was in the old Hanchett district, near downtown San Jose, around the corner from my sisters' school, in an area stepping over into middle-class. The records of the Santa Clara County clerk don't reveal how Dad could have possibly bought that house. They show only that it cost $24,400—the price, then, of a two-bedroom home on a small lot in an average neighborhood—and that the house had a second mortgage.

There's no hint of the hustle or the con job Dad must have used. He didn't have enough credit to get a credit card. Nonetheless, in two and one-half years we had gone from camping in the Mojave Desert and eating cold instant mashed potatoes to sleeping in our own house. We could look through the two tall windows in our living room at a pretty street where the neighbors planted pink azaleas along the sidewalks. I marveled at Dad's skills and his resilience. But I couldn't really trust in our continued success any longer, not without knowing the reason for our past failures. And, fundamentally, I could not put away my anger at our parents.

Mom and Dad settled in and relaxed more than we'd ever seen. Mom joined the parents' group at St. Leo's and was thrilled to go to the meetings and discuss the most minute and commonplace school issues. Dad started a business, Cypress Construction Company. Most evenings he was home, at ease in his big reading chair by the tall windows. He joined the Book-Of-The-Month Club and subscribed to *The New Yorker* and to *Commonweal,* the liberal Catholic magazine with a tiny circulation, especially among door-to-door salesmen. My parents began to have a social life with some neighbors and a few men Dad knew from his work. None of it was remarkable, unless you knew how anxious and private they had been before.

On the surface, life in California was as good as they'd told us it would be. Even so, there was that loud, low-pitched humming from the vibrating tension in our house that could never be explained. It came from my parents, cut off from the normal world but trying to raise a family in a nice house on a pretty street, with piano lessons for Mary. They were fretting one minute about the lawn needing a trim and the next minute about the Danger showing up on the front steps.

Since it felt better to stay away from home, and high school wasn't working, I found refuge at the public library or West Side Billiards. Or at San Jose City College, not only in the library anymore but roaming the campus. I joined in with students to talk politics, or about what they were studying in sociology, or anything. It felt elevating just to be around those, to me, smart college kids, who seldom spoke about their families because they thought they had much bigger things to discuss. At seventeen, and technically still in high school, I should have been an outsider. But I finessed the details and slipped into the groups sitting on the grass in the quad and at tables in the student union cafeteria.

A great number of students at City College, which was a two-year school, were taking vocational courses. Bookkeeping and auto body repair were popular. But there were also junior poets and musicians and people who explored different classes while they decided what they wanted to have as a major. They were the misfits, so I fit in.

On Friday nights, an English teacher named George Greene, who liked dark turtlenecks, showed an art film in a small auditorium. The movie, which we called "the flick," was always either in black and white or foreign. A foreign black-and-white film with a few scratches was the best. I met Judy at the Friday flick.

I FIRST SAW her from across the auditorium. She was tall and lovely. Long auburn hair and green eyes so bright they reached across the room. She laughed with friends before the film. There was an open, happy link between her and the others. Afterward she was thoughtful in the discussion of Charlie Chaplin's popularity in France, saying it might come from what the French thought Chaplin was saying about the United States rather than their reaction to his comedy. That was an interesting new analysis for me. She seemed *substantial.*

When she stepped out for a cigarette, I went right behind her with a light. I was stumbling trying to say something impressive, or at least something not stupid, and keep the conversation in motion. From the things she said, it was clear she was searching for a way to get beyond City College, not sure how to begin. That was what I was doing, too. The difference was she admitted it and then laughed at herself. I could also sense she had troubles of her own, which made me feel closer to her. She asked, "So, what classes are you taking?" and I thought the conversation might end if I said high school classes. But I wanted to tell her the truth. "So what if you're in high school?" she answered. "Maybe you shouldn't be. I don't care, anyway."

Judy shared an upstairs apartment on Laswell Avenue, two blocks from the college library. Her friends were early hippies. I thought they were cool. Like the groups on the edge of society in Mexico who took me in, Judy's friends, coming and going and broadening into a network, let me join them. I started spending less time in the library and more time with Judy and her friends. It really was *very* cool, until the surprise.

PART TWO

TWENTY-ONE

CONFIRMATION CAME WITH Judy's phone call: "Mike, the doctor says it's true. It's *true*. What are we going to do?"

I did not want to believe she was pregnant. We'd been together for a few months, but I'd only recently turned eighteen. My panicked response was "You've got to get another doctor. Is this guy a real doctor? He's wrong."

It was a heartless response to a young woman free-falling into black space, aghast at the implications of her news. But then, I was trying to change the facts because I couldn't begin to understand what to do either.

Neither one of us could see how big the catastrophe would be, or how deeply it would change my relationship with my family.

Hard to believe, but we had never thought about Judy getting pregnant. We had both been too enchanted by the adventure of new horizons. Then, we were captivated by each other. We had been thoughtless about the obvious, immature, kids.

We saw each other right after Judy's doctor visit. Her head was up; bravado, I knew. Her shoulders were square. Then she seemed to fold into herself and began sobbing. "I'm keeping the baby," she said. "And I'm staying in school. I don't know how, but that's what I'm going to do."

Judy was more than three months along when we found out. During that time we had not stopped drinking gallon jugs of Red Mountain Burgundy, or smoking, or screaming about on a pitching motorcycle. If we'd known she was pregnant, we still would have been too ignorant to know how to keep the baby healthy, but we'd have tried. At least Judy would have gotten more sleep and drunk more milk than wine. And there would have been a doctor to warn us about how much damage the baby can suffer when the mother is exposed to measles early in the pregnancy. Our son would pay for our youth.

With the baby coming, I was half-hysterical twenty-four hours a day. I slept in a panic and woke up scared to death. *How can we be parents?*

And then there was the more immediate problem, which I knew was going to cause another crisis: What would I say to my parents? For all my anger at them and my rebelliousness, they were still very powerful in my life. At first I thought that perhaps I could become a responsible father. Judy would stay in school, with me working, and my parents would not have to know. I thought on that long enough that even I saw it was irrational. I had to tell them.

It was in the afternoon; Mary and Fiona were at school. My parents were in the kitchen, looking serene, so for a moment I thought—self-servingly—that it would be unfair to tell them until later. But when I came to the doorway, it tumbled out, stumbled out. At first I wondered if I'd said it in a way they could understand, because Mom seemed nonchalant, as if she hadn't heard me. But that was her way when things were too terrible to absorb. Then Dad became a volcano. I'd never seen him half as angry. It was as if I had betrayed him and our whole family. He stalked out of the kitchen, rubbing his hands across his face and back over his neck. He paced in circles around the living room, bumping into furniture. Then he leaned forward, pushing his face into mine.

"*Bullshit!*" he yelled, his jaw trembling. His lips pulled back from his teeth and he spit as he talked. It was terrible to see. "This whole thing is bullshit! You don't know what women will do to get a man. I've seen it happen too many times. Then your life is over, it's *gone*—you're a kid in high school and your whole life is gone. So forget it. That girl has somebody else's baby. *Forget* it! That's an order from your father." I understood why Dad was upset, but the degree of his frenzy shocked me. I wondered at the time whether there was some connection to his unspoken past.

It took some time for me to get there, and I made Judy suffer along the way, but eventually I arrived at what I had to do. I'd been raised with too many "standards" to "forget it." I would not deny the baby was mine. I would stand by Judy in any way I could, which was much less than she needed. My only skills were in picking fruit, and my grasp on common sense was extremely slippery. But I did not tell my parents. I told them Judy and I had broken up.

In June 1964, about a month after learning that Judy was pregnant, I graduated from Del Mar High. The administrators overlooked my attendance records and my grades, which were both dismal. It was like when the men at Juvenile Hall had put me on the bus to Texas; they'd had all they could take and didn't know what else to do.

Judy and I had no money. She was in college, working part-time in a sandwich shop. I was unemployed and still living at home. We heard about a state medical school program in San Francisco where student doctors saw women from prenatal care through delivery for $175. Judy's brother, Don, got the price down to $150 by donating a pint of blood. Then Judy's parents and our friends helped pay the rest.

Her parents were not going to be able to do much more than that. They had come with the surge of people who fled the Depression to work in San Jose's canneries. Her father was from a substantial family in a small place in Missouri called Malta Bend. After they lost all their money, he spent most of his time drinking or saying he wasn't drinking or trying not to drink. Her mother smoked cigarettes and stared out the kitchen window. They did not like what Judy had done, but they loved her as they could.

ON SEPTEMBER 17, 1964, about seven months into the pregnancy, I borrowed a car to get Judy to her regular checkup at the clinic. Twenty minutes up Highway 101, just after Moffett Field Naval Air Station slipped past on our right and about an hour from the hospital, Judy said she felt funny. Something was wrong. Five minutes later, she was sweating from the abdominal pain and trying not to scream. Then she was almost throwing herself out of her seat. She grabbed my right wrist so hard the car jumped into another lane.

"Mike! The baby must be coming, the baby's coming!" She spoke in spurts, trying to handle the pain.

"No, no, that's not it," I said, feeling desperate. "It's probably something you ate for lunch. What did you have?" We both knew the baby was too young to be born.

The pain subsided for a few minutes, then came back stronger. Without realizing it, Judy had chewed through my shirt and was going at my shoulder. The hospital was near Golden Gate Park, a long way through the city. The parking lot attendant saw our car bouncing off the curb, heading straight toward him, and he jumped out of the way.

I screamed: "It's a baby! It's a baby! The baby's here! *Get the doctor!*"

Judy was half passed out. People in hospital gowns ran out with a gurney. When I saw their expressions, I was even more afraid.

We got Judy up on the gurney and rolled her toward the hospital. We hadn't gotten inside the door when someone said, "There it is."

I told him, "No, it can't be. We're not ready yet."

A little while later, a doctor came out of the delivery room shaking his head. The baby was alive, he told me, but he was so small that the doctor doubted he'd make it. I should prepare myself for the worst. He said, "Should we tell the baby's mother?"

I said, "No, don't tell her, it's way too much already." I sat down and stared at the floor.

JUDY NAMED OUR baby Sean, because it had a nice sound. She didn't know it was an Irish name. He stayed in the hospital for six weeks. First they had to save his life. Then they had to keep him alive after the surgeries on his immature digestive tract. The doctors said it was Judy's measles that had caused most of his problems.

When we went to see Sean in the neonatal intensive care unit, he lay there in his wheezing incubator, silent and still under the blue bilirubin light. The bandages and tiny tubes were in different places almost every time we went.

I got a job making fruit cans at the Continental Can Company, on the swing shift. I worked a double seamer, the machine that puts the bottoms on the metal tubes that become cans. The factory was so loud you could hear the old-timers walking up to the plant from a block away, yelling at each other through dead ears.

One night about two weeks after I started, I finished my shift at one in the morning and walked over to see how Judy was doing. Sean was still in the hospital in San Francisco, and she'd taken a single room in a student area near San Jose State. I didn't know that the police had an undercover stakeout on her block to catch a serial rapist.

As I approached the front of Judy's building, a man in a knee-length green jacket jumped out from behind me and grabbed me in a neck lock, saying only, "Hold it, asshole." It seemed like a strong-arm robbery or an attack by some lunatic, so I fought him. I had him down and was kicking his ribs when he grabbed something that looked like a badge and said, "Look at this! I'm a police officer. You're under arrest!"

He's lying, I thought. *Why would he jump me if he was a cop?* I kept kicking. When he pulled a gun, I kicked it away and went after his head with my work boot. I kept picturing the man dragging my dead body out of the green-and-yellow Pontiac parked next to us and dumping me at low tide on the Alviso mudflats at the south end of the bay. I had a lot to be angry about in those days, but I was also trying to stay alive.

Fortunately for us both, several police cars flew up. I thought they'd saved me from a crazy man, but his badge turned out to be real. The cop I'd beaten was very angry, and so were his friends. They said that I'd been trying to kill a police officer.

It was daylight when Dad bailed me out of the Santa Clara County Jail. I found him at the long ramp that led from the door of the jail to the parking lot. He was seething, about to quiver out of his skin, but there was more fear than anger in his eyes. I told him that it was a misunderstanding, but he couldn't calm down.

I was limping from the beatings they'd given me in the back of the police car and in the booking cage. The left side of my face, from my temple to my chin, looked like half a ripe eggplant. There were hard welts across my back, and both knees and elbows were swelling badly from the blows of the nightsticks and flashlights. I started to tell Dad what had happened, but he wasn't hearing me. All that mattered was that I'd been arrested. "You have to find a way to settle this mess, right now," he said. "There is more at stake here than you know. The truth is not important; it's a lot bigger than that."

It means something when your father sees you dragging your way out of the county jail at dawn, beat to shit, and he can't afford to notice.

The police lied to the assistant district attorney, of course. They said I had attacked the officer for no reason, just came off the swing shift and assaulted an officer with my bare hands on East Williams Street at 1:15 in the morning. According to the charge, I'd had intent to commit murder. I could tell the assistant D.A. knew it wasn't true. I could tell he didn't care.

We were in his little office with the law books fanned out across the shelves behind him. He said he had a deal for me. He said he'd have mercy on me because I was too small-time to worry about. "Forget about this shit," he said. "Take the deal and get out." All I had to do was promise not to make any claims against the police for holding me down and beating me with cuffs on my wrists and their knees on my back, pressing my face into the concrete floor of the booking cage. Sign the release and forget it. Or, he said, he could put me in a state prison for a few years. He had the paperwork all ready. He showed me the form. All he had to do was check the box that said "Prosecute" and my life would change forever. It was all up to me, whatever I wanted to do.

It was not up to me, not even a little bit. My family and its secret were at stake. I signed the paper and hoped it would be enough for them to leave us alone. In court, when the assistant D.A. asked the judge to dismiss the charges, he said it would be "in the interest of justice." I was so worried about the jeopardy I'd put my family in that it took a couple of days before I saw the joke in that phrase.

I realized that whatever the Danger we were running from was, it meant we had only two choices when we came to the attention of the authorities: We could run, or we could accept whatever they did to us. Justice was not part of the discussion about which choice to make. I didn't know the truth back then, so I blamed my parents.

A few weeks after the court date, Judy and I went to pick up Sean from the hospital. I was capable of looking about one hour into the future—any more, and the picture went fuzzy. The nurses looked worried as they wrapped Sean to hand him over to these kids who were his parents, ready or not. They were worried about what they saw when they looked at us. It wasn't the bruises on my face; they were fading anyway. It was my wide-eyed, stiff, overwhelmed expression. And Judy, who had dressed as well as she could, seemed withdrawn, nervous, was too quiet. Her eyes were down, almost studying the floor. Anyone could see that we didn't know what we were doing.

Judy was fussing with Sean when a short man in a shirt and tie stepped out of an office and said pleasantly, "Come on inside so we can talk about the charges."

He must be mistaken, I said. "We already paid a hundred and fifty dollars and a pint of blood."

No, that was for a normal delivery, he explained. He opened a dark blue file folder full of columns of numbers, too many to comprehend. With intensive care and all the surgeries, the man said, the bill was nearly $17,000, and he wondered about how I planned on settling it. He said this so nonchalantly that at first it seemed like a reasonable question.

I told Judy, "Let me have Sean for a minute and maybe you can explain to this man." And then I took off and tried to steal our baby. I stepped into the hallway, edged over to the elevators, and rode down seventeen floors to the lobby. The glass doors to the parking lot were just ahead when the telephone rang on the guard's desk. He said, "Excuse me. They're asking about you up in Newborns."

Back up in Newborns, they had Judy trapped in the man's office. I told them that I was never, ever going to have $17,000, so they could arrest me or let me go, because it wasn't going to make any difference. I said, "You can lock me up for ten years or you can give me an ice cream cone and let us go home. I can't pay that money. And we're keeping the baby." I guess I said it to shock them into giving in, because I didn't know what else to say. There seemed to be no chance they would arrest a father for taking his son.

I saw all the sad eyes staring at this pathetic couple. A nurse couldn't stand to watch anymore and left the office. The short man called someone on the phone, spoke quietly for a minute, looked back around at us, and said, "It's canceled." They gave us some boxes of Pampers and a few cases of Similac powdered baby formula (with iron), and hoped we didn't drop the baby before we got to the car. A nurse said, "Be sure you sterilize the bottles every time."

ALL MY LIFE, I'd known that keeping our family together was the most important thing. Whatever our parents' failings, the family was the unit that suffered together, triumphed together, stuck together to face the unjust world. But now, with Dad's absolute rejection of Judy and the baby, that had changed completely. Judy had so few people to count on that she *needed* me.

She was trying to learn how to be a mother, with no guidance beyond Dr. Spock's *Baby and Child Care* in its cheerful pink cover. Her own mother was not much help. But the book didn't tell her why Sean cried so much. It didn't have a chapter on babies who are too small to be born, who spend their first month at the edge of death and the next month trying to recover. The index didn't have an entry for babies who saw a terrified young woman peeking at them in their secondhand crib, a mother who was sure that she'd probably do something to ruin them forever. Judy stayed awake at Sean's side for days at a time, afraid of what would happen if she slept.

I let my parents continue to think that Judy and I had broken up, though I knew the deception couldn't last. I spent about a month feeling first that I was betraying Judy and Sean and then that I was betraying my parents. I thought Mom would eventually agree to my helping Judy and that Dad would follow. But if that didn't happen, I would leave the family and, in doing so, break off a piece of it and throw what was left into emotional chaos.

The collision came just after ten at night, in our kitchen. I had to go to Judy's to give her a break, I told them. Silence. Then Mom spoke. "You can't possibly take on that child—you're a child yourself." She was backed up against the kitchen wall, twisting a dish towel in her hands.

Dad's mouth wasn't working; it opened and closed like a goldfish's. Finally he sputtered, "That woman! That *woman*! That woman is— That child is not your child." It was now obvious that the scene would be as bad as I'd feared.

"Dad, he *is* my child," I said, as if we could have a reasonable conversation.

"Ridiculous," Dad said. "We cannot allow you to ruin your life. She is laying a trap for you, and *you*, my young man, are falling into it. I am your father and I must not . . ." He ran out of words. Silence, again. Then he ripped off his glasses and said I'd have to fight him to get out of the house. I could see the little grooves on his nose, lighter than his tan. I stared at them a moment, to gather myself for what I needed to do.

Then I turned and went out the back door. Dad didn't fight me. As I drove off to Judy's, I felt sad and alone and guilty, but most of all, *free.* I loved my parents and cared deeply about my little sisters, but I'd felt the weight of the family's problems for so long that it was a joy to get away. Maybe run away.

I would miss them, but I barely spoke to anyone in the family for three years.

TWENTY-TWO

MARY BELIEVED IN the American dream: that if you work hard, you are guaranteed to do well. Of course, she got that from Mom and Dad. Strive for the horizon, they said—you have your future in your own hands. For Mary, that meant excelling in school. All the while I was drifting at the end of a tether, confused by my teachers, angry and bewildered by our life, Mary was doing her homework. As I slipped away from the family by inches, Mary stayed the good daughter. The dutiful child. Until suddenly she was not.

When she went to the all-girls Notre Dame High School—the one Dad approved of because it banned makeup and jewelry—she did very well. She was tall, a bit thin, and reserved. I wondered why she loved school when it was so awful for me. She had wonderful grades, edited the yearbook, and never crossed the nuns. She assumed that in return for her hard work she'd be able to go to the college of her choice. She chose New College, a small, prestigious, and expensive school in Florida, which she planned to enter in the fall of 1967.

But abruptly and for no logical reason, as far as I could tell, Mom and Dad said the family was moving to Mexico, again. This time to Guadalajara.

In the months before their move, my parents and I had partly reconciled. They accepted the fact that I was going to be with Judy and Sean, though neither they nor Judy were ready to meet each other, and they had seen their grandson only once, from a distance. Judy, Sean, and I were living in a three-room apartment in San Jose. I was attending City College. Judy was taking prenursing classes. When Mom told me they'd decided to go back to Mexico, where Dad was working on a few deals, I

took it as a new symptom of their recurring insanity. There was no reason to ask for an honest explanation.

It began as an orderly retreat. Dad found investors in California to
lend him money to buy a tourist magazine in Guadalajara, one of those
monthlies that live on hotel and restaurant ads and run stories about
what to see and where to buy memories. I have no idea how he got anyone to back the magazine, especially since he had never published anything and never made an investment bigger than a set of used office
furniture. But Dad's gift was to inspire confidence.

He went to Guadalajara to set things up. On the night he returned,
Mom called me to say that they were leaving the next day, much sooner
than expected. I didn't know what it was, but something had spooked
them.

Surprised at the sudden departure, I went over that morning to say
goodbye. Mom was as bubbly as a homecoming queen awaiting her ride
in the rented limo. As I stood in the driveway with her, looking at the
trail of boxes and furniture from the front door of the house to yet another trailer, she said, "Oh, Michael, won't it be so wonderful? Can you
only imagine?"

For me, Mom's surreal optimism only made it worse. I turned away
from her, my insides twisted with pain. It was a physical reaction to the
emotion of the event. Pain from the inexplicable, unstoppable tragedy.
They were going within the hour. If this was their life, I thought, the farther they got from me the better. Because it hurt too much to watch.

To get back into Mexico, they would pretend to be tourists yet again,
though tourists generally don't load a trailer with beds and chests of
drawers. "No problem at all," Dad said. "It's not a trailer, it's a camper.
Look up in the front. There's the window I installed this morning."

They would tell any inquisitive border agents that Mom was a
renowned concert pianist. Mary's piano was loaded in the back of the
trailer for easy viewing as absolute proof. They would be touring Mexico in a camping trailer at the invitation of the Mexican Ministry of Cul-
ture, so that Mom could bring her art to the masses.

Güero, our rugged parrot, had disappeared the year before from the
tree in the backyard—stolen, we thought. But now there was Duchesse,
Mary's little dog with the build of a small pig and the glossy black fur of
a seal. And Samantha the cat and her three brand-new kittens, all four in
a clothes basket on the backseat. Just the typical the entourage of any
concert pianist.

Mary was worried, dark, silent. She did not want to go. She was seventeen and wanted to stay in San Jose to make money for college. Our parents' promise to cover her tuition and expenses seemed unlikely to be fulfilled now that they were refugees again. When Dad insisted that she go with them, she compromised. She would stay with friends for a couple of months, earn what she could, and then join the family in Guadalajara. She would see shortly that her plan to get out on her own for good and earn what she needed for college would have been immeasurably better.

When Mom and Dad pulled out of the driveway, the rear end of the car clipping the gutter from the weight in the trunk and the shaky, rattling trailer, they had been on the run for more than twenty years.

After they drove off, the deserted house would become something I'd see later a thousand times over, from Central America to the Balkans, wherever war made refugees run for their lives. Sudden flight to the unknown forces a family to choose between the sentimental—photographs, souvenirs—and the essential, like food or blankets. You can gauge the panic of the flight by what the family has left behind. For my family, San Jose was not Kosovo. There were no Serbian artillery rounds shaking the ground, spraying terror with molten chunks of metal. There was no fan of black smoke approaching, with people checking it by the minute because it marked the advancing line of enemy troops, where stragglers were being murdered and houses plundered and torched.

But my family was flying in full panic from 1208 Mariposa Avenue, from the nice white house just down from Sears and around the corner from St. Leo's Church. From that pretty street lined with poplar trees, where the neighbors thought all was always well.

As I walked through the house after they left, I found the debris of an abrupt disaster. Furniture was pulled out but left because at the last minute something else seemed more important. Mounds of clothing yanked from closets, considered and then abandoned. Fiona's school papers, collected in scrapbooks bound with green ribbons, had made it as far as the living room, next to Dad's reading chair.

A line of small pieces of furniture and boxes of clothes was still sitting behind where the trailer had been parked because there'd been no room for them. I knew without thinking that there was no need to get them back inside. The house, like my parents' life in San Jose, would be deleted from their thoughts. In three months the bank filed for repossession, but the house had already disappeared for my parents. They would never mention it again.

Dad made sure they got to the Mexican border after the drowsy overnight shift came on. Mom pretended to be asleep. Fiona, without being told, laid a pillow over the clothes basket to hide the four cats. Then she put her head on the pillow and closed her eyes, too.

In Guadalajara, Dad really did get his magazine, *Spotlight on Guadalajara*. After Mary arrived, she helped with the layout, something she'd learned from editing the yearbook at Notre Dame. Copies were given away at hotels, car rental agencies, restaurants. Every cover had the price, ten pesos, crossed out and COMPLIMENTARY COPY stamped across the front.

There were enough advertisers for *Spotlight* to make money, though not enough for Mary's tuition at New College. Dad refused to disappoint her on something so big. He arranged to barter the tuition in exchange for free printing of the college's forms on the *Spotlight* printing press. In September, on schedule, Mary went off to the school she'd dreamed of. As Dad said, "All you need to make it is a good idea and the confidence to pull it off. That's what made America great, and it'll work in Mexico, too."

Their home in Guadalajara was a big two-story house with huge windows flooding in light. It became a social center for the expatriate American crowd. People like Selena Royale, an actress in a beret and long slit skirt, who was proud of being chased out of Hollywood by the blacklist, bumped cocktail glasses with the retired U.S. consul general Adolph Horn.

Dad had fought alcoholism for decades, usually, I think, through abstinence. I saw him drink once in a while in Texas and Mexico, but I don't think I ever saw him drunk then. Still, Fiona later told me, once they felt safe in Guadalajara, he mistakenly thought he could manage a few drinks, once in a while.

Just about a year after they'd arrived, Dad lost *Spotlight*. He said it was because his legal status as a tourist meant he had to register the magazine in the name of a Mexican friend. When the business prospered, the ex-friend simply took it over. Dad went to the office one morning, he said, and the locks had been changed. It was a plausible explanation, though I suspect now that alcohol played a part in losing the magazine, as well as other times when his business faltered.

For Mary, who was thriving at New College, it was the one reversal of fortune that she never forgave. Dad was no longer able to print the college forms, and he couldn't afford to pay the tuition. Near the end of her second quarter, a college administrator called Mary into his office and told her that her parents owed too much money. She was being expelled.

It wasn't possible, Mary said. Her parents would never let her down like that. Besides, they had *promised*.

The school was very sorry, the administrator said, but she would have to leave, right away.

Mary telephoned Mom, who said something about a problem that Dad would be straightening out soon. Mary instantly knew better; she was finished in Florida. She retreated to San Jose, where Judy, Sean, and I were. But we were so perpetually, completely broke that we couldn't help her. However, a Notre Dame teacher named Madeline Spencer, a former nun, took her in. Mary found a job doing layout for the Hillis Printing Company, and eventually her own apartment, saving every dollar she could. New College refused to release Mary's transcripts because Dad couldn't pay her back tuition, which meant that she'd be entering the University of California at Santa Barbara—in September 1969, two years after she'd gone off to Florida—as a freshman. And since Mary was still a minor and her parents no longer lived in California, she'd have to pay out-of-state tuition, which amounted to several thousand dollars extra each year. She'd have to find a way to get that money on her own.

This became the time of Mary's awakening. She decided that she must have been wrong about everything important in her life up to that point, blinded by believing what our parents had told her. *They were liars,* she thought, liars and incompetents who could not be trusted. She did not want to talk to them or even think about them. She was done with them. I told her she was being far too harsh. She told me I was blind to the truth. Now I think we were both right.

As our family disintegrated, as Mary churned in anger, I was relieved to be far from the pain that came with our parents. Like Mary, I was so disillusioned and exhausted that I didn't want to think about what had gone wrong.

And Fiona was about to give up, too.

IT WAS SIMPLER for my youngest sister. She had not been so beguiled by Mom and Dad in the first place. By the age of thirteen, she saw that she shouldn't expect much from them, so she wasn't as disappointed when they didn't come through. Any hopes she had for a reasonable life dissolved when *Spotlight* was lost. To save herself from the heartbreak of being let down by her parents, she accepted that her mother would earn a little money from sewing while her father drank a daily bottle of cheap tequila. It got as bad as you can imagine for a family of fugitives living illegally at the bottom of a third-world country—living with no supper tonight, and only a cracked brown briefcase full of plans for tomorrow.

Dad became a broker between Mexican companies and private lenders in the United States. There were only a few small deals, but he was sure the business soon would grow. Somehow he kept enough income trickling in to keep going for another four years, but there were months with no money at all. Every time Fiona came home from school, it seemed that another piece of furniture was missing, sold. The couch. The piano. The beds. They went from one apartment to the next, a step ahead of landlords looking for the rent.

Fiona attended the Butler Institute, which my father thought was the best private school in Guadalajara. Dad kept telling Frank Butler that the back tuition payments were coming, but he was running out of things to sell. Almost everything was gone except that fifty-four-volume Great Books of Western Civilization, with the genuine veneer bookcase and the unique guide. Dad had clung to those books. They represented his respect for intellectual discussion and, so, his self-respect. But finally he had to give the Butler Institute something beyond promises, so he gave the books. It bought a little time, but only a little. Before long Fiona was asked to leave the school.

By 1970, Fiona had decided she was no longer the child in her family; she was fifteen. At that age Mary and I had still trusted our parents' faith in themselves. We'd thought Mom's rule about using napkin rings onerous, but by 1970 the O'Connors didn't have a table and there was nothing left to connect the harshness of Fiona's life with the glamour of our parents' visions. She decided that they no longer had any power over her. She withdrew permission for them to be the adults. She decided that she was more responsible than they were. That's a terrible thing for a child to realize. She allowed them to pretend to be in charge of her, as long as they were not demanding.

Dad's letters to me remained incessantly optimistic, of course. He said that life was great and about to get better. When he wrote that he was sending Fiona to live with me, he explained that she needed to be "rounded out" at an American high school. He did not say she had been expelled from the Butler Institute because he couldn't pay the tuition. When she arrived with her stories about the misery of their life in

Guadalajara, they seemed like a teenager's wild exaggerations. I still saw Fiona as my very young sister, so I didn't believe her. I told myself that whatever the family's problems were, I couldn't fix them, and at least I had finally escaped them.

Until Dad drew me back to the meat grinder.

TWENTY-THREE

IN LATE 1970, my father called with "a small problem."

It was six years since I'd left my parents to help with Sean, three years since the family had run to Guadalajara. Judy and I were married. Our lives were taken up with trying to get by, like those of everyone else who lived on the poor side of east San Jose. But we were also trying to earn degrees. Judy was studying to be a registered nurse.

Four years before Dad's call, while I was installing gasoline tanks into Mustangs on the assembly line at the Ford plant in Milpitas, near San Jose, I had decided to become a Latin America correspondent for CBS News, then the country's most respected TV news organization. I thought my time in Mexico would give me an advantage in Latin America. Realistically, it was a silly idea. I was a semi-skilled laborer with an embarrassing school transcript. But I'd inherited Dad's big ideas and his capacity for self-delusion. I decided to make my own future.

I switched my classes at San Jose City College from history to journalism and went on to San Jose State College, a four-year school. Then, disappointed by the undergraduate classes, I thought I should try for an advanced degree. By 1970 I was working one or more jobs, trying to finish the B.A. and get into grad school. Judy and I mostly saw each other coming and going, and we mostly talked about Sean. He had been diagnosed as nearly completely deaf, the result of Judy's measles. Sean was confused and angry at being cut off from the world, and he suffered with emotional problems, too. There was little room in my life to worry about my parents. It seemed that was probably good, since there was nothing I could do for them. When I thought about them and my sisters, I felt only confusion, pain, and guilt.

Dad's telephone call was collect. He said there'd been a minor delay in "the deal of a lifetime" with a lender in Houston. He and Mom would be traveling there shortly to sign the papers, "and after that we'll be all set." In the meantime, he needed me to buy him a car.

He was on a pay phone, on the street, the traffic banging behind him, talking about his latest gold mine. To keep things light, he said the car would be "partial repayment for your first eighteen years." It didn't need to be anything special, "just reliable," he said, with unintended irony. "It's only for a few weeks." He said he was coming up by bus to get the car and to take Fiona back. He'd arrive in three days.

It was too much for me to absorb. What did he mean, buy him a car? On an average day I had a grand total of about twenty dollars. It was an adventure each morning to see if I could start our own ancient Chevrolet, and I was buying gasoline five gallons at a time because that was all I could afford. I thought of myself as a student but spent most of my time working in canneries or factories or gas stations, sometimes getting food stamps or student loans, never sure if there would be enough to pay the rent.

But when your father is down so far that he has to call you collect to ask you for a car, you get him one. You save your doubts for another day. Judy, though, was sure Dad was hustling me.

I worked with a fellow at the Standard Station on North First Street whom no one on the crew liked because he was too nice to both the customers and the boss. He was leaving for the Air Force Academy and wanted to sell his 1956 yellow-and-white Chevy automatic, an old lady's car passed on to him by his parents. He said he'd bring the price down to $165 if I moved fast. Fast was good for me. There wasn't a thing under $175 prettier than that Chevy at any nearby car lot or junkyard.

I showed the vultures at Household Finance my stack of pay stubs from about a dozen companies. The stubs went back for years, as regular as the pages on a calendar. Sure, my furniture was worth more than $300, I lied, and they could have it all if I was late on a payment. They called T. G. Johnson, my manager at the Standard Station, who told them he was not thinking about firing me, unless they knew of a reason. They gave me $160 cash, repayable in twelve installments to be made in person before the fifth of the month at something like 34 percent interest per annum, compounded, including special fees, office assessments, and life insurance that only paid off the loan.

Driving home in that pretty Chevy for my father, I felt satisfaction; I'd fulfilled my duty as a son. Then a noise started banging low in the engine, followed by a nasty vibration. A mechanic friend found a bad main bearing—along with extra heavy oil in the engine, meaning someone had tried to cover up the problem. My friend put a shim in the bearing, something to keep it quiet for a few miles, but the engine couldn't last long without an overhaul and there was no money for something that big.

THE NIGHT DAD was to come had been tense between Judy and me. She was afraid of him, which came out as dark anger. It was not just because he'd done everything he could to get rid of her not so long before. She feared him because she saw his dreams as hallucinations but knew that he still had power over her husband. The disaster with the Chevy had made it worse, because now Dad would have to stay longer. I realized how silly I sounded when I tried to persuade her that this time his plans might possibly be reasonable.

Dad arrived late, knocking on our front door around ten that evening. I was sitting in the living room; still, somehow, I didn't hear him. Judy went toward the door from the kitchen, and Sean, who knew Dad was coming, ran over to let him in—and there was my father in the doorway, with the face of today's lottery winner, though his hair was tousled and his shirt pocket torn. "God bless all in this house," he said, trying to start things smoothly. "The greeting of a weary traveler." He carried a small plastic beige suitcase and a white cardboard tube about three feet long. There was a black smudge on the front of his pants, by the cuffs, and he was wearing thong sandals, his toes wagging at us in excitement.

He'd had trouble at the Los Angeles bus station, he said. "I was so beaten up from that awful ride from Guadalajara that I fell asleep. When I woke up, well, just look. Someone had stolen my shoes. Try explaining *that* to decent people. All you get is hard looks and sneers. Sometimes it seems that there's not a bit of Christian charity left in the world."

Judy recoiled as he spoke. She told him that he could not stay with us, that he couldn't even come into the house. I didn't expect that. She looked surprised, too, so maybe she didn't expect she'd say it. But she meant it. I wanted to do something to help the pain I saw in her while sparing my father further humiliation. But before I could figure out how to intervene diplomatically, he said, "Oh. I wouldn't dream of crowding in. Not for a moment. I've been looking forward to a nice room at the Y. I hear it's a wonderful Y."

I explained about the Chevy automatic sitting on the street, waiting for him. It took a while for me to get out what was wrong and for him to understand how completely screwed we were. When we drove the car a few blocks, it sounded as good as when I'd paid for it. But I knew it had an invisible mortal wound. The car was like my family, I thought. At first everything seemed good, even better than in other families. But there was a secret hidden inside us, something broken that could not be fixed.

As we sat there stymied back in front of the house, Dad grabbed the cardboard tube and pulled out big sheets of thin paper with architectural drawings. "I have to show you the project," he said. "The plans are ready. You'll be impressed with your father when you see—*look.*" Under the streetlight, in his ruined clothes and thong sandals, he splashed the drawings across the front seat and said, "This is what we've been working on, your mother as much as me. It's been a long haul, but it's almost over."

The plans showed an apartment complex called Condominio Colín and a shopping center, Centro Comercio Colín. It looked real, with little people on the sidewalks, cars on the streets, and pages of construction details. There were more pages of financial statements and charts of how the profits were to be distributed. Dad beamed. "We get ten percent of it. That's the family's, forever. But first we get one percent of the loan that goes to build it, a commission of one percent."

The next night, after work, I took the Chevy down South First Street, trolling past the used car lots, looking for an ugly car they might trade for my pretty one with a blown-out bearing. I had to find a dealer I could cheat before the knocking started again. In the last row of cars, on a lot at the corner of Martha Street, I saw a dirty '53 Ford, banged-up blue, not reflecting a speck of light from the bare bulbs strung overhead. It looked just right. The salesman was around thirty, with a gut and a bolo tie. I thought he was probably crooked enough for me to cheat without feeling bad about it, and dumb enough for my plan to work. I shouted to him, "Say, what's that old Ford like?"

The Ford started quickly, with not too much blue smoke coming out of the tailpipe. I didn't even try to drive it. I explained to the salesman that he could help me solve a small problem and come out ahead at the same time. I said my father had to get back to Mexico with my sister, but we were running short on spending money and gas was going to be a problem. We were looking for a good car with a stick shift and a six-cylinder engine, one that got better mileage than the beautiful little Chevy I had. For the right car, I said, I was offering a straight-across trade, no cash either way.

The salesman liked my car, but he wasn't buying my story. He wanted to check the engine. He got behind the wheel, revving the engine high and throwing the transmission through all the gears until that *knock-knock-knock* started thumping out of the bearing and I knew I was busted. It was like what Nannan used to say when she caught me in the middle of doing something wrong: "Little Michael, you standin' der naked as a worm."

I rushed to get back home before Dad arrived, but he was there already, pacing the sidewalk in humiliation at being barred from his son's house. I told him about my latest failure. He said, "Michael, you had an excellent idea for the times we are in. We'll just refine it and we'll make it work. That Ford seems like the right car to you?"

"The best I could find tonight."

"'S okay, 's okay," he said. "We never stop trying. When it's all said and done, we have only our own actions to account for, so we must always try to persevere." He told me to get Fiona and her suitcase, say goodbye to Judy and Sean for him, and tell Judy she was always welcome at the O'Connor compound he'd be building in Guadalajara. Then he said he'd take the Chevy and follow me back to the used car lot.

Neither the salesman, who was Latino, nor I could believe I'd come back, while Dad acted as if I'd never been there. He brought out Fiona and soon had her telling the salesman in Spanish how much she missed her friends in Guadalajara. The man's grandfather came from a town near Monterrey, so Dad told him about the wonderful memories our family had of northern Mexico. Then he brought out the cardboard tube with the architectural drawings and spread his dream across the hood of that ugly blue Ford.

And then my father pounced. Did the salesman ever think about having his own business back in Mexico? Did he ever think of how sweet life would be there with a car dealership of his own, a place where the help worked the night shift and the owner went home early? Didn't it seem that the corner of Centro Comercio Colín, right where Dad was pointing on the drawing, would be just the ticket? For the right man, of course— a man with vision to see beyond tonight's sales figures.

The dance went on for fifteen minutes, Dad enthusiastic but soothing, the salesman wary but then eager, peering at the drawings, watching

Dad's arms wave open to welcome the future. The salesman wanted to be part of it. Dad knew his project in Guadalajara was going to work, and the man believed in him. Ready for the kill, Dad said, "But the whole damn thing hinges on me getting back to Guadalajara ASAP, *rápido*, to get that paperwork ready for the signing in Houston. Did you ever have your whole life resting on what happens in the next few minutes? That's where you and I stand right now. This Ford is important enough for me to promise you a very nice spot in the shopping center for, let's say, one-fifth of the market rate for rent. And we can put it all on paper right now in your office."

That was how my father got a car for reduced rent for a place on a drawing he carried around in a cardboard tube. The salesman was neither nasty nor stupid as I'd first thought. He just wanted to believe. My father truly believed in his dreams, and now the salesman did, too.

With only two small suitcases and the white tube, Dad and Fiona were loaded into the Ford in a minute. I gave him as big a hug as I could find in me, because I loved him but it hurt too much to see what he was doing to himself and my mother and Fiona. I needed him to leave so I could forget our life together.

A minute later was the last time I saw him. I was standing on the sidewalk in front of the car lot, craning my head to watch him slip away under the streetlights of South First, off to clear up a few small details and then to close the big deal. Even then I thought he might do it. Hell, he'd done bigger things a hundred times. Not three miles from where I was standing, he had made a whole house appear for us on Mariposa Avenue. How many times had he woken up in a new town and come back with a good job by dinner? Who else had his imagination? His drive? There were times when the check didn't come or maybe it bounced, but he always showed up with his charm and his love for us and enough money to bail us out.

Yes, the scene at the car lot was pathetic. If you looked at it logically, you'd feel pity for everyone, even the salesman. But Dad still had his certainty, and I was still the son of a family where fantasies helped us survive. And I still worried deep down that if I ever stopped believing, then all of us—Mom and Dad and my sisters, and Judy and Sean, too—might plunge and crash to earth. Like Tinker Bell, when the children doubted she could fly.

TWENTY-FOUR

IN THIS HOUSE IN GUADALAJARA, food was often scarce. Fiona was out of school—there was no money for a private school, and since she and Mom and Dad were in Mexico with the legal status of tourists, they didn't even have the right to be living there, let alone have Fiona go to a public school. She was sixteen. She told herself that she had to get into a high school because eventually she had to go to college. She met an Episcopal minister, Reverend Dannelly, from St. Mark's Church, near the house. He realized that she was marooned in Mexico with parents who could not help her.

The reverend knew of a fundamentalist Christian group in Tuscola, Texas, just south of Abilene, that took in kids with troubled families. The group gave the kids room and board and enrolled them in the local public high school, so conservative that it forbade dances. To Fiona, it sounded like the environment might be oppressive, especially for a girl who by then was used to a lot of freedom. But she didn't care. She wanted to go to school, so she went to Tuscola.

And so the three O'Connor children were dispersed: Fiona in the backwoods of West Texas, but delighted to be freed from her parents; Mary in Santa Barbara, still so furious with Mom and Dad that she couldn't talk about them coherently; and me in San Jose, juggling my course work with the overtime at some gas station that we needed to get by for another week. Meanwhile, Judy was pregnant with our second son.

It may not seem reasonable unless you grew up in a family like ours, but Fiona, Mary, and I didn't talk about what was bothering us, not to one another. We almost never phoned or wrote. It was as though we wanted no contact with anything that reminded us of our life with our parents.

That's when the family that began with so much love and optimism near a refugee camp in Germany, that had grown and flourished while struggling to overcome its troubles, became simply three isolated children cut off from the couple who were their parents.

Dad and Mom, by contrast, still believed that all would be healed by their imminent triumph when the Houston deal closed. But the deal kept getting delayed. Dad flew to Panama to meet with some of the lenders. He drove that '53 Ford to Houston for more meetings. He was told that everything was fine, the money was coming. By then there were a half dozen wealthy Mexican businessmen who were also trying to get financing through Dad. He was elated about all of his pending deals, but the businessmen began looking at the thousands of dollars in fees they were paying to the brokers in Houston, plus expenses for the meetings. They became suspicious.

The Houston financial company, Investments Universal, was headquartered in Zurich and run by a Texan named Millard Gaskill. To assure everyone that the money was coming, Gaskill asked Dad to check the company's books and meet with its banker, John Furze, who was visiting Houston from his base in the Cayman Islands. The man Dad met was an elegant Brit, who had what seemed to be an impeccable pedigree. He had been in private banking for many years and had worked for the British government and Barclays Bank. He was a founder of the Cayman Drama Society. He would later be invited to Buckingham Palace and named a Member of the British Empire by the queen for his work with poor children. When he told Dad that the money was about to be released, my father believed him because Furze seemed so cultured and so smooth. Dad went back to Guadalajara and told everyone to be patient, to stay focused and believe. They did—and kept paying the fees to Gaskill.

I wouldn't know what happened to the deal until I got the court records thirty years later, but a fool could have seen it coming. Millard Gaskill, the man behind Investments Universal, never had money to lend, only fees to charge. The company had no home office in Zurich. The branch office in Panama, despite its brightly stamped incorporation documents, was just another phantom enterprise in a country whose laws were designed to help businesses hide their money, or help them hide the fact that they had no money.

On January 21, 1972, a U.S. criminal grand jury returned a fraud indictment against Gaskill. He was arrested by the FBI. The grand jury said that Gaskill had defrauded a group of businessmen in Oklahoma City of $45,000 in advance fees and expenses by falsely committing to lend them $9.3 million to buy an office building.

Gaskill was released on bail in a day. A week later, with other fraud cases mounting, he put on a pair of gray-and-white-striped slacks, a checked shirt, and a golfer's cap, and drove to the Addicks Public Shooting Range in Houston. He sat on a bench, put the barrel of his hunting rifle to the left side of his chest, and killed himself.

TWENTY-FIVE

THREE WEEKS AFTER Gaskill was buried at the Restland Cemetery in Dallas, Mary called me from Santa Barbara. I was on the white wall phone in my kitchen. It was early morning. I was going to be late for class if I spent time talking to her. But her voice was empty, so I knew I had to. I started pacing, nervous about the class and about what trouble Mary might have to make her sound that way. She spoke in fragments: Dad's sick . . . cancer . . . hospital . . . Houston . . . Mom's there.

It was nonsense, I was sure of that. Mom and Dad were in Guadalajara, working on the Houston deal, which I still thought was possible. Cancer? How? There'd been no word about cancer, or even an illness. I studied the dark red-and-brown pattern in the linoleum on the kitchen floor, trying to accept Mary's words. She sounded as if she believed them.

Just after dawn that morning, the U.C. Santa Barbara campus police had searched through university records, found Mary's address, and driven out to give her a piece of paper with a telephone number. It was an emergency.

The number belonged to Nannan. Nannan, who'd been out of our lives for years, on the other side of so many things by then. She told Mary that Mom was at her house in Houston and that Dad was gravely sick with cancer at a local hospital. Reeling, Mary asked, "Are they going to operate?"

Nannan said, "Well, he'd have to get a little better first."

In fact, when I spoke to Mom at Nannan's, I knew it was already too late. It wasn't what she said, it was what she couldn't say.

I learned later that Dad had started coughing a few months earlier. He'd said it was a cold or allergies or nothing at all. As it worsened, he'd said it was improving. He saw a doctor and came home declaring that everything was fine. He had to put all his time and strength into shepherding the Houston deal, he told Mom, and after the money came through, he'd get a complete medical checkup. Finally, when he was almost too weak to walk, he allowed her to take him on a plane to Houston to get to a hospital.

For Mom, who had always been so nervous about driving into the United States from Mexico, arriving by air was much worse. You couldn't slide through immigration checks at an airport as you could on the border. You couldn't smile and say you only went over to Mexico for lunch. The officials would know where Mom had boarded the plane and would want to see some papers that she didn't have. But after Dad collapsed on the plane and was taken off on a stretcher to a waiting ambulance in Houston, Mom, hysterical, climbed in with him, telling the immigration inspectors she'd be back. Dad looked terrible. It was okay. They understood.

My father may have been dead when they took him off the plane, or on arrival at the veterans' hospital, or shortly afterward. The cause was lung cancer, aggravated by self-delusion and a corrosive desperation to prove himself. He was fifty-seven and had been running since 1947, close to half his life.

I can't recall much about what happened when my sisters and I gathered at Nannan's house with Mom. As much as I look for the memories, they stay hiding. There are flashing snatches of scenes, more snapshots than anything else. I remember Nannan, big and warm, but her face drawn in sorrow, saying, "Mah, Michael, you so big now. I tought you mus' be in prison by dis time. Good you here for you momma."

And Mom leaning against the wall in Nannan's kitchen, head down. Mary and I lay on the table the two grocery bags they'd used for suitcases. We pull out their clothes and fold them. There's an envelope with five twenty-dollar bills. "That's the lot," Mom says. It's all they have. They'd borrowed the five twenties.

I wrestle with the picture of our family without Dad. I can't make the picture focus. For several years I've been glad for Dad to be away, in Mexico or anywhere he could play out his tragedy without me watching. But this time he is not coming back, with his stories, his charm, his plans that gave us all something to hold on for. There's the deepest sadness, a wide hole under me, when I think about his decades of fruitless striving. *His plans are done with now,* I think, chastising myself for believing that the parade of big plans could ever have had a rainbow. Then chastising myself for not having faith in my father, when faith was what he wanted most of all. Despite his self-deception and his lies.

Especially his lies about us: that nothing was chasing us. Now my father will never tell me the truth, which was what I most needed.

Aunt Eleanor comes from Boston with a tall woman, who she says is our aunt Mary. Mom must have called them. People sit in a room for hours and can't talk. Aunt Mary says, "What will happen to your mother, Michael?"

"I don't know."

Someone, probably Mom, says that she and Fiona will go to England, to Burnley, her hometown, because there is nowhere else. Not back to Mexico. She can't stay in the States.

A man who they tell us is our uncle David calls from Boston to say that Dad should be taken there to be buried with his mother. "Why not?" I ask my sisters. "There's no place else anyway. We don't come from anyplace, so there's nowhere to go back to when we're dead."

Aunt Mary and Aunt Eleanor say that someone named Pa will pay for it.

"Who's Pa?"

"That's your grandfather."

Later, at a service at Our Lady of Fatima Church, Father O'Sullivan says sinners who don't repent will burn in hell for eternity. He means Dad. Afterward he asks how we are and shakes my hand.

Mom is afraid of Boston. There's something waiting there. Something so frightening that she won't attend Dad's funeral, just as Dad had been afraid to go to his mother's funeral eighteen years before. Sensing the danger, we three children will not go to Dad's funeral either. *Keep moving; don't ever go back. Back is where it's waiting for you.*

Aunt Mary and Aunt Eleanor gave Fiona bus fare to get her clothes in Tuscola, where her classmates raised another hundred dollars for her. Then she went to Guadalajara to retrieve what little was left in the house, but mostly to deal with the two dogs. Alcibiades, the Pekingese-Maltese, she gave to the mailman. He'd always liked Alcibiades. But Duchesse, the fat black one they'd brought down from San Jose, was twelve years old. There were no takers. So Fiona asked an American medical student who lived nearby to give Duchesse something to put her to sleep. There was a small ceremony. The medical student dissolved a pile of Seconal pills and injected Duchesse. They dug a grave in the vacant lot across the street. The neighborhood's unofficial security guard,

an old man with a khaki uniform and a bicycle, made sure with a coup
de grâce from his pistol. The shot rang against the cheap, flat-faced cement buildings, then stopped. And that was the end of Guadalajara, and
Mexico, and all the great plans and marvelous things to come for the
O'Connor family.

In Houston, after Dad had died, I asked Mom, "Now that he's gone,
you can tell us what we're running from. What did we do?"

She said, "No, Michael, there's nothing. Just a little trouble a long
time ago. Nothing to talk about now."

TWENTY-SIX

IN EARLY 1973, with a new M.S. in mass communications research from San Jose State, I somehow got the news director at KPIX, the CBS affiliate in San Francisco, to see me for ten minutes. I told him that my goal was to be a CBS News correspondent in Latin America. He didn't care about that. Neither was he impressed that I spoke Spanish, nor by my master's thesis on prejudicial pretrial news coverage. But he did like the fact that the only time I'd ever called in sick on a job was when my leg was in a cast, from a motorcycle accident, and that I had excellent typing skills.

I worked the night shift—making coffee, keeping the news wire machines in paper, and trying not to piss off the producer of the eleven o'clock show by making it necessary for him to rewrite my copy. The pay was ninety-three dollars a week, or twelve dollars less than I'd been earning pumping gas.

The people at KPIX said I couldn't write grammatically or spell worth a damn, and that I dressed like a hick—all correct. But they admired my curiosity and my knack for getting strangers to speak to me frankly on the telephone. My first promotion was to produce the noon newscast, where I spoke only to people in the newsroom. I created so much flying chaos on the air each day that the show's anchors seemed afraid to come to work. So the news director promoted me again, to assignment editor, which put me in charge of what the reporters and camera crews were doing. This was surprising, especially to me, since I still didn't know what *I* was doing for long hours every day.

Eventually, I convinced the news director at KTVU, in Oakland, that I could become a reporter. He said he saw promise. But after a few stories, the general manager saw disaster and told him to fire me. Instead, the news director made me the weekend reporter but said not to appear on camera for a couple of months, hoping that would be enough time for the general manager to forget about me until I learned to be smoother on the air. I dressed so badly that a perpetually disheveled cameraman named Gerry Koch decided to be my wardrobe guru. He took me to secondhand clothing shops in Berkeley, where he tore into piles of brown corduroy jackets and green ties discarded by U.C. professors. Gerry's theory was, if you don't know what you're doing, dress like a professor, because at least you'll look intelligent.

That worked for a while—until the news director deduced that my real problem was not my wardrobe. When he watched me on camera, he said, I looked like I was afraid of something. "O'Connor, you don't want people to see you. Why are you trying to hide?"

I dodged the question—but he was right.

I fell in love with journalism. Finally I had something to believe in. It was the romantic belief that telling the truth about people with troubles would help them—even help us all. My news career was an extension of Mom's attachment to social justice, and of Dad's theory that good things come from hard work. As a journalist, I worked so hard in those days that close friends called me crazy.

I was probably the most aggressive reporter when it came to hunting for government deception or looking for people who felt cheated. Or looking into secretive groups. People with something to hide, politicians or street crooks, cops, the good ones and the bad ones, knew they could trust me to be honest with their stories. Perhaps they sensed that I, too, was running on the wrong side of some kind of line.

There was, for instance, the left-wing group in Northern California that was so extreme they gave other leftists the creeps. It was the New World Liberation Front, with their principal tactics of mailing bombs to public officials or putting bombs in public buildings and utility facilities. They did it scores of times, and while most attempts failed, there were a lot of explosions and a few casualties and a good deal of fear in Northern California. The FBI's antiterrorist unit never found the group.

However, I spoke with the bombers a lot. They said they knew they could trust me. (The FBI agents said they trusted me also. In fact, nearly thirty years later, one of them, Pat Webb, helped me with advice when I began my investigation into our family's past.)

There was news value in all those secret things I was learning about, so my bosses let me explore them. But I was driven by wanting to find the secrets and then tell the public about them. I was relentless in looking for what had been concealed—except when it came to the O'Connor family mystery, which I tried to put out of my mind.

I also became driven by the belief that journalism plays a crucial role in our society. I believed there was a binding contract without signatures between journalists and the public. People let us go around finding out things in the public's name, and in return we had to look for everything that was important to the public and tell them about it honestly.

But even if I was on TV, I was still hiding. When I went to work for KRON in San Francisco, I gave them only a P.O. box for an address, which also was the address for my telephone number, an arrangement through a friend in the security section of the phone company. We lived on the top of a hill in Marin County, up a long, narrow road where I could watch approaching cars. My car had what were called "no hit" license plates; thanks to friends at the San Francisco police intelligence detail, I got plates that did not even appear in the state's computers. Of course, none of this was rational. It just made me feel better.

Judy and our two sons seldom saw me in those days. I was out early and home late, and weekends were what other people took off. I was away, as my father had been away. Like him, I thought I had good reasons. There were times when my sons, too, had an incidental father. When they grew up, they told me they were jealous of my job and very proud of it at the same time. They also say they always knew I loved them. Though they both wondered what was driving me.

TWENTY-SEVEN

CBS News hired me in 1983 to cover the wars in Central America, where Washington and Moscow were using proxies to fight each other. It was then America's biggest foreign story. It was a fabulous first assignment, and there were secrets hiding everywhere, beckoning a journalist to find them.

The new job meant the end of our marriage. It didn't cause the marriage to end; Judy and I had changed in different ways since the days when I was a high school truant. But because I was to be based in Miami for CBS, we had to look at how fair it would be to move everyone to the other side of the country if there were doubts the marriage could still work. It became clear that it wouldn't work no matter where I was based. I kept trying to make that Judy's fault, but I couldn't.

After the marriage ended, I convinced CBS to move me to El Salvador, and I jumped so deeply into covering news that it took me more than four years to finalize the divorce. I stayed in contact with my sons, visiting them, and I brought them to stay with me in El Salvador for a short while. They loved that, because none of their friends had ever been to a country at war. All that was not enough, but they said they understood. I wasn't sure that they really did.

The wars in El Salvador and Nicaragua were still quite hot when CBS decided to slash its foreign coverage to save money; that was 1987. CBS was profitable; they just wanted more profits. They closed many bureaus and laid off more than 10 percent of the reporters, including me. When I left El Salvador, there was not one CBS reporter permanently assigned to the expanse that begins at the Rio Grande and ends at the South Pole.

I knew I could get another good job; that wasn't what tore me up. It was that CBS News, the very best, had coldly reneged on its responsibility to journalism: The public needed to know what was going on, but CBS wasn't going to tell them. I could not understand that. Naïve, I know. Foolishly, I had believed that the great CBS had the same ideals about news that I had. I told my friends that if CBS could turn its back on the public, then any TV news organization could, and everyone would. That was an accurate prediction.

Within a couple of weeks I was rehired by KRON in San Francisco. The money was good, the life was easy, but I hated it because local TV stations were also starting to carve away at the quality of news coverage. Before long, KRON was saving so much money by cutting back on coverage that there wasn't enough left to call it "news."

There was still a beacon of responsible local coverage at KCBS in Los Angeles. So I went there in 1990. But there, too, continuing budget cuts came alongside news managers who didn't think news was worth anything. Southern California is a huge, throbbing, complex place full of real news that we did not cover. There were important events, trends, and issues, but you couldn't find them on our newscasts. There were giant sections of the area, where the poor lived, which were hardly covered, unless there was a murder or a riot. By contrast, Hollywood was a favorite subject. TV journalism had lost the journalism and was only TV.

They knew better than to ask me to cover the silly stories, but I told my boss I felt like the piano player in a whorehouse. I told him I was quitting at the end of my contract, but my body quit before that. I simply lost my voice. It was similar to a nasty case of laryngitis. The doctors couldn't find why my voice kept croaking and going away for days until one said it had to be psychosomatic, nothing else explained it. Looking back, I know he was right. I felt that the newscast was a fraud on the public, and my throat was not going to participate.

I didn't want to speak. You can't be a TV reporter if you can't speak. After I left TV, my voice came back.

By then I was married to Tracy Wilkinson, a reporter for the *Los Angeles Times*. When Tracy was assigned to the *Times*'s Central America bureau in 1992, I thought I would go there and do the occasional freelance story for National Public Radio and mourn the death of television journalism. Then someone told me that *The New York Times* had been calling around to find me, that they needed someone part-time in Central America and they'd heard I was going there. I thought they must have had me confused with some print reporter named Mike O'Connor, not the one sullied by TV. When they reached me, I asked the man if he was sure he had the right person. He still offered me the job.

Working for NPR and *The New York Times,* I was fulfilled professionally as I had never been before; here were serious organizations that wanted honest reporting on important stories. When Central America became too calm, I followed the blood to the former Yugoslavia. There would be a string of awful wars: in Croatia, Bosnia, Kosovo. The stories were of people murdered or maimed, and I ran the risk of the same. But what scared me the most in all those places, what spiked the most, what made me drink too much to get to sleep and then fly out of bed before the alarm clock went off, was the fear that I'd miss the first artillery barrage or the next mass grave or the best quote or not understand something. That I would not get the real story.

Tracy saw those traits. In their best manifestations they are part of what propels a good foreign correspondent, but Tracy thought that in my case there was more. She and I had met in a war, in Nicaragua in 1986, with death and chaos all around us—not so different from the backdrop in Italy 1944, where my parents fell in love. She was slim and beautiful. Brave and tough, but unlike some tough people, she was gentle, too. She was also intense when it came to covering news, and had been only twenty-two when she took over the UPI operation in Chile and Bolivia. Then five years later she got the big story, Central America. She and I were part of the small knot of reporters who jumped around those countries covering the news. Life feels larger and extremely crisp when you're covering big events, often brutal events, where you also confront danger and have to get around all the obstacles to get the story. Camaraderie is natural, but I found myself standing next to Tracy at the news events and the parties. We started going out, and without meaning to or realizing it, I fell in love. Tracy knew what was happening, but then she's smarter than I am. We were married in 1988.

Our second time in Central America was from 1992 to 1995. Then we went to cover the wars in the former Yugoslavia—Tracy for the *Los Angeles Times* and me for *The New York Times* and NPR. Tracy thought I was too driven in getting the story, all the stories, even with the wide latitude granted to quirky foreign correspondents. I thought I was only doing journalism, that was what it looked like, but she sensed I was on fire for other reasons.

Tracy began urging me to accept Fiona's challenge after Mom died; I was the journalist, and so it was up to me to find out what our family had been running from. At first, Tracy cast the effort as journalism; whatever I found would make a great story. When I resisted, she said the answers might bring me peace. Solving my family's riddle might help explain why I didn't trust people, especially people with power. Maybe I'd learn why I felt that nothing in my life was settled or permanent. Why I felt better on the road, covering news, than at home. "I see you repeating the patterns from when you grew up," she told me. "We're both successful in our careers, but you think it will all vanish overnight."

Tracy was right about my perpetual mistrust and the idea of nothing being permanent. But that seemed natural to me, at least natural *for* me. I suspected she was right about the other things, too, but I didn't want to solve the puzzle of my past. I didn't want to even think about it. I thought it would be impossible to figure out and dangerous to try.

After all, something very bad had made us run in the first place.

PART THREE

TWENTY-EIGHT

THE NEWS CAME on the phone. I was in Sarajevo, on assignment for *The New York Times*. My apartment had holes from sniper rounds across the front, and the phone line was bad. Through the crackling and echoes, I could only make out Fiona saying, "Our mother is dying." Then something about a cancer Mom had not told me about, and the name of the hospital. When I called there, someone in her room held the phone for her. All she could manage, so weakly, was "Oh, Michael, is that you? I've been waiting for you to call." She had been waiting to say goodbye. It took me two days to get to San Clemente, California. She was gone before I got there.

When I arrived for my mother's memorial service, in September 1997, I expected to shove my family's tormenting, unknowable mystery into the deep past. Mom was free from it now, and I wanted to be free, too. I quivered to get moving, back to a war, any one would do. There's always one around.

But the old strategies didn't work after Fiona and I found the cigar box that Mom had saved for us with the photos and documents, and the diary. Mary was in Spain, unreachable until a week after Mom died. Fiona, diplomatically but insistently, came at me with the idea that now was the time to investigate our past. That was precisely, absolutely, the opposite of what I had in mind.

"That's an interesting idea," I told her when she kept pressing. "Maybe I should." But I didn't mean it. I pointed out that whatever had happened, it had begun so long ago we'd probably never find it with certainty. My little sister said, "I bet *you* could find out." Then she told me something that would make it much less likely that I would dodge away from the mystery.

· · ·

AFTER DAD DIED, the Boston O'Connors paid for the tickets that took my mother and Fiona to Burnley, England. Fiona hadn't liked Burnley, a town that had been sustained for centuries by weaving mills until it lost them all to overseas competition, and that now looked in vain for a future. Fiona had spent most of her life on the move, adapting to new places. But Burnley felt moribund. She spoke Spanish like a native and English like a Texan but was surrounded by relatives with north of England working-class accents she often could not understand. More important, as a foreigner in her mother's country, she couldn't get permission to work. She needed to earn money to go to college. Within six months she wrote Aunt Eleanor to ask if Eleanor would arrange for Fiona to stay with people in our new extended family so she could work and eventually go to school.

Mom's sisters and brothers had been happy to see her marry an American officer and once upon a time had shared her optimism about a future in America. But now she was coming back broke, a failed romantic. Her siblings took her in but made her pay for her sin: an ambition that reached beyond their town. Her sister Ann Helena chided her, "Jess, you know that no one ever really leaves Burnley."

Mom had gone in a big circle and come back to the beginning. Her life was a romantic tragedy, certainly, but don't think for a second that my mother would have traded her life with my father for one without him.

In 1973, Mom decided to return to the United States. She rankled at her family's condescension, and she missed her children. To stay in the United States she needed a visa. So she went to the U.S. Consulate in Liverpool, filled out the forms, smiled politely, and answered the interviewer's questions. On May 31, they gave her the visa.

She came to San Jose, where I was living with Judy, Sean, and our second son, Gabriel. She got a job as a nanny for a fourteen-year-old boy, Gary Shannon. His mother, Virginia, was a high school counselor who had also recently lost her husband, a California Highway Patrol officer. When Virginia no longer needed help with Gary, she asked Mom to stay on. After a while, Mom was getting small monthly supplemental security income checks from the federal government. She lived with Virginia and Gary for nine years in their ranch house in the robustly middle-class neighborhood of Willow Glen.

She moved to Orange County in 1982. While living frugally in a trailer with her income from the SSI check, she always seemed cheerful there, a quality that drew other women her age to her. She put swatches of bright flowering plants outside her trailer, with potted cactus inside. She made her morning rounds to trailer park neighbors, left saucers of food for stray animals, and read a lot. She lived in the trailer and then nearby in a pleasant government-subsidized apartment building for the elderly for the rest of her life. She would not take money from her children. "I have all I need," she would say. "You know, Michael, I'm really quite happy here." And she was.

I was overseas during most of that time. She clipped my stories from *The New York Times* and kept an ear on National Public Radio for one of my reports, following her son secondhand. I called every couple of months, visited once or twice a year. But even that was tough. It always made me anxious. It revived something that seethed inside me, and I didn't know why.

On my visits we walked and laughed down the quaint streets of San Clemente, under baskets of geraniums hanging from old-fashioned lampposts. As her pace slowed, my arm steadied Mom among the skateboarders and tourists. She'd peer into an antiques store at an armoire that reminded her of England or a table lamp that recalled Italy. Then we'd stop at the bookstores for some audiotapes; though her eyes were going, she still wanted her books. She liked historical biographies, contemporary American novels, and, of course, mysteries.

We looked normal and we acted normal and we never talked about why we were not.

Gazing at the dapple of red-tile roofs scaling the green hills, she would say, "Well, Michael, it really is beautiful. It reminds me so much of Italy and Mexico, don't you think?"

Mom had long before reconciled with Judy, and our sons loved their grandmother. They were living with their mother in Marin County, north of San Francisco. They visited Mom, sometimes alone, sometimes with Judy. My sons had a modern, divorced, dispersed family, with a father who tried to stay an important figure, even though he was overseas and there were many months between his visits.

At last Mom was at ease, no longer the woman so wary of strangers. She had learned well how to hide the dangerous things. She could hop-scotch around pieces of truth and manage the handy deceptions so well that none of her many friends saw what was missing. For the first time in decades she felt safe enough to relax. She had defeated the truth.

· · ·

AFTER HER MEMORIAL service, Fiona and I sat in Mom's living room looking through her stuff, and the past came back with a great slap. A loud one. Fiona mentioned our two half brothers, Terry and Jack, and their mother, Helen.

I was stunned. Silent. Groping to understand the facts, and then the consequences, of what she had just said. Fiona wondered why I was surprised. She was certain she had told me about this other O'Connor family, which had begun near Boston many years before us. I guess she did tell me. But though there must have been other times, I only recall seeing her twice between when Dad died and when Mom died; that had been twenty-five years. I was still running. In blessed oblivion.

Fiona had met Dad's first sons a few times since leaving Burnley to live in Boston. *Damn,* I thought, *this is the crap you get when you go looking into the past.* Suddenly I had two brothers.

The story got worse. Fiona said that Dad had left his first family without support. That was hard to believe about the father I'd known, for all his faults. But it helped explain one thing: why Dad had been so frantic when I'd told him about Judy being pregnant. Had Dad been reliving his own feelings of entrapment? In any case, it seemed that he had not found an honorable exit and had abandoned his children.

I could now see why my parents had probably run away in the first place. Still, leaving a family wasn't a serious crime, not one to dog you forever. But Fiona had another intriguing new detail. Our aunts Mary and Eleanor had told her that years ago the FBI had been looking for Mom. And that the Immigration Service had also been trying to find her.

Then Fiona said that in Guadalajara, in the early 1970s, Mom had told her something similar: that federal agents began looking for Mom after she attended left-wing political meetings at a church in Boston and had gotten on some "bad lists." But it seemed to me that all three women had been feeding one another's imaginations. Or, more likely, inventing a false trail to cover up the true and reprehensible reason for us being on the run.

After all, how could Mom have gotten a U.S. visa, and then SSI payments, if she was wanted by the federal government?

It took little of Fiona's nudging for me to feel that it was a good idea to make a quick visit to the Boston area and meet my father's relatives. For one thing, it would give me the chance to get to know Fiona again.

Over the years, I'd had no interest in meeting my father's family, but after Mom died I couldn't think of a reason not to see them. It would be foolish, I thought, not to at least stop by. Of course, I could have stopped by anytime in all those previous years, but now it seemed okay, even good. And doing so would take care of Fiona's questions. I wouldn't have to do much, I thought. I'd meet the relatives, ask a few good questions about our past, and get the answers to solve the puzzle.

THE FIRST THING a stranger notices about Randolph, Braintree, and Holbrook, a trio of towns just south of Boston, is that Irish-looking faces are everywhere. As I checked in to the Braintree Sheraton, I thought I saw a close relative three times, someone who'd come by to say hello. But no, it was just another Irish face, like mine. The hotel was in the style of a faux Irish castle, with a bar called the Tipperary Pub. Everyone working there, even the busboys and kitchen help, seemed to have freckles.

When my grandmother Catherine died, back in 1954, Aunt Mary and Aunt Eleanor had taken over running the clan. After Aunt Mary died of cancer in 1987, it was Eleanor alone who interpreted and enforced the rules. Rule number one: The clan stayed together. Rule number two became clear when Eleanor called my hotel room before my suitcase was on the bed. Rule number two was: Everyone always listened to Aunt Eleanor. After a warm greeting, she issued her orders. The first one included an already-issued order to my uncle Tom, who'd been told to pick me up. Eleanor said, "He'll take you to his house for coffee with his wife, Margaret—they live the closest. I'll meet you there, and afterward we'll go out for supper." The day was gone, controlled by an elder relative. *This,* I thought, *must be what it's like to be a member of a large family.* The next day belonged to Aunt Eleanor and my cousin Pat, Uncle Tom's daughter. Eleanor said, "On Saturday we'll have a family get-together at Karen's on the Cape. Now, some people think that's too far to drive, but Karen has the nicest house and we'll have it there."

Karen is a cousin. At her house I stepped into a Norman Rockwell painting called *New England Family Afternoon.* There were about seventy-five strangers waiting for me, mostly cousins and spouses and their children. There were twenty-one O'Connor cousins in my generation, and I couldn't count how many kids they all had. Half of them seemed to be named Kevin or Cathy, and initially they all looked as nervous about meeting me as I felt about meeting them. But within minutes, the whole family took me in completely. A load of people whom I'd never seen, whose names I lost track of as soon as they stepped away, was replaced by other strangers who also hugged me and pulled me into their warmth. I had all the credentials I needed; I was my father's son. And every other one told me I looked so much like my uncle David, who had died two years before, and that it was tragic he was gone before he could see the family resemblance.

I had no way of knowing how a person was supposed to feel or act at a big family gathering. What confused me was the strong sensation of pleasure, even joy, in the room. There was a shared spirit, an invisible wire, a happiness running through my relatives. They got it just by being together, by hugging and teasing and simply talking with one another. I was struck by how much we'd missed out on during all those years we'd been hiding.

It was bewildering. I couldn't keep track of who was married to whom, who'd just called to say they were on their way, whose kid had stayed home with a cold. For my relatives, I realized, life went in cycles, with a calendar of comforting family events, from church holidays to anniversaries to the World Series that you'd watch with your cousins. For us, in hiding on the road, life had been only linear, always forward, with no rhythm from the past. Christmas would arrive each December, but we had no guarantee that it wouldn't be in a brand-new place where we knew brand-new people, or no people at all.

Aunt Eleanor was the ringmaster, moving me through the crowd, finding any possible link between a given relative and something in my work or travels. Uncle Tom kept things light, joking about how Little Mary, Aunt Mary's daughter, was outwitting some Yankee businessman who was trying to cheat her company.

Puzzled, I said, "But isn't everyone here up north a Yankee? Aren't you Yankees, too?"

Tom laughed and laughed, and said, "Oh, Gawd! Oh, for cripe's sake! Did you ever hear anything like that?"

Eleanor said, "No, Michael, we're Irish and Catholic. The Yankees are Protestants, English. Different people."

Of my grandparents' six children, three were still living. While Eleanor and Tom stuck close to me at the party from the start, I first saw Uncle Larry from a distance, against a far wall, by himself. He was a tall man, good-looking, elegant in dark slacks and a light sweater. But I sensed the tension in him from two rooms away.

Larry raised his drink in a big greeting and casually walked over, look-ing as if he wanted to look at ease. "It's damn good you finally made it—we've been waiting for you for years," he said, laughing. "How's your sister Mary? When's she coming home?" He was joking, but he was not comfortable. I guessed that he must still be ashamed of whatever Dad had done to get all this started, and that he hoped we wouldn't be getting into it.

Then there was a buzz in Karen's house. Something that said everyone was suddenly very edgy. In a flash of paranoia, I thought, *It must be the police. What a dumb bastard you are! Here your father kept away all that time, and you come right into the middle of the whole deal, and someone, somewhere, calls the cops. What did you expect? If Dad ran, what makes you safe?*

But then someone, I think one of Uncle Larry's sons, Jimmie, said, "Yeah, it's Terry." My new half brother.

I did not want to face Terry or his younger brother, Jack. Maybe it was my shame for the murk of our family history, or my embarrassment to be one of the children that Dad had chosen instead of them. But here was Terry, ready or not, and it wasn't reassuring that the others also seemed nervous.

As a lame joke, I asked Tom, "Do you think he's got a gun?" I didn't like it when Tom had to consider a moment before saying no. "Is there some reason I shouldn't see him?" I asked.

Tom said he couldn't think of one, but he was thinking of something. He and Larry walked quickly to the front steps. Eleanor stayed with me and put on her brave face. Outside the window, a gray-haired man in his late fifties walked slowly but directly toward the door, smoking a ciga-rette. A pretty blond woman walked beside him, speaking to him calmly. Rosemarie, Terry's wife. His head nodded as she spoke.

Tom and Larry went to the front door. After a few moments of quiet talk, Tom said, "It's Terry!" as if he'd just discovered him standing there.

Terry was bubbling, or maybe burning, in a familiar way. I'd seen that look before in myself. We chatted. I don't remember the details of what we said, but I was grateful that it didn't blow up. Maybe, I thought, there were too many people around for him to start any trouble.

After the party ended, I drove with Eleanor back to Braintree. At sev-enty-six, my aunt was an impressive person, a devout Catholic, but not at all stern about it and very down-to-earth. She joked easily, with a crisp wit, but now she turned serious. The reason Terry seemed so angry, she said, was that my father had indeed abandoned him and his brother and mother, with no contact and no money.

How could he have done that? *What a bastard!* I felt deep, deep sorrow for the abandoned ones, and anger at the man who'd hurt us all. I hadn't really known my father at all. *What else didn't I know?*

It was too much to take in, and I hoped that there was something more to Dad's story, a big piece still missing that might explain it.

And according to Eleanor, there was: the U.S. Immigration Service. Somehow they thought that Mom was an illegal alien. My grandmother and Uncle Larry might have been involved with that, she said.

That doesn't make sense, I thought. Why would Mom be in the U.S. illegally? She was from Britain, our closest ally in the war. It should have been no problem for her to enter the country.

Aunt Eleanor couldn't explain it, but she thought it was best for me not to tell Terry or Jack that our grandmother and uncle had possibly been involved with the government investigation. "Let it all lie, Michael," she said, looking over at me to be sure I was hearing her.

Then, she continued, there was also the FBI. Agents had interviewed Aunt Mary twice about Mom and me.

"What the hell was that about, Eleanor? Maybe that's the reason we were running."

Eleanor said, "None of us could ever understand why the FBI might be interested in your mother. Maybe it was something small. Who knows? What happened was such a shame, but we'll never have the whole picture."

The pity now, she said, was that Terry still couldn't get over his father's disappearance. She said that Jack had put it aside long ago, but Terry always seemed angry at something. He was still digging into the past when everyone else was satisfied that they knew all they would ever know. Aunt Eleanor saw no use in Terry's questions. There were tragedies that only became worse when people tried to exhume them.

"So," she said, with authority, "keep all that in mind. It would be wonderful if you and Terry and Jack finally got to know each other. But let's all go on from here instead of looking around too much in the past."

THERE WAS SO much new to absorb in those few days with my relatives that I didn't notice what was missing. As for Immigration and the FBI, I doubted there was anything to it. I'd seen similar tales as a reporter, family stories that got told a hundred times and twisted badly in the retelling. What continued to shock me was my father's unforgivable treatment of his first family. Did we run all those years because Dad was in hiding from Terry and Jack and Helen? Or from the shame of having abandoned them?

They were vexing questions, but at that point I was happy to take Eleanor's advice and returned to Bosnia. After another fourteen months in Bosnia, Kosovo, and Serbia, Tracy and I moved to Israel, she as the *Los Angeles Times* bureau chief and I for NPR. Though she occasionally pressed me to look into my family's story, to come to grips with what kept me running and searching, I wanted to spend all my time covering the Israeli-Palestinian conflict. More interesting, I told her. But, gradually, I won the battle with myself. I came to believe two things: First, that however bad the truth was, it was better to know than to avoid. And second, that it wouldn't be so hard to find the truth. After all, that's what journalists do.

To clear up any doubts about the supposed federal agents, in the summer of 1999 I filed Freedom of Information Act requests with the FBI and INS, asking for anything they had on my parents or me. If there was anything, the cases were old enough for the files to be made public. But the government responded by saying there was nothing at all on any of us, except for my mother's application for a visa in 1973, which she'd needed to come back to San Jose from Burnley, and the immigration file that showed she'd been granted permanent residency and, shortly before she died, had applied for U.S. citizenship.

I knew that you couldn't trust government agencies to tell the truth just because you had the legal right to get it, but in this case their written responses were believable. First, if they had anything from a fifty-year-old case, why would they conceal it? More important, there was the fact that Mom had had a current INS file and was getting the SSI benefits. It made good sense that there wasn't anything else.

If I was going to find the reason behind my family's running, I concluded, it would be with the people who knew us when it started: Dad's siblings. They might need some prodding to remember, or some cajoling to stop trying to forget. But they had to know.

In 1999, two years after my mother died and I had met my father's family, as the fall foliage turned in New England, Tracy and I flew from Israel for a week's visit with my newfound relatives. I thought Tracy would like them as much as I did. I was also optimistic about solving the mystery. The first time around, I'd been too full of mourning for my mother, stunned by what I'd learned about my father, and overwhelmed by all those cousins-out-of-the-blue to do a proper job of getting answers. This time it would be simple, I thought. Tracy and I would sit around for a few days talking to a few folks. We'd just pull out our reporters' notebooks and get this thing figured out.

And maybe I could spend time with Terry along the way.

TWENTY-NINE

TERRY WASN'T SURE he'd ever seen our father. He had a picture in his mind of a man storming out of their family's apartment—early in the morning, perhaps before dawn, hard to be sure. The man is arguing with Terry's mother. There are suitcases and tears. Down the stairs the man goes, almost running, to a yellow taxi, where a woman holds an infant. The man throws open the door, just short of violently, then jumps in and leaves.

Sometimes Terry can remember his father taking him to a parade on the Fourth of July, or perhaps it was a large O'Connor family party. He thinks he remembers that they were happy.

What fogs Terry's memories, aside from the fact that he was so young then, is that he grew up with a lie. Everyone O'Connor, every adult he loved and trusted completely, would tell him that his memories couldn't possibly be true because his father—my father—had been killed in World War II. "I always got a simple declarative statement that didn't explain anything," he told me. " 'Your father died in the war.' "

In September 1999, I went with Tracy and Fiona to see Terry at his home in Holyoke, Massachusetts. He and his wife, Rosemarie, were extremely gracious. She said he had been waiting for many years to talk with me. Terry was charming, with a strong sense of humor, but just below the laughs lay suspicion. It wasn't hard to understand. First his father had disappeared to raise another family. Then the people closest to him had lied to him and his brother for years.

But something made me uncomfortable with Terry for our first hour or so together. He looked too much like my father. He had the prominent O'Connor nose, Dad's hands, Dad's shoulders. Even the way he held his cigarette reminded me of Dad. I was supposed to be the only son, but here he was, and his damn brother, too.

We began by telling each other about ourselves. He'd heard an outline of my life from Fiona when she moved to Boston from Burnley, but I filled in the persistent sense of danger and mystery, the isolation and sudden departures that left everything behind, the periodic poverty. Fiona joined in to laugh and tell Terry, "You had to live without Dad, but believe me, life with him was tough. Who knows, you and Jack might have gotten the better deal." He smiled at that, but barely.

What I did not tell him was that through all those tough times growing up we always believed our parents loved us and did the best they could for us. I didn't tell him that we were a strong, united family before it all fell apart. That would have been unkind.

We were both impressed by what Mary and Fiona had done with their lives after they escaped our family.

Fiona, though she'd gotten only to ninth grade in Guadalajara for lack of tuition money, was accepted by the University of Massachusetts in 1973. She majored in economics but left without graduating to work full-time in a government antipoverty program. In 1992 she earned an M.B.A. from Simmons College in Boston, her first diploma ever. By then she was married, with a five-year-old son. She became a manager with NeighborWorks America, a national, federally funded organization that helps people buy their homes.

Mary kept doggedly excelling in school until she'd earned a Ph.D. in anthropology from U.C. Santa Barbara, where she won a Fulbright Scholarship. She married a professor at the university and teaches there between field research trips among Mexican Indians.

Terry told me about his two sons from previous marriages, one in college and the other a trooper in Washington State. When I was in television news, Terry had been a radio reporter and a talk-show host before starting a successful advertising and marketing firm. But for now he brushed his work aside, because he wanted to talk about our aunts and uncles, and especially our grandmother, the matriarch called Ma, and how all of them had embraced Terry and Jack when they were young boys. Despite their great deception, they had tried, he thought, to make up for the father who was gone, and they'd done it lovingly.

As the hours passed in that first long talk by the fountain in Terry's large backyard, with the two of us pulling hard on cigarettes and slugging back small glasses of whiskey with ice, the wall between us began to shrink. Terry told me that he'd learned his father was still alive around 1955, when he was fifteen years old. He and Uncle David were driving from the O'Connor family home back to Medford, just on the other side of Boston, where Terry and Jack grew up. Terry asked his uncle the question that had been chewing at him for as long as he could remember. If anyone would answer him, it would be Uncle David.

David was the youngest of my father's siblings, only ten years older than Terry. He was also the closest thing Terry had to a father. From what I was hearing about him, Uncle David was the exact opposite of Dad. He was born in the O'Connor family house in Holbrook and lived there until the family moved a few blocks away to Mill Street, in Randolph. He married Libby Lannen, who lived five hundred yards up Mill Street. She moved in with David and Uncle Tom and our grandparents. She and David had six children while living there, and David died in that house, in 1995. Libby was still there, and five of her children had settled within a few miles. Her son Bobby, my cousin, lived across the street.

That was stability, I thought.

Uncle David had worked as a carpenter, then as a high school shop teacher. He was home for dinner every night and went to Mass with Libby and the children every Sunday, embracing the routines that had made my father so desperate to get away.

So, back in 1955, the year of our first flight to the Villa de Santiago, when Terry and David were driving to Medford and Terry said, "My father's alive, isn't he?" David at first ducked the question. Then he said he didn't know for sure, but he believed that was true. And he told Terry not to say a word about it, to anyone.

For Terry, David's answer meant two awful things. Two things that Terry had feared but suspected. Things that he needed to know but could not stand knowing. It meant that his father really had abandoned him, just as he'd always dreaded. And that meant that the O'Connors had kept a terrible secret from him and Jack. Terry was afraid to ask anything else because he thought the next answer might be worse.

Looking back on that moment, staring into it from decades away and feeling shaken once again, Terry explained why he couldn't tell anyone else. "David had told me the darkest secret in the family—how could I turn that against him? How could I betray the man who was closest to me? And how could I go to my mother and ask her if she'd been lying all this time? It would mean that she wasn't a widow, as she always said. It would mean that she'd been left by her husband and then was lying to us about it. I couldn't humiliate her that way."

Terry was tortured by his family's mystery, as I was by my family's. And, like mine, his search was blunted by the fear of even darker revelations. Perhaps he'd find that his mother had driven our father away, that she was not the saint he'd thought. Or that Dad had chosen his second set of children because his first sons weren't good enough. In any case, Terry believed that confronting his mother would have been pointless. She would have fallen back on the old family myth: *Your father died in the war.* "That's the way she handles it," Terry told me. "That's the way she has to believe. Every time I got even close to the question, the curtain would drop. *Bang!* She would give the party line."

Later on, David gave Jack the same tidbit of information: *Your father may be alive. Don't tell anyone.* David told neither boy of the telegrams and letters and phone calls over the years from Dad, or of Aunt Eleanor's visit to Houston. Perhaps, as the youngest of the siblings, he did not know about those contacts. Or perhaps he simply let the boys believe that no one knew where their father was.

Once Terry and Jack learned that their relatives had been lying about the most important thing in their lives, they couldn't let anyone know that they knew. They couldn't even tell each other. So the O'Connors kept on lying, and Terry and Jack kept on pretending to believe them. Everyone choked down his share of the deceit and behaved as if there were nothing wrong in the first place.

Then, in 1972, Dad really did die, and no one was ready for that. To keep the secrets secret, Aunt Mary and Aunt Eleanor rushed to Houston without telling anyone besides their brothers and their father. In their mourning and regret, they maintained the old fiction even after they brought Dad's body home. My grandfather arranged for a priest to meet the plane, along with a hearse from Hurley Funeral Home, whose owners were discreet. They quietly brought Dad to St. Mary's Cemetery, half a mile from the house where he grew up, to a grave quickly dug next to his mother's. The priest would keep the secret. Dad's father and brothers and sisters and their spouses were at the burial. His sons Terry and Jack were not even told about it. Neither was Helen, who still considered herself married to Dad.

Finally, Uncle David was designated to go to Helen, hold her hand, and say he was so sorry to tell her but Dad had died many months earlier—and to apologize for the fact that, despite what she had always been told, actually, some of the family had been in touch with him, on and off, since 1946. Without using the hurtful words, he was telling Helen that she and her sons had been shut out all those years by a calculated conspiracy among the people she'd trusted absolutely.

David told her all of this in the modest apartment on Orchard Street in Medford, where she'd taken her sons some twenty-five years before to wait for Dad to come back to her. It was where she'd raised the boys on her own, always certain of the O'Connor clan's unconditional acceptance and love. She considered herself part of the family; after all, wasn't she an O'Connor, too? That was what she believed until David told her the truth.

It's hard to imagine which news was worse for her—that Dad was actually dead, or that she'd been so deceived for so long. But when Terry and Jack found out, they knew what cut the deepest for them. They learned that everything they'd told themselves couldn't be true, or shouldn't be true, was undeniably true. Their own family had lied to them about their father from the time they were toddlers. They found the dishonesty unforgivable.

As Terry told me, "It was like everything I was afraid was true from when I was eight years old was proven to be true when I was thirty-two. We were just hung out to dry, absolutely, by the people who I thought loved me." I realized at that moment that Terry had lived the kind of truth that I had been trying to avoid: The more he learned about the family's secrets, the more it hurt. It drew me closer to him. Though I hardly knew him, we really were brothers. For Terry and Jack, the worst deception was their exclusion from their father's burial. They'd guessed that Dad was loping around the fringes of society out west, or maybe in Latin America, still out of contact with the family. Instead, he'd been lying next to his mother in St. Mary's Cemetery, and they had not been there when he came home. They blamed Uncle David in particular because they'd trusted him the most, but they broke off contact with all the O'Connors.

For twenty years after our father died, as my sisters and I wrestled with our own isolation, trying to forget how we got that way, Terry and Jack did the same. They gradually came back to the family, but it wasn't until David was dying—two years before Mom—that they were fully reconciled.

I couldn't comprehend how the O'Connors, who seemed so honest and wonderfully human, could have acted so callously toward Helen and her sons.

Terry thought he knew why: The O'Connors were convinced that my mother and father were running from the federal government. The family feared that if Helen and her sons learned where we were, they might tell Immigration or the FBI.

The mystery had circled back to the feds, again.

Then Terry, with a stark, puzzled face, asked me something that he obviously couldn't hold back any longer. "Why were they running?" That was, of course, the question I had come to ask him.

MY ORIGINAL PLAN—in which I'd find the quick and sure truth about my parents from my relatives in Boston—had failed. Aunt Eleanor had given me the most details, but not enough to explain what had happened to make us fugitives for all those years. Besides, her account of federal agents didn't square with the FBI and INS files. More important, if Terry, who had been tormented with finding the truth of why his father left, had found out nothing substantial from our relatives, either they didn't know enough or they were not going to tell it.

The new plan was what I'd hoped to avoid from the outset: to attack the mystery as I would a big, complicated investigative news story, a saga that began half a century or more in the past, that twisted from Europe to Canada to the United States and Mexico, with federal agents most likely involved somehow along the way. It was a story with more human drama than I cared to digest. A father who'd deserted his first two sons, a cabal of loving aunts and uncles betraying their nephews' trust, and then all the lies by my parents to me and my sisters, beginning from the time we learned to speak.

I saw that monster project coming at me that night at Terry and Rosemarie's dinner table. It was not something that Fiona or Tracy had to push on me, not any longer. It was something I had to do for myself. I wanted to hunt down the truth about us. When I told them I was going for it, Tracy, Fiona, Terry, and then Jack and Mary were all eager. I'd need their help in fitting the pieces together. And, from my brothers and sisters, I'd need their memories. We all knew that might be the hardest part.

HOW DO YOU learn about people with a secret? You can start with documents, in this case my mother's diary, and the papers and snapshots we found in the cigar box. You talk to everyone you can find who knew them, study every document you can think of that might hint at what they were about. And you don't try to do it all on your own, especially when you're emotionally involved. You ask smart people to help you find things and to analyze what emerges. In this case, I turned to a chorus I knew well from my years as a journalist: former federal agents, an ex–CIA operative in domestic intelligence, local police, and others with deep access to federal files. Plus, to get a balance of perspective, a motorcycle gang leader who knew how the feds worked, but from the other side.

Within months of my evening with Terry, I had traveled around the country to speak to each chorus member directly. I knew that if I explained my search in person, they would help as much as they could. Though the FBI had said that they had no record of my family, and the INS came up with only Mom's paperwork from 1973 on, I asked some of my contacts to begin back-door searches to see if there was anything more. I asked others to find out whether my mother or father had ever been charged with a crime or wanted as a suspect.

Meanwhile, I began looking for anyone who had known my family in our travels or had been close to my parents before they met. Ultimately, I would travel back and forth across the United States, through England and Germany, and deep into Mexico, searching for people and documents. I even researched at the Holocaust museum in Jerusalem for records of the refugee camp Dad ran when I was born. But my first journey was to Canada, to the village on Prince Edward Island where I was told my father was born. The place called Tignish, on the northeast tip of the island, where it plows into the Gulf of St. Lawrence. I needed to see that place, and to see with my own eyes the local records that confirmed that my father was born there, and that the couple I'd been told were my grandparents were indeed my father's parents. I was through believing anything I couldn't be sure of.

It was the beginning of finding who our parents really were, what our family's real story was.

PART FOUR

THIRTY

WHEN MY PARENTS MET, they almost snapped into love. It was on the *Queen of Bermuda,* an ocean liner converted to a troopship carrying several thousand American and Canadian soldiers in July 1944, along with a handful of British women with ENSA, the British USO. So the odds were very bad for John O'Connor, but bad odds didn't discourage him.

He'd seen her first from a distance, through hundreds of olive drab uniforms. Then he found her at a railing looking at the sea. He was an Irish American talker, which helped, especially because she pulled back a bit in new surroundings. He could talk when she was quiet, and that would fill the spaces until she felt at ease.

He was six feet tall and solid, but slim, with thick arms from loading and driving trucks. He had a self-confident way about him, just this side of brash. He knew that he made an impression. She was small and looked even smaller next to him, a bit over five feet tall, a bit over one hundred pounds. But her attitude, her spirit, seemed so much bigger.

Years later, when they told people about that first encounter, they both said it must have been a miracle that they'd met, with all of those men hoping to stand at the railing with one of those very few women. And soon it seemed there was no one else on the ship as it lunged and slid through the waves toward the fighting in Italy.

They didn't know how it happened, and they certainly didn't expect it. Romance accelerates in wartime, but this was so sudden for them, and so complete. One day they were two people, alone. Then they were a couple.

"We were both desperately in love," Mom wrote in the first entry of the diary I read after she died. "We recognized a kindred spirit in each other. We could have met anywhere with the same result but everything about the voyage leaned to the romantic. The war was at its critical stage and there was an uncertainty in the air—even a possibility of not reaching Italy, whilst the moonlight on the Mediterranean is calculated to make any heart beat faster and ours were no exception."

He was close to thirty, she was thirty-one. They had lives behind them already. But at that ship's railing, their pasts had no meaning; there was only the now. And despite their different backgrounds, they had one powerful thing in common, even if they didn't notice it at the time. Both had been boxed in by stern social constraints, and both had resisted the restrictions. Their journeys to war were part of an effort to break loose.

My FATHER WAS born in the Canadian village of Tignish in 1914. It was his mother's birthplace, and her mother's, going back to the time her family arrived on Prince Edward Island from Ireland in the 1840s. The unyielding rules from that village stayed with my father to the day he died.

Tignish is a lonely and remote place of low hills and small bays, of family farms and fishing boats, where the wind flies off the ocean like a sharp blade and sends the squirrels hiding on the lee side of the birch trees. It was a place of rigid propriety, where whispers about some neighbor family's misbehavior from a half century before were repeated over dinner tonight. So respectability meant everything.

Catherine, my father's mother, was born in 1886. Her family had an eighty-acre potato farm with a few dairy cows and a small kitchen garden. "The land was so poor," she told her children, "you couldn't raise an umbrella on it." They lived on the verge of disaster. A failed crop, a winter that set in hard in October instead of November, a feud with a neighbor—any of these could bring ruin. Their harsh life made people conservative and clannish, and careful to follow the rules of their rural society. Families stuck together in the face of a brutal world. The rules were set by the Catholic Church, by the village priest and the nuns at school. Traditions were absolute because they had always been. The family guaranteed survival, and the rules guaranteed the family.

A handful of poor Irish families—the Farrells, the Hogans, the McCarthys, the Ryans, the Mackies—staked out land around Tignish. My grandmother was a Mackie. Her people probably came from County Wexford, in southeast Ireland, about the time of the potato famine. The starvation in Ireland reminded the Irish of Tignish how close they were to not making it through the next planting season. For generations they'd lived by pulling potatoes out of the ground and jerking fish and lobster from the deadly cold waters around their island. Most live the same way today.

From almost the beginning, those who found the poverty too much tried to get to Boston, a city filling up with Irish. It was a place where an Irish woman from a rural Canadian village could hold her traditions close. In 1905, Catherine Mackie borrowed twelve dollars from a neighbor family, the Champions, bought some material to make traveling clothes, and took the train to Boston. When she left, Tignish had about thirty extended families, about what it has now, and, for the most part, they're the same families.

In her new clothes, Catherine Mackie stepped off the Boston & Maine Railroad car and passed through the three-story archway of old North Station into the crowds on Causeway Street. She arrived less than two miles from where Boston's original immigrants, the Puritans, had landed in 1630—to create a society so sure of its righteousness that outsiders were excluded.

Though the Protestants' intolerance would ebb over time, the Irish Catholics swarming in were seen as enemies of the correct religion and the way things should be. Many of the Irish—impoverished, badly educated, victimized by discrimination—kept their backs together against outsiders. They clung to one another, drank at Irish-only bars, took care of one another on the job, and listened to their priests. They made a place, apart from the rest of Boston, where their own Church and traditions were revered. And so, while Catherine joined a world of tenements and pushcarts on crowded streets, completely different from her village— in what people thought was important about life, in their values—it wasn't so different at all.

My grandmother found jobs as a waitress and a hotel maid. Then she married a fiery, witty Irish American truck driver who knew she was the boss. Thomas Aloysius O'Connor's contribution to the well-being of the family that ultimately included six children was to protect his job at the Railway Express Agency. Catherine's contribution was to infuse the family with the deepest sense of duty and decency, with a reverence toward tradition.

"There are two kinds of people in this whole wide world," Thomas would tell his children. "There are the Irish, and then there are those who wish they were Irish." Perhaps so. But Catherine knew there were different kinds within the Irish as well, the ones who had standards and the ones who did not, the ones who worked hard and the ones who got by. She would make sure that her family was the very best kind.

In 1913, with Catherine pining for her village, she and Thomas moved to Tignish. He opened a poolroom called Tommy Pool. It gave him a chance to use his charm on the public. But a poolroom must not have felt respectable enough, because on official records he listed himself as "Grocer." The First World War sent most of the village's young men—Tommy Pool's customers—to the army and damaged the island's economy. Just before the business went broke, John Jeremiah O'Connor, my father, was born, on September 10, 1914.

He was baptized ten days later by the priest who would run the parish for fifty-six years. At the time Dad was baptized, the redbrick St. Simon and St. Jude Catholic Church, which boldly jumps up from the deep green grass of Tignish, had already loomed over everything else in the parish for fifty-five years. It still dominates the village physically today. The strongest force of morality now is another parish priest.

With their business bankrupt, my grandparents moved back to Boston. But as Catherine waited at the train station on Prince Edward Island, she did something that shows how deeply she felt the need for proper appearances. The family story is that there were two friends from Tignish behind her in the ticket line, so she spent most of what she had on first-class tickets, because it wouldn't do to be seen in second-class if you could help it. There were a lot of debts to friends after the business failed, but Catherine spent years paying them off a bit at a time to keep the family's reputation.

In 1926 the family bought a house in the southern suburb of Holbrook. The town was known for not welcoming the Irish, and Catherine was never completely comfortable there. But it was a good house for the money, and she always said that frugality brought success. The deed to the house, the mortgage, and the small loans taken out on it were signed only by her.

Catherine's children learned the lessons taught in Tignish and repeated in the immigrant experience in Boston: Be practical in all things; keep your dreaming to songs and poems; follow the One True Church; and keep loyal to your own kind, to your family, for they are your strength. Then there was the unspoken corollary: You must never fail your family in the important things. Because they are always with you, your honor is theirs, too. Or your disgrace.

Catherine took her children back to Tignish every summer, and they kept returning as adults with their own children, just to be there. Into their eighties, Catherine's children would stand on the barren piece of reddish land where the family farm used to be, stare through the wind at the ocean, and talk about the family's great tragedy: It was the odyssey of the son who had broken the rules, who had failed his family and could not come home.

FOR MORE THAN half his life, my father did what was expected of him. Like his brothers and sisters, he went to the one-room school across the street from the home in Holbrook. He learned his lessons faster than anyone, charmed his teachers, and at night helped his sisters with their homework. He was the prince of the family: the oldest, the smartest, the one bound to make them all proud. Their only fear was that John was too much the dreamer. While he was devoted to his mother and ached for her approval, Catherine worried that he didn't understand that a wise person takes small, secure steps, not leaps.

Though my father did not graduate from high school, he started businesses when still a teenager. He cut blocks of ice from the lake near home and imported fish from Prince Edward Island. His plans failed, but he kept going. In 1934, at the age of twenty, he got a job driving a truck for the Boston Railway Express Agency, just like his father. Still living in the family home, he bought a flashy car. He liked to show off, but he was settling into a life that fit with everyone else's.

When he was twenty-two, he met Helen Goncars, the cashier at the café across from the Railway Express office. She was a good-looking blonde, witty and petite, with blue eyes that had a spark in them. On his next visit to Tignish, he wrote her gushing love letters: "I didn't know it was possible to want to see a person as badly as I want to see you right now." And "I've got to stop this or I may not be able to swallow the next big lump that comes into my throat."

In May 1937, when he was not yet twenty-three and she was twenty-five, they married. Her family was stolidly Catholic but Polish, a shortcoming that my grandmother could accept if it made the prince happy, his brothers told me. He lived with his mother until the day he married, then moved with his wife to an upstairs apartment twelve blocks from home.

My father was doing everything he was supposed to do—the steady work, the Sunday dinners with Helen's parents—but it wasn't enough for him. By the time they had a son, Terry, in 1940, the marriage was stumbling badly, at least from Dad's point of view. He told his mother and siblings that he felt smothered. "Helen is a good woman," he said to his sister Eleanor. "There is nothing wrong with her. It's me. I don't know what's missing."

His family saw clearly that he needed something more. They also knew there was nothing more. He was married, and that was it. Under the rules, marriages did not have to be happy, they only had to be forever. Among all his relatives, among all the Boston Irish Catholics seeking respectability and acceptance and welded to the Church, marriage was sacred. None of the relatives knew how to help, so they just watched it go to hell. His mother, adamant, told him, "Snap out of it. My God, son, look at all you've got!"

He found reasons to be away from home: weekend trips with a boyhood friend, driving his mother to Tignish. He spent long hours at work and with his buddies afterward. He drank too much. If there was no other escape, he'd wait at the train station for Eleanor to return from work at the Wausau Insurance Company. She once caught him sitting there, staring past his knees, mumbling to no one. He looked up, his smile suddenly back in place, and asked her over to his home for dinner.

Eleanor had plans and wanted to beg off, but she knew that her brother was torn between his sense of responsibility and his yearning to escape from what he felt was a noose. She went home with him, as she did all the other times. After dinner he would plead with her to stay a couple of hours more, anything to avoid being alone with his wife. It went on for years, getting worse.

In April 1942, he wangled a job running a steam shovel at an American naval base in Newfoundland that shipped war supplies to England. It was big money for him and a way to get out of Holbrook. Four months later he joined the Canadian army, likely on impulse. Army records show that, as a U.S. citizen, he refused to swear allegiance to the Crown but swore to obey army orders, and that was enough. He quickly impressed his training officers. According to their reports, he had "superior learning capacity" and extremely high test scores. His file also shows that he lied about his education. It says "Boston University—2 yrs. on a B.A. course." But no one checked, or if they did, it didn't matter, and shortly he was recommended for officer's training.

Helen, perhaps sensing that her husband was sliding away, took Terry and rented a cabin near the army base in Canada. But as Dad was about to be sent to Europe, he told her it was over. He was not coming back to her. She didn't believe him. They might not have known she was pregnant at the time, but seven months later Jack was born.

My grandmother didn't believe Dad could leave his wife either. Catherine counseled Helen to be patient. He would come around, she said, because that was the way she had raised him.

THIRTY-ONE

As the *Queen of Bermuda* continued toward the war, John and Jessica could not stop talking to each other. They stood close and held hands, but that wasn't enough. They touched each other by talking, by revealing themselves in a passionate flow of language and confession. He told her that there was trouble in his past. She said she didn't care. She told him about her hometown, Burnley, England, and its own deadening uniformity. She told him how she, too, had defied her family's conventions and escaped, and that she was eager to move into the world beyond what she knew.

There were days when it did not rain in Burnley, a town of 110,000, or drizzle a constant mist. There were days in summer when the sun showed how deeply green and lush the hills were, with their oak trees and pools of wild buttercups and pink snapdragons, and white grazing sheep. Burnley people waited for those rare days as they lived through the long sieges of harsh rain and dark, low skies. When summer came—that brief summer of Lancashire County in northern England—Burnley people still kept sweaters and raincoats close by.

It was the weather that first made my mother, Jessie Lawson, yearn to leave Burnley. It was in 1923, when Mom was ten years old. She was a slight, dark-haired girl, smart and rebellious, determined but quiet. She looked at the gray sky through the window of the Barden Lane school and thought, *I am going to get out of here. I must and I will.* When she told her sisters, Ann Helena and Zilpha, they didn't believe her. Don't be daft, they said. They knew that no one left Burnley.

Well, in a way, some left. But they took much of the town with them.

In early July the cotton-weaving mills shut down, and the coal mines, too, and most of the stores. Thousands of families took a forty-mile train ride for a holiday on the beach at Blackpool. Under the same leaden skies as at home, people sat for five days on the sand with a neighbor family on one side and a mate from work on the other. Then they got back on the trains and returned to Burnley for another year of ten-hour shifts.

In the world of mill workers, Gertrude Fitzgerald, my mother's mother, was an extraordinary woman. By her early twenties, she had somehow struggled her way out of her cotton-weaving mill and into a profession as a schoolteacher. She joined the campaign for women's suffrage, a social movement of mostly middle-class women, not the likes of Gertrude's family. She even bought a home at 13 Stoney Street, a tiny and decrepit mill worker's house but a remarkable achievement for an unmarried woman in that time and place.

Gertrude's next-door neighbors were the Lawsons. The eldest Lawson son, James, had been working in the mill alongside his father and grandparents since he was twelve. When he and Gertrude married, he moved into her house. Six years later, with three children, Gertrude sold the house and bought the corner store at 20 Kirkgate Street, four blocks away, with quarters for the family in the back and upstairs, where two more children would be born. My mother's family had climbed one short rung up the social ladder. The new place was imposing for the neighborhood, where the others lived in houses called "two-up, two-down": two rooms upstairs and two rooms downstairs. They could also have been called "two-across," because the rooms were small enough to cross in two short paces.

As with the O'Connors, Mom's mother was in charge. She ran the house and the store, and sent her husband around the neighborhood with a wicker basket selling their baked goods door-to-door. She squeezed what she could from a small business in a poor town because she was damn determined to see her family rise above the rest.

She told her children that they must think for themselves. She was strong and independent, and her daughters would be, too. "You've got to have a trade in your fingers," she told them. When they left school at fourteen, as children did in Burnley, they were all apprenticed to companies that taught a skill. "You can't be sure what the world will bring you," Gertrude told her girls. "Men may have to tend a house, and women cannot always count on their husbands." Apparently, she did not count on James Lawson. He helped with the store, but he seems to have

been more a shadow than a father or a husband. He was further evidence
that a young woman must think on her own.

The best days for Burnley peaked about the year my mother was born,
1913, when Lancashire County dominated the world trade in cotton
cloth and the weaving industry employed more than half of Burnley's
workers. But weaving was already moving overseas, and the town began
a steep decline.

From her corner grocery store, my mother watched her town falling
apart. The household began work before daylight, baking bread and
cakes and mincemeat pies. My mother—Jess to her family—was slow at
it all, even a little defiant; she had other things on her mind. It would still
be dark when Gertrude began calling, "Where is Jess, now?" Or "Jess,
pay attention to your work, don't dawdle."

From the store my mother saw the daily parade of those mill workers
still employed. On the darker mornings she could hear it before she saw
it, with the slap of wooden clog shoes—cheaper than leather, with metal
taps to make them last longer—striking the cobblestones. In every neighborhood, the men left in their dark uniforms, pulling down the brims of
their flat caps; the women in long aprons tossed dark shawls over their
heads and shoulders. Everyone the same.

Elderly local people recalled to me how, a few blocks down the hill
from the grocery store, the steam engines started up at the Witham and
Thornber mills on Plumbe Street, where the people of Jessie's neighborhood worked. Steam from the boilers thrust the gigantic, shining shafts
from their cylinders, then pulled the shafts back, spinning huge flywheels
seventy revolutions a minute. Smoke from the coal fires to heat the boilers at every mill in town coiled upward from huge stacks, then folded
back to cake every building in soot. Burnley disappeared in the smoke.
By the time the sun was up, the town was gone. Farmers on hills two
miles away could not see it. People called the place Burnley-in-the-Smoke.

In drab procession, the workers walked with their neighbors to the
mills, where they labored under dim light from gas mantles. The place
rumbled with noise that was felt as much as heard. Along the ceiling,
over each row of looms, was a driveshaft connected to the steam engine
by a series of banging, creaking, screaming bevel gears. Workers jumped
among rows of looms placed inches apart. They ducked the leather drive
belts looping down from the ceiling and dodged the "picking sticks" that
lashed out from the sides of the looms to send the shuttles back and
forth. Weavers stood in their wooden shoes in pooling groundwater and

machine oil, inhaling a mist of drifting cotton dust. At night the procession reversed direction.

By the time my mother was in her late teens, the British cotton trade was moribund. A study by the British Ministry of Labour found that the number of industrial workers in Burnley had been cut by nearly three-quarters in a few years. It was over that quickly.

The collapse of the weaving industry propelled many in the socially conservative population in new and radical directions. It connected Burnley with the ideology that brought the rise of the Communist movement and the Spanish civil war. When she was a teenager, seeing the effects of a growing world depression and a collapsing cotton industry, left-wing politics began to pull on my mother. And there was the tug of one of her brothers, Alfred, two years older.

Alfred was a rigid, dogmatic, angry young man who strode through their home and corner store with his own sense of righteousness. He was an organizer for the Communist Party of Great Britain, which preached a radical line but generally with polite, British tactics. It called for things like a national health-care system, a welfare state, and government ownership of major industries, but it also advocated debate and elections to bring these changes about. The idea was to get influence in Parliament, not start something so untidy as a revolution. The Party's solution to the mill workers' avalanche of misery was to help lead them in a series of strikes. Uncle Alfred took Mom along as he organized workers. He may not have had to ask more than once. His political work must have seemed exciting and important to her. She began helping him by selling the Party's newspaper on the street.

My mother never joined the Communist Party. There is no hint of her in the minutes of the local Party meetings. The surviving Party members from those days all remembered Uncle Alfred well, along with his sense of duty to the poor and his obstinacy. The members were cordial, inviting me into their small homes, serving cookies—"biscuits," they called them—or, often, small sandwiches of tuna and butter or cucumber, sliced into delicate triangles, and pots of fresh tea they fussed over. But only Mary Abbot, a former leader of the weavers' union, remembered Mom, and then only as "that little girl Jessie, that were Alfred's little sister, and she helped him with things like the newspaper and setting up dances."

As the mills continued to lose business, Burnley's streets were often filled with people on strike, or coming off a strike, or whipping themselves up for the next strike. The local newspapers were clogged with stories about the upheaval. The weavers, the shuttle makers, the spinners, and the tacklers were all fighting the mill owners over something. Thousands of strikers would besiege a mill and intimidate those who had crossed the picket line. Hundreds of police would guard a mill manager's home. Mounted officers patrolled the town in knots, ready to charge workers as they followed the weavers' marching jazz band and defiantly sang "John Brown's Body." With fewer than one hundred members in the area, the Communist Party and Uncle Alfred were but a tiny part of the turmoil. In fact, Uncle Alfred's Party comrades told me they had been worried the workers were becoming too aggressive and beyond the control of any organization.

Burnley's mayor declared that the town was coming apart. On the same weekend that the Grand Theatre showed *The Finger Points,* with Clark Gable and Fay Wray, and the Empire featured Ronald Colman in *Arrowsmith,* the police arrested a number of citizens for inciting to riot. They included a mother of six—with her youngest in her arms—a fifty-one-year-old widow, and Harold Smith, the Sunday school teacher at St. Andrew's Church. The vicar of St. Stephen's, my mother's family church, warned of civil war.

Ultimately, the strikers lost most of their fights. Still, the mills lost, too, because within a few years most were out of business. Long before that, though, Uncle Alfred and his little sister began to quarrel. Alfred unswervingly followed the Communist Party line from Moscow. My mother was committed to something she called "a better world for us all," but she rejected the Party's doctrinaire politics.

Then my mother met the people who would help her get out of Burnley. David and Sadie Gibson lived in Glasgow and were dedicated to the Independent Labour Party, a popular socialist political party with a strong pacifist strain. The Gibsons, who have died, considered the Communist Party of Great Britain only a front for Stalinism, their friends told me. Mom recounted to Fiona that after meeting the Gibsons at a conference in Wales, in 1936, she went to live with them in Glasgow. The city was then a massively overcrowded place of heavy industry, with a deep history of leftist political thought. Sadie Gibson ran a small post office and gave Mom a job.

The Independent Labour Party headquarters in Glasgow shared its building with the umbrella organization for British pacifists, the Peace Pledge Union. The building, on Dundas Street, was a hub for young idealists, for a flashing energy that flowed up and down the stairways and through the disorderly offices. Tom Fulton, a member of the Independent Labour Party at the time, remembered my mother for her north of England accent and shy manner. And she told Fiona that she enjoyed the boisterous frankness of the urban Scots, who seemed to live life more vividly than the dour folks of Burnley. Jessie Lawson was on her way to becoming a pacifist.

Refusing to fight in the Second World War was much easier in Britain than in the United States. The British were more tolerant of unpopular views and more lenient in offering alternative service on farms or in government offices. Even so, some conscientious objectors refused alternative service on principle, while others refused to cooperate with the system at all, in some cases hiding from the authorities.

There were small, informal groups in Glasgow that helped those in hiding stay a step ahead of the police, sheltering them until the officers stopped coming around. Helping these men was against the law, but there is no record of anyone arrested for it, according to Bill Hetherington, the archivist for the Peace Pledge Union. My mother belonged to one of those groups for a while, she told Fiona. But soon Mom's beliefs were changing once again.

She decided to help the war effort and joined ENSA, the British USO. She put on a uniform. She helped stage events for soldiers much as she had helped her brother Alfred organize dances for the Communist Party in Burnley. In July 1944, she was assigned to a post in Rome, which had just been liberated by Allied forces.

On July 16, she boarded the *Queen of Bermuda* and left for Italy. It was the next day, when she stood at the railing to look at the sea, that an Irish American officer made his way through the mass of olive drab uniforms and started talking to her.

THIRTY-TWO

My mother was based in Rome while my father moved through northern Italy with his Canadian tank unit. But they saw each other whenever he could hustle a leave or a pretext.

People who have not felt it may not believe this, but there is a cleansing that can happen amid the atrocities and chaos of war, even a sort of liberation. Wars are perfect places for people with a lot to forget. They can fill you with such terror for your life—and such horror at what people can do to one another—that they strip your mind of what came before. With the help of World War II, my parents became welded together, their pasts obliterated.

In her diary, Mom wrote of their time in Italy:

The front was somewhere near Florence, but Jerry [Dad's nickname] managed to dash down to Rome quite often and indeed, despite of the terrific odds, we saw quite a bit of each other throughout the whole campaign. We also saw a lot of Italy together and learnt to love it for its blue skies, sunshine and picturesque villages.

War can also make you fall in love. With bullets spraying at any time, nothing to eat tonight or to prevent you from freezing by dawn if the weather keeps turning colder, you take a narrow view of things. When nothing is safe, the future becomes a vague promise and the past a vaguer memory. Even when you are outside direct danger, life turns unpredictable. Nothing is secure, and who you were may disappear. If you can reach over and find someone like yourself, someone equally desperate to escape the past, and you can steal a few days and nights with such a person in a city like Rome, you won't ever want to let go. If you can find a coconspirator to cheat the war for a few moments, someone to hold so tightly that you forget to breathe and to hold more tightly in your dreams when you are apart, which is most of the time, nothing else has any meaning.

Near the end of the war, my parents wanted to find a way to stay overseas. They heard that the Allied governments were creating the United Nations Relief and Rehabilitation Administration, or UNRRA, to take care of refugees. Dad applied for a job. While he waited to hear, his unit was sent back to England, and Mom followed from Rome. She wrote in her diary:

> I returned to the UK at the same time. Having wangled the trip home so that we could be within reach of each other. I left Rome on the anniversary of the Russian Red Army my memory of that morning is still coloured by the scene in the square in front of Mussolini's old Palace which was a stone's throw from the club in which I worked situated, as it was, in the old Roman forum.
>
> Russian, American and British troops had gathered to the strains of a military band and the blue skies and the huge white Victor Emmanuel monument looked down on their brass shining in the sun.
>
> At the beginning of April Jerry managed to get a leave which we spent partly in London and partly in the Red Lion Hotel in Thursday, Surrey, where the nightingales in the nearby wood sang us to sleep in the lovely Spring nights.

In August 1945, Dad was released from the army to join UNRRA. He was assigned to run a refugee camp in the German village of Empelde, near Hannover. It was only three months after the war's end, and there was no legal way for Mom, now an ordinary British civilian, to travel through occupied Europe. Though pregnant and beginning to show, she went every day to a military airfield in London to beg for space on a flight to anywhere in Germany. It was rash and desperate, and it didn't work.

Dad had better luck. He persuaded the Belgian Foreign Ministry to have their embassy in London issue Mom a visa for a trip to Brussels. There was no official reason. He just talked them into it. He was good at that.

He went from the refugee camp in Germany to meet her in Brussels, but you couldn't just drive around Europe in those days picking up pregnant English women and carting them through military checkpoints and across borders. You couldn't get a gallon of gas unless the trip was for military reasons and you had the right paperwork. But these were foolish details for a couple in love. They found a uniform for a British army nurse and stuck on some new shoulder patches. Then they doctored my mother's ENSA identity and travel documents to make it look like she had permission to travel in Germany.

The refugee camp in Empelde was a converted Nazi slave labor compound where about four thousand prisoners had worked at an I. G. Farben explosives plant, making ammunition for pistols, rifles, and anti-aircraft guns. Most of the refugees were Polish, but there were also about 850 Jews, 400 Yugoslavs, and a number of others, including 84 infants. My father's problem was to keep them well and in the camp until they could be sent home. The Empelde camp seemed relatively benign. United Nations records show that it had doctors, ample food, a school, a small band for dances. There was a library with ninety-seven books.

Three miles to the west of Empelde, the village of Gehrden was on a slow rise from the camp. Peter Bauer lived there when my parents arrived. The morning after he first heard the clank of American tanks in the village, then ten-year-old Peter and his father, Curt, walked cautiously to the mayor's office. White sheets flowed out of the village windows in surrender. Most people stayed inside, afraid, but Peter and Curt felt a bit braver. As Peter told me, it seemed to them that Germany had been conquered by the Nazis and liberated by the Allies. The Bauers spoke English, and they wanted to see what they could do to help the Americans.

More than five decades later, Peter still saw the scene clearly, like something from a postwar movie. While his father went into the mayor's office, he told me, he "stayed outside to look at the tanks. Then a very pleasant soldier was in his jeep. He gave me something I had never seen: chewing gum."

Peter's father came out of the office deputized as an auxiliary town policeman, and the bottom floor of their home was requisitioned for Allied officers, with the Bauers moving upstairs. First there were three French military doctors, attached to the American forces, then two British officers. In late November 1945, "a wonderful couple" arrived, Peter recalled. "They were so unified and strong together. They stood next to each other always. It was like the birds, the lovebirds, cuddling next to each other. That is the picture I have when I think of them."

There were obvious inconsistencies that Peter did not recall. Here was my mother, a British woman in occupied Germany, wearing a military uniform but quite along in her pregnancy, a notable contradiction. But Peter doesn't remember the inconsistencies, because they didn't matter for my parents. All they cared about was being together. That was the image they broadcast. Peter said they did what they could to have a normal home, with my father off at the refugee camp most of the day and home at night with Mom.

The Empelde camp was a place for victims who would continue to be victims. There were suggestions from the Allied military government to make conditions harsh enough to encourage people to go home, to the destruction left by the war and now occupied by the Red Army. The UN records include an order from the military government, labeled SECRET, demanding that at my father's camp "maximum effort must be made to insure NO decrease in the number of Poles willing to be repatriated."

The United Nations Administration was pushing to pack the overcrowded trains and trucks and keep them moving east. My father, perhaps brashly, sent a memo back saying "There will never be a successful repatriation campaign while the DPs [displaced persons] . . . must endure considerable hardship in order to go home to decidedly uncertain futures." There was organized resistance to repatriation in the camp, which was patrolled by sixteen Polish soldiers on the outside and a police force of thirty-four Poles inside. Gangs of young Polish men slipped from the camp into the defenseless local villages for revenge and plunder. In the only wartime detail my father gave me, he killed a gang leader in a shoot-out after the man had killed my father's deputy.

A few miles from the camp, the city of Hannover was so badly damaged that 200,000 residents had left for the nearby countryside to survive by subsistence farming. On top of that, the trains from Eastern Europe coming to take the refugees home brought thousands of destitute ethnic German people who'd been expelled by the Soviet army. The devastation and wretchedness were nearly universal, but that was not what my mother saw. She looked past it.

We are spending a delightfully happy time in lovely surroundings. Our house is situated at the top of a hill leading from the quaint town of

Gehrden and is built on the edge of a lovely pine wood of which the big
windows in the spacious rooms command a wonderful view.

In February 1946, she wrote:

Michael and a new day were born at the same time but whilst the day
dawned noiselessly, Michael heralded his arrival with a sneeze and a
lusty yell. I was conscious at his birth and was amused to note how
ridiculously like Jerry's was the shape of his head. When he opened his
eyes they were like two big smoke-pearl buttons in his little face and he
sucked his thumb from the beginning. Jerry and I could hardly believe
that he was actually ours, that here, at last was the wee mite we had
longed for since those seemingly far off days in Italy. He was ours and
nobody could take him away from us—incredible.

Jerry was very concerned and so was the doctor, particularly as
Jerry had threatened to shoot him if anything went wrong and as he
had accidentally left his pistol lying on the table, the poor doctor was
petrified to see it there as though in wait when he arrived at the house.

The third Sunday after his birth Michael was christened in the village church whose parish dates back to 1600. It was a beautiful crisp
morning with the snow on the tree-tops all around glistening in the sun
and everywhere carpeted in white. All the members of the UNRRA
team arrived at the appointed time—a little late perhaps—and poured
out of trucks and jeeps and what have you.

By June 8, the refugees were gone to whatever was to abuse them next
and the camp closed. Mom wrote, "We feel now it is time to look to our
future and to this end Jerry has laid the foundation of an import and export business with representatives in most of the European countries,
Canada and America." My father's hustle and the company name, San
Lorenzo Enterprises, were the new firm's main assets. But for my parents, that would have been enough.

The first leg on their route to certain success in America was a drive
back to Brussels. Dad had a legitimate movement order showing he was
"Returning to Home Station." But Mom had nothing; she wasn't supposed to be there in the first place. So they phonied up some UNRRA
documents to show that she was a UN nurse and I a refugee orphan
whom she was taking to my grandparents. It didn't work this time. The

military police at the German border didn't buy Mom's fake papers and turned us back. But in the pattern they would follow for the rest of their lives, my parents got around that. As Mom wrote:

> It was decided at length to risk smuggling me through in the trunk of the car which, fortunately was very large, and to hide Michael under an army overcoat and hope that he kept quiet. We waited until it was almost dark and by this time a terrific thunderstorm was raging. When we were within a mile or so of the border I was bundled into the trunk where a coil of wire scratched at my face and tore at my hair and to add to my discomfort Jerry put the spare tyre and some bits and pieces of luggage in front of me as a precaution against possible inspection. As can be imagined, we approached the border with some intimidation and the knowledge that if Michael and I were discovered we should all be in the soup—and pretty hot soup at that! My one fear was that Michael should begin to cry when the car pulled up.
>
> What a relief it was when the guards merely glanced at the documents and gave the signal for us to pass. We were not yet through the danger zone however, as the Dutch guards a few yards ahead flashed their torches in a signal to us to stop so that a search of the vehicle could be made, as smuggling goods out of Germany was rife. Jerry ignored them and zipped right through, dashed to the trunk to let me out and then proceeded to wind in and out of the country roads, which at that point were a network, in order to shake off the pursuing guards.

After busting the Dutch border like moonshiners on methamphetamines and eluding the police over the twisting roads, they stopped at a restaurant and asked the owners to warm a bottle of milk for the baby.

Don't misunderstand, my parents did not disdain the law. My father's upbringing had ground respect for rules into each of his corpuscles. My mother was raised sternly, with British middle-class aspirations. She may have strayed a little in Burnley or Glasgow, but only up to the edge of what was acceptable in those places. As they ran through postwar Europe, they would have felt more proper having all the right papers with all the right stamps. But if they had to choose between being legal and being together—well, that was no choice at all.

My sisters tend to the opinion that our parents came to like the thrill of beating the law. But I think there was a lot more panic than excitement in them as we dodged around eastern Holland hoping to outrun the border guards. If over the years they came to seem to enjoy running, it was like two shipwrecked people in a life raft who say they just love to row.

We went to England, stopping in Burnley for Mom to say goodbye and to show off her American officer to her family. Of course, he was actually a Canadian officer who was an American, but in Burnley they saw him as an American officer, and that was what was impressive.

A niece of Mom's named Sheila was only eight years old when we arrived, but the event was so big that it stayed with her: "Me mum said, 'Our Jess is coming with her American and her baby.' Well, we all were simply squirming with anticipation. We went 'round to Grandmum's and there he was. He was so tall and elegant. Auntie Jessie was so proud; we all were. I thought he must have been a major."

But the real wonderment, Sheila said, was that somehow her aunt Jess was leaving Burnley for good: "No one did that, you know. I didn't know people could live somewhere else." And they were going to America! In Burnley, Sheila said, that was a prize too big to dream about.

Dad was the man with big ideas, who always wanted more than the people he grew up with. Mom was the idealist, determined to get out into the world with him. They had a plan and a little money, they had each other, and—*whoosh!*—they were launching. They would hold hands, swing their arms in unison, and leap to success, powered by my father's all-American certainty that you can make it if you try and by my mother's unreserved faith in her man.

THIRTY-THREE

IN JULY 1946, my parents and I arrived in New York from England on the SS *Gripsholm* and went straight to Toronto to start Dad's import-export business. It failed within months, and we quickly moved to Boston. My parents finally had to confront the big problem. I'm sure that they had tried to pretend it away. That was their style. And, with the drama and romance of all they had lived together, it would have been easy to push it aside. But my father could not delay it any longer; he had to ask for a divorce from Helen, Terry and Jack's mother. The law did not allow him simply to end their marriage—she had to agree. Mom and I were hidden away near Boston with friends of Dad's while Dad went to Helen.

Helen refused a divorce. She could not comprehend why Dad was asking or how he even could. It was not possible. In her love for him, in her Catholic faith, Helen could not agree. He tried a second time, and she still said no. From that point on, he waited for her to change her mind but refused to see her or their sons. He left a suitcase in the O'Connor home in Holbrook and told his mother he'd be staying with a friend in downtown Boston, to make it easier to look for work. Sometimes he went back to Holbrook for a few days to sit and talk with his mother, imploring her to accept a son who had rejected his wife. Catherine, busy in the kitchen and with her youngest child, David, listened but could not approve of what he was doing. She was responsible for the entire family, for its reputation and its road to heaven. She turned the guilt back toward herself. The unpardonable failing was not his but hers, because she had not taught him the proper ways of life.

It would have been even worse for my grandmother had she known the whole story, about my mother and the new baby: me.

Mom got work as a housekeeper for a woman in the Jamaica Plain section of Boston, where she and I lived in the small apartment above the garage in the back.

When Dad wasn't out of town working as a door-to-door salesman, he'd sneak over to see us. Unable to be a good son, a real father to any of his children, or a true husband, he felt useless, remorseful, and most of all, trapped. While he needed a divorce for legal reasons, he also needed his mother's approval for his own sense of worth. But Catherine counseled Helen to hold tight. What Dad wanted was simply wrong, she insisted, and with time he would surely see that. The dilemma festered.

In late 1946, Dad finally told his sisters about Mom and me. He had made his choice, and he needed them to understand. That was a lot to accept in those days, especially in a working-class Irish Catholic family. It put my aunts at odds with their religion, their upbringing, and most dauntingly, their mother. She was granite-hard on matters of God and propriety. "I don't think we knew anyone who was divorced," Aunt Eleanor told me. "It was not what good people did." When Dad took his sisters to meet Mom, they were impressed with her intelligence and her spiritedness and saw how smitten she and Dad were. "They looked like two twenty-year-olds, hugging and pulling on each other," Eleanor remembered. "Well, that was it for us. He was our big brother, our hero, so we thought we should keep his secret, because he was sure he could straighten everything out with Helen before long."

Then came the surprise that left them grasping for an explanation. It was just before Christmas 1946. Mary, then twenty-six, was at her job as a clerk for the Internal Revenue Service in downtown Boston. Two FBI men came onto the floor. They strode up to Mary's desk, in front of "the other girls," as Eleanor called them. The men spoke loudly to Mary, abusively. She was humiliated. They were looking for Mom, and Mary couldn't understand how that could be. *Why is the FBI looking for Jess?* The agents, grim-faced, told her they knew she was hiding "that O'Connor woman and her kid" because they'd been investigating us—and if Mary didn't tell them where we were, the FBI would investigate her, too.

Mary was not hiding us, but she did know where we were. Eleanor laughed at that point in the story. Not because it was funny. Because it was a terrifying moment in her sister's life. For Aunt Eleanor, that ball of emotions came out as a troubled laugh. "Mary almost fainted," she said.

"But she recovered enough to send them on their way without a shred of information."

Mary told only two people about the FBI visit: Eleanor and my father, who said he had no idea why the agents would be looking for Mom. They hoped that, somehow, it was a mistake.

Though my grandmother wasn't told anything about Mom and me, she knew my father was hiding something. She could not make him return to Helen, and he refused to live at the O'Connor home. He would not listen to reason, her reason. He was nervous, jumpy, he disappeared for days. He was not the person she had raised.

In April 1947, four months after the FBI was at Mary's office, my grandmother resolved to find out what was really going on. She told my father's brother Larry to follow Dad. Larry thought his mother's order was reasonable. He thought Dad was being irresponsible toward Helen, and besides, Uncle Larry had been raised to do what his mother told him. Dad was driving a large maroon Packard he had from before the war. It was easy to follow. One evening Larry tailed it to the apartment in Jamaica Plain, then reported to Catherine that he'd seen Dad greeted too warmly by a woman there.

My grandmother was furious but wily enough to wait until the next day, when she expected Dad would be gone, to have Larry take her to the apartment. She was going to fix this problem. She would save her son from further sin and reclaim her family's self-respect.

They went up the stairs and into our apartment, Catherine first, propelled by righteousness and the fear of what it would mean if she failed once again. As soon as she heard Mom's British accent, Catherine realized that she might be able to intimidate this foreigner. She told Mom that she had to leave the country, that day or the next—it didn't matter where she went. There would be no discussion.

My mother counterattacked. Finally meeting the woman whose standards and rules still held so much power over Dad, she refused. She was staying. The two women who loved my father collided, and they shared no common ground.

Then my grandmother gasped—at the sight of me asleep in my crib in the corner of the room. Larry hadn't known there was a baby. My grandmother did not step toward her grandson. To acknowledge the baby would have been to accept it, and she had come to eradicate Dad's mistakes, not sanction them. She said that I would have to go, too.

Again, Mom defied her. We were not leaving.

"He is a married man," my grandmother said firmly. "He has two children. He has responsibilities. Who are you? He is married before God."

Mom blazed back, "Do you think I am any less married because some man did not sign a piece of paper?" By "some man," she meant a priest. She was not against religion but didn't agree that only a priest could sanction a marriage.

My grandmother's order was refused, but she tried to show Mom how Dad's life was already complete. He was in line to get his full-time job back, she said, driving trucks for Railway Express. He had his brothers and sisters and the whole O'Connor clan. How could Mom want to take him away from everything he knew, everything that was good for him?

My mother answered that she was all he needed and he was all she needed. I can see Mom's small fists squeezed tight, her elbows back, her face forward, close to my grandmother's. But Catherine pushed on. Her long hair, turning white by then, framed a face as stern as ice. She pressed again. Mom would not yield.

Furious with Mom as well as with Dad, crushed by her own failure as matriarch, Catherine turned to leave, telling Larry to follow. They crossed the driveway to the back door of the main house, where Catherine asked if she could use the telephone. She called the Immigration and Naturalization Service and reported that a foreigner was trying to break up a good Catholic marriage. She insisted that an INS agent come immediately. She said she'd wait. She was going to get things in their proper order. When an immigration agent came, she made her report to him.

Catherine and Larry drove home hardly speaking as they considered the brutality of what they'd just done. Catherine told Larry that it was unavoidable and proper, that she had solved the problem because Mom and I would be deported.

Still, Larry and his sisters wondered how seriously the INS would investigate my grandmother's complaint, assuming that the government had more important issues. In any case, Catherine's intervention did have one immediate, tragic effect. Her own family fell into opposing camps and began to lie to one another. Smiles at the breakfast table, evasions all day long. This entrenched a pattern of deception within the family that would continue until after my father died.

Dad was devastated. He was furious with Larry and at one point, drunk, threatened to shoot him. He still tried to bring his mother around, but he stopped trusting her.

My aunts, meanwhile, were appalled by their mother and Larry. They cared about Helen and my father's sons and hated what was happening to them, but they also believed that they had to support Dad's choice and help him if they could. They helped Mom get a series of jobs as a house-keeper or a nanny in quiet towns around Boston, despite the INS, the FBI, and their own mother. My aunts did not tell anyone in the family what they were doing. In fact, the men of the family did their best to stay out of the conflict, not wanting to know what was happening around them.

It grew worse. In between Dad's futile appeals to his mother, he left for months at a time on his sales jobs. Finally, in 1949, three years after he'd come home from the war, with Helen still refusing a divorce, he just disappeared. He took me and Mom, and left without telling anyone. My aunts and uncles did not know what finally made us go, but they believed it had something to do with the FBI. That was who Dad was afraid of; he'd told them so. They just didn't know why.

WE VANISHED ENTIRELY until 1953, when Dad, yearning for his lost clan, went to the Western Union office in Uvalde, Texas—a safe three hundred miles from our home in Houston—and sent a telegram to his sister Mary. There was no name at the bottom of that yellow telegram, no return address, but Aunt Mary knew it was from him. It told her he was still alive, not in jail, doing all right.

He sent a handful of other telegrams, signing them all "Tex." Mary told Eleanor, but they kept it to themselves. A year or so after the first one, he called Mary from a pay phone. He probably bragged a little be-cause we had moved into our place on Mobile Street by then. He gave her our home phone number, but with the sternest warning: Never call except for an extreme emergency, and then only from a pay phone. He said he was doing better financially and in a few months hoped to start working on "the police problem." When that was settled, he would try to cross the chasm between him and his mother.

In 1954 my grandmother—still in her sixties—began forgetting things. Her children thought she was despondent because Aunt Mary had moved a hundred miles away when her husband, Bill, got a teaching job in Westfield, Massachusetts. "It's not right," my grandmother kept saying. "A family stays together." Soon, though, her symptoms grew worse. The doctors found a brain tumor, and Catherine died that November.

The O'Connors gathered at the house for her wake. Her coffin sat in the small living room, with chairs in front and candles throwing shadows on the blessed heart of Jesus, pierced by thorns and bleeding. My grandfather was beyond despair. No one could imagine what the clan would be like without Catherine. And not knowing what the clan would be like, no one could be sure what *they* would be like. In the sorrow pressing down on them, Aunt Mary confessed in a whisper to Tom and to Larry that she had spoken with Dad and even had a telephone number for him.

The siblings agreed that they had to tell him about his mother's death. Dad could never win back his mother's respect or acceptance, but at least he could come home to say goodbye.

"We went down to the pay phone at the train station to call him," Uncle Larry told me. "We thought the police, or somebody, could be listening on our side, still." Tom made the call—a short call, because after Dad heard the news he couldn't speak long. He could not attend the funeral, he said; it would be too dangerous. "He was afraid the FBI would be waiting for him," Larry said. "He thought it would be like Al Capone coming back to town. He didn't want to take the chance."

So Dad was still hiding when he said goodbye to his mother from across the country.

The next event my relatives remembered was two years later, in 1956, when Aunt Eleanor came for that brief visit to Houston. There were a few letters from Dad after that, but then they stopped, with no explanation, in 1958. We had disappeared again—to the Villa. By then my parents were too afraid to tell anyone where we had gone.

Then, in the mid-1960s, Eleanor said, the FBI confronted Aunt Mary again. It was similar to the time in 1946 when they came to the office where she was working and loudly demanded that she tell them where Mom and I were hiding. By the second visit, Aunt Mary was a schoolteacher in western Massachusetts. Two agents went to her school's administrator, who called her out of the classroom. She told Eleanor about the long, long walk down the hallway to the main office and how humiliating it was to be questioned in front of her boss. This time, the agents wanted to know where Dad was. She told them she had no idea. That was the truth; we had dropped from sight.

THIRTY-FOUR

WHEN I MET with Fiona and Terry at Terry's house in Holyoke in September 1999 to open the discussion of how we might examine our past, they both told me straight out: Don't expect much from our aunt and uncles, the clan's elders. They don't want to disturb the past.

That seemed bizarre to me. Why wouldn't everybody involved want to pool what they knew? Then it would be easy. We'd just come up with the answers. That was naïveté on my part, which came from not knowing how the dynamics of a big family can work. Then I got smarter. I saw that, to get the information, I'd need to treat my own family like any other group with a secret, whether it was a street gang, isolated villagers, a guerrilla band, or an office of bureaucrats. Just be honest, don't push, and spend as much time with them as you possibly can. It almost always works.

With the O'Connor elders, it took a little longer.

My relatives would talk to me anytime I asked. They wanted me to stay in their homes. They treated me more warmly than I'd imagined possible. But one after the next, they told me that they couldn't remember anything to help me understand what we'd run from.

It was two years after we met when Uncle Larry finally confided to me how he'd trailed Dad to where Mom and I were hiding and brought Catherine there. He recalled the apartment's address: 3 Agassiz Park, just off the Jamaica Pond in Boston. He could remember with precision the small driveway between the main house and the apartment over the garage. His description was so good that I found the place easily, without a wrong turn. But he could not remember what my mother and grandmother said when they confronted each other.

The first time he tried to remember, he sat in a chair, breathing heavily, looking out a window on the other side of the room. Then he bent down a bit, stared at the floor, put his hands up to cover his ears, and said, "I'm trying, but I just don't think I heard anything."

I couldn't imagine anyone not liking Uncle Larry. He was charming and emotional and flayed himself for his mistakes. He'd been divorced twice, but his ex-wives liked him so much that he stopped by to see each of them several times a week. We spent a fair amount of time together, and he believed me when I told him that I held no grudge.

The day he started to remember things, we were drinking stingers at a bar in Falmouth, on Cape Cod. It was four years after we'd first seen each other at the O'Connor family gathering where I'd met my relatives. After close to an hour, Larry started talking about the day he'd led my grandmother to my mother. "You were just a little baby, in a crib in the corner of the room—I can see you now," he said. "I really didn't know all this was going to happen to your mother and you. Christ, Mike, I had no idea."

I just let him talk.

"Look, Mary and Eleanor always said that I did it because I was just a kid, seventeen or eighteen. But I was twenty-something. I'd been in the war in the Pacific. I was a year away from getting married. I was no kid. They say Ma made me do it. Well, I wouldn't have done it unless she told me to, but I could have said no. I followed your father to that apartment because I thought it was right. I knew that your father was making a mistake—he had his whole life here. He had a family. What in the hell was he thinking about? I still ask myself that. He could have gone back to driving for the Railway Express. They were paying something like thirty-eight dollars a week, steady pay. But he had his head in the clouds."

Larry was sounding more sure of himself than he looked. His shoulders were hunched, his face still and flat, not nearly as animated as usual. "Things were different in those days. When you got married, that was it. What was he thinking of? He was the star. We all looked to him. I did it. There are things you feel all your life. You have to just put them away or they'll eat you up."

Larry was silent for a minute, and then he began to cry. It might have been the stingers, or his Irish genes, or his pain for the needless pain of so many others. It was all of those things that made me cry with him.

AUNT ELEANOR, WHO had never married, became the matriarch after my grandmother, and then Aunt Mary, died. When there were frictions between family members, she intervened. If a marriage or a child was troubled, she gave advice. If the advice was not followed, she gave orders. It was up to her to guarantee that family rituals were done properly, all the weddings and graduations and birthday parties, the visits with the bereaved and depressed, the trips to Tignish. She became the keeper of the family lore, the protector of all they did to stay close—and, with that, the custodian of the family honor. I knew she was worried that the answers I was looking for would call that honor into question.

Eleanor passed on to me what Catherine had told her about the shoestring farm on Prince Edward Island, and how Catherine's father, Paddy Mackie, had bravely captained the schooner *Maggie Macbeth* with its produce and lumber through the Gulf of St. Lawrence. She retold stories she'd heard sixty years before in the O'Connor living room—how Catherine and her sisters had spun the thread and wove the cloth for their clothes. How my grandmother, to make the story live, had mimicked the snap of the spindle and the swoosh of the loom. The smallest details sprang from Eleanor's memory. She was also eager to explain how talent and intellect had made Terry and Jack successful businessmen, Terry with his ad agency and Jack with his huge party-goods store.

But for a long time Aunt Eleanor couldn't remember why my parents were afraid of the FBI. And she was vague about those awful days when she and Mary helped Dad hide Mom and me from our grandmother and the INS. Gradually, though, she began to recall more details. But it was clearly difficult for her, and she summoned the words in small gasps. "There was actually a break within the family. . . . Your Aunt Mary and I didn't talk about it that way. But that is what happened. . . . Larry and Ma made one choice, and we made another. . . . We felt we had to help your father and Jessie. . . . We had to keep it all a secret from Ma; that was the hardest to accept." That time, all those decades ago, was still wrenching for her. There was no right thing to do, only a choice of whom to betray in a family where unity against the outside had always been paramount.

And then a breakthrough: Eleanor said she'd recalled something about Mom getting on "bad lists" from her visits to the Community Church of Boston. "Bad lists" was the same term Mom had used some thirty years earlier when she had told Fiona about what had happened after she went to lectures or seminars at a church near Copley Square in Boston. The Community Church faces the square.

The fact that it had been so difficult to get that information from

Eleanor made the story more difficult to dismiss than when I had heard it from Fiona some four years before.

Over time, in her tiny writing desk, Eleanor began to find letters and photographs from Mom and from Dad. You wonder how those things could have been misplaced for so long in those two small drawers. Early on she found a letter Mom wrote to her in 1955. It explained why we'd run to Mexico the first time. Dad had been detained for selling door-to-door without a license.

Mom wrote, "He was arrested in Harlingen on a charge of neglecting to obtain a salesman's license for that city—a minor charge actually but they took his fingerprints as a matter of routine and hinted that they would be sent to Washington for investigation." Not mentioning the panic we all felt, Mom matter-of-factly told Eleanor: "Within a few hours we were en route for Mexico, the car stuffed with everything practical we could carry."

After a couple of weeks in the Villa, Dad was returning alone to Houston to get what he could carry from our home and bring it back to the Villa—where we were to start a new life. On the way, he stopped at his apartment in Harlingen to clean it out, too. Mom wrote that he ran into the police chief, who remembered Dad from when he had been taken to the police station. The chief said he'd been wondering if he'd see Dad around because he wanted to tell him that the officer had been overzealous—there was no cause for any further investigation or for sending Dad's fingerprints to Washington. Case closed.

It was a great letter to have. It solved one of the early mysteries of our life: why we had run to Mexico the first time, and then why we had suddenly gone back home.

But it said nothing about what we were running from. That mystery, the big one, was still alive.

In the New England spring of 2001, three and one-half years after I had begun asking Eleanor about my family's past, she and I were sitting on her deck with coffee and the Sunday papers when she casually began to tell me how my being sent to Juvenile Hall in San Diego had led my family to run from Mexico back to Texas and ultimately to California, a story Mom had shared with her a few years before. Mom had told her about the letters from the San Diego County juvenile authorities, who were suspicious of a family in which the parents refused to retrieve their son from custody. Those letters made Mom and Dad feel the law was getting too close.

Dad's occasional letters to Eleanor and Mary had stopped suddenly in 1958, when we'd run to Mexico for the second time. His sisters kept trying to reach us at the house on Mobile Street, but their letters were not answered and then the phone was disconnected. Fearing the worst, initially they thought perhaps we'd all been killed, though they didn't dare check with the police to be sure. They could only hope that we were running again and wait for Dad to feel safe enough to contact them. It was a painful wait.

Dad didn't resurface until 1971, in Guadalajara, where he thought he was about to close the Houston deal. Eleanor showed me the letter he'd written to Aunt Mary. It was the most complete review of our history that I had seen. In it he tried to explain more than two decades of failure—and, in particular, the latest leg of my parents' long journey, from California back to Mexico. He began by recalling our flight from Boston, twenty-two years before:

It's been a long twenty-odd years. Most of it spent in subdued apprehension, enlivened by moments of acute panic. Every time we'd get established a little man with a brief case would show up, and we'd hit the road again. We left furniture, clothes, houses, cars and pets. I've made good money usually, but never enough to compensate for the periods of enforced idleness.

We'd usually head to Mexico, and I'd sneak back to work in the States, never at a job but as a self-employed contractor or salesman. The kids never knew, they just thought we were nuts.

One advantage is that when I got set to move them back, they came to their school as if they had lived in Mexico all their lives, thus breaking the trail. Of course they all speak Spanish like Mexicans, in fact, better than most Mexicans because we've always been, one way or another, able to keep them in good schools.

We've lived, and got partially established, from Houston to San Francisco. I know the streets in every town in the South and the West, from Gila Bend, Arizona to Hangtown, California. This does not mean we were on the bum, we were just more mobile than the average wage slave. For example:

We moved from Monterrey, Mexico to San Jose, Calif. started out broke, stopped off for eight weeks in San Antonio, Texas, put the kids in school, and I went to work as an estimator-salesman for a building company, accumulated $2,000 in eight weeks and we went on to San

Jose, as the building company was making noises at me to fill out the tax forms for them.

We had six good years in San Jose, and I fell into the trap of thinking we were safe. We bought a house—Again! I was doing well in my endeavors as an estimator-consultant to the building business. Mary and Eleanor—she has decided she likes Fiona better—were in Catholic schools. Mary graduated from Notre Dame High School in '67. She was valedictorian and had offers of scholarships from half the colleges in the country. I had just been offered a job at $36,000 a year, complete with Social Security and tax deductions. Of course I refused it, because I know how long that would last. The next step would have been a long stretch in the Stoney Lonesome for me, and a boat ride for Babe. Anyway, it made us feel good, because I know the work.

By this time we were really in the rat race: big house, two cars, checking accounts, and I was trying to figure out some way to do something for Terry and Jack, when the ax, as it always did, fell.

Mary had answered several of the scholarship offers, and, innocently, had filled in forms giving information on me. My work, income, etc., and then gotten a query from the California State income tax board, who were having a little trouble finding my returns. That meant the honeymoon was over again.

This part of Dad's letter corroborated what Mary recalled about what had happened in 1967, as she was close to graduating from high school and had applied for federal and state loans and scholarships. After all, that was what normal middle-class people did. Neither Mom nor Dad knew about the applications until the state of California wrote back to ask for more information. Though the letter was routine, it panicked our parents, because Dad had not filed state or federal tax returns since he'd fled Boston. Fugitives don't tell the government where they work and where they live.

The day they received the letter from the state of California, Mom took Mary up to the second floor of the house on Mariposa Avenue, still unfinished under the new red Spanish-tile roof. It was quiet up there, and Fiona, then a curious twelve-year-old, would not hear. Mom spoke quietly but very seriously. She was so scared that she broke her own sacred rule. She told Mary something about why we were running. Initially, it was the way Mom spoke that made Mary afraid, and it took her a few moments to understand what she was hearing. First, Mom brought out what she called "the family Bible," a big one with a laminated gold cover and an oval picture of the Virgin and Baby Jesus in the middle. She told Mary to put her hand on the Bible and swear before God that she would not tell anyone, *no one,* what she was about to hear. Mary didn't tell anyone until after Mom died and we began investigating our secrets.

Mom said that Mary could not follow through on the scholarship applications because doing so might alert the FBI that Mom was in the United States. She didn't say why the FBI was interested, and Mary didn't ask. As Mary later described it to me, she saw only the fact that her future was disappearing.

"Your father and I will make it up to you," Mom told her. "We will get you into that college."

But first they were going to run away to Mexico, one more time. The routine letter from the California tax authorities prompted the run to Guadalajara.

On the one hand, it seemed absurd for them to run from the doorstep to success and respectability on the flimsy theory that a scholarship application would get the house surrounded by federal agents. On the other hand, my parents had lived on the thinnest edge of instant catastrophe for so long that paranoia was part of their DNA. And they would tell each other that they must have been right to run all those other times, because they were still free.

Mary did get into the college. But with that deal our father made to barter printing college forms on the press of his magazine in Guadalajara. When Dad lost the magazine and couldn't do the printing, the college expelled Mary. That was part of why she was so angry with her parents, why for years she didn't even want to talk about them, much less see them. She thought, *First they live so irresponsibly that they get into trouble with the FBI, so I can't apply for scholarships and college loans. Then, after promising to cover my tuition with the barter deal, they screw up and lose the magazine.* She thought, *They make ridiculous mistakes and their children pay the price.*

Dad continued in his letter to our aunt Mary with the news that he was about to become wondrously successful. He said he had found a company based in Zurich, Switzerland, with offices in Houston and Panama, to finance the construction of a condominium and a shopping center for a total of $5.8 million. These were the building plans he'd brought to San Jose when he came to get Fiona and a car. This was "the Houston deal." This was how he explained the poverty that he and my mother and sister were living in. The deal had swallowed "two years and cost $30,000, half of it from me," he wrote.

> We've been living for one year on a budget of $40. per week, and that ain't easy, even in Mexico!
>
> This is the big turning point, at least in this branch of the O'Connor family. What lies ahead is not just a quick killing, but wealth. From my point of view it's the first time in 20 years that I do not have to plan on a possible midnight flit.

After all those years on the margins, my father thought he had found safety and prosperity in Mexico.

Then he echoed something I'd heard from him in the Villa de Santiago many years before, when he was planning his hotel for American tour groups. He told Aunt Mary about his hopes to create a place where his Boston people could visit, where bygones might be bygones. Where he could become the loyal son and good brother once more, and the caring father to Terry and Jack:

> I had thought of setting up a sort of H.Q. south for the entire family, although I did not know if they'd react to my sudden reappearance with scorn or disgust. However it was worth a try.
>
> What Babe and I had, we still have, and it's stronger than ever. The realists laugh at enduring romantic love, but we know better. I know that the choices I had were all bad, and I took the only possible one.

It was a good reprise of our lives, and of the man who'd guided them—in parts rueful, hopeful, grandiose, paranoid, and self-justifying. Dad was wise enough to worry that his children would conclude that the family's life was so bizarre and difficult because their parents were crazy. That's exactly what happened. I blamed them. Who else was there to blame? With what I had found, and with the letter, I could understand that there was much more to the truth than what I used to believe. With that, my anger began to go away.

Still, there was one crucial thing missing from the letter. It did not say what we were running from.

THIRTY-FIVE

SINCE 1997, WHEN WE WERE GOING through Mom's apartment after she died and Fiona brought up the "bad lists" from Boston, which Mom had told her had made the FBI want to find her, we'd considered the theory that Mom somehow had been snared by McCarthyite hysteria. I'd kept it in the back of my mind, though it seemed far-fetched to me. I thought of my mother as a sentimental humanitarian, not a political activist. I took it to be a whimsical story to hide a much more sinister truth. However, by the summer of 2000, we were running out of solid new leads in any direction, so it was time to look more closely at *whether* the FBI had been chasing us.

By that point Mary, Fiona, Terry, Jack, and I were talking to one another regularly. Tracy and I were still living in Israel, but I was going to the United States a lot to search through records, consult with the former federal agents and others who were advising me, and spend time with my relatives in the Boston area.

I expanded my research to the period of my parents' lives before they met. And began retracing our family's path from Houston all the way to Guadalajara, interviewing anyone I could find who might know something. The trouble was that everyone knew us as what we pretended to be: fairly ordinary folks with an unusual past. My family had been successful at hiding in the open.

My siblings and I were going over our memories, comparing them, stitching together newly recalled facts. We reshaped the story as I learned more from my mother's family in England and public records there, and from long talks with people who knew her in Britain in the 1930s.

Taken with the project, my sisters and I were speaking with one another more than we had in many years; we were growing close again. We had learned a lot about our parents, but we still didn't know what had been chasing them. With Fiona's certainty about what Mom had told her concerning the Community Church meeting, and the O'Connor elders' conviction that the FBI and INS were somehow involved, I went back to the agencies' responses to my Freedom of Information Act requests.

If government agents *had* been hunting my mother for political reasons, I thought, getting my parents' records would be even more difficult. I didn't trust the FBI or the INS to do honest searches of files. Some of that was the natural suspicion a journalist develops about government agencies doing an honest job when the result could be embarrassing. Their responses to my requests in early 2000 added to my doubts. Though Mom had first entered the United States in 1946, the INS had said they had no record of her until 1973, when she applied for a U.S. visa in England, where she'd gone after my father died. Maybe they had simply lost the earlier records, but maybe not. Meanwhile, the FBI response was full of double-talk. I'd asked for anything they had in their files, anywhere. They'd replied that they had thoroughly checked and found no record of either of my parents. The response was couched in a way that made it seem as if they had reviewed all their files, but actually they were saying they had checked their "main indices." Could there be, I wondered, some records not referenced in those indices? What about records that had been classified, decades before, as secret? What about records at the FBI field offices?

To help me double-check the official responses, some of the former federal agents who were advising me had made their own discreet but thorough checks of FBI and INS files. They found nothing as well. But they warned me that not finding any records didn't mean they weren't there, especially if the case was mired in the postwar Red Scare.

In June 2000, I hired a Washington, D.C., law firm, Meyer and Glitzenstein, specialists in Freedom of Information Act requests. I asked them to formally appeal the INS and FBI responses on whatever grounds they could find and to keep pushing and appealing until we were sure the government had searched all its files. The law firm warned that while the law required the government to comply promptly with a request, some agencies almost always found ways to delay, and it might take several years to get a definitive answer . . . and that answer might still be that they could find nothing on us.

As the lawyers made their appeals, I kept looking for people who had known my family. It should have been a straightforward investigation for any experienced journalist, yet many mornings found me tentative, uncertain. Should I call my attorney in Washington or the former CIA man in California? Or should I review my notes on what Aunt Eleanor had told me? My confusion deepened when I tried to concentrate on sifting through my memories, and I wound up depressed or with a savage migraine. I was an expert at finding hidden links between people and events, yet the patterns to my own life eluded me; I saw only a jumble of odd and disconnected incidents. There were days when I couldn't focus well enough to read the newspaper.

In July 2000, nearly three years after my mother's death, I was about to drive into Mexico to talk with people who had known us there when I stopped cold at Laredo. For two days I stared over the border, trying to make myself cross the bridge into Mexico yet finding a dozen other things to do in town instead. A part of me wanted to sabotage this mission. Deep down, I wasn't sure that I wanted to find the truth. I was afraid of the truth.

When I could not delay any longer, I drove hard toward the bridge until it lay dead ahead, then I pulled off the road. I looked at the immigration posts at either end, at the people walking on the bridge, and flashed back to the first day of the Korean War, when a radio news bulletin had turned my all-powerful parents into a pair of fearful fugitives. I felt the panic again as I sat there, immobilized and furious with myself.

It took me half an hour to cross that bridge.

FOR THE NEXT couple of weeks, the attacks came suddenly, then retreated. As I traveled south through Mexico, there were times when my vision blurred or my concentration wobbled so that I had to pull off the road to recover. Then my panic might well up and leave me panting, staring fixedly at the windshield, buffeted by passing cars while trying not to throw up. I could almost feel a warning hand on my shoulder, a voice urging me to turn back from the danger and pain in front of me. When I persisted, the hand became fierce, yanking me to a halt. It was my parents' old taboo, and my own sense of treachery for breaking it. *Not all mysteries were meant to be solved. Some were created by people wiser than you to keep you safe.*

I suppose the closer I thought I was getting to an answer to our question, the more troubled I was about looking for the secrets my parents had believed should be kept hidden. Mexico, a mysterious place in itself, had always seemed to harbor some of the truths about our secrets. It was worst when I reached Guadalajara, where my parents' dreams were finally destroyed. I spent one afternoon in a comfortable restaurant with Carlos Oceguera, my father's partner in the disastrous Houston confidence scheme. After Fiona, Carlos was the person who knew my parents the best. I thought that he might have figured out why they had been running or, better, that they may have hinted or even told him.

The other customers in the restaurant were middle-class Mexican women, backs straight on their chairs, wearing quiet suits and subdued jewelry, having small snacks with coffee or tea.

I felt relaxed that day. A Mexican investigator, a man who'd also worked for U.S. government agents, had looked into Carlos's past for me and found an honest history. Carlos had nothing to hide, no reason not to be candid. He was, at seventy-one, a distinguished-looking man, well dressed, with wavy hair still streaked with blond and a thin, precisely trimmed mustache. He spoke in a low voice, almost softly.

As we began talking in generalities about Mexican politics, a pianist in a white suit played Latin American standards. He played "Perfidia" with such passion that the customers went silent. When he finished, the formal waiter—black suit, white napkin hanging from his arm—could hold back no longer. The waiter lifted the musician to his feet and embraced him. The gentle applause was for both the music and the waiter's exuberance.

I remember that moment clearly, because it was just afterward, as Carlos began to tell me about Dad's final, desperate efforts to secure his future, that my right hand stopped working. I could no longer take notes. Carlos was saying, "He believed that Mexico was a good place for American investors. He really believed he could make our business work here. . . ." I stared at my hand, resting uselessly on the notebook on the table. It held my pen, but it would not write. It refused. It lay still for a good ten minutes. *Very troubling,* I thought. I felt disconnected from my body. Carlos didn't seem to notice, and I tried to ignore it.

Later that day, my mind stopped taking orders as well. I called James Kuykendall, an old friend and a former top agent with the Drug Enforcement Administration, now advising me on my search. James had heard from my private investigator, a man named Gerald Colca, and there was news: "Well, it looks like our friend in Houston has found a bunch of lawsuits against your father. Looks like they're for fraud and so on. First signs are not too good."

I don't remember what else James said, or what I said to him. I put down the phone and looked at nothing for a long while, until the sun set and my hotel room was black. I had found what I'd most wanted not to find: that we'd been running all those years because Dad was a crook. A thief. A failed chiseler.

Then I was on a wrought-iron bench in the plaza, facing the cathedral with the raised bandstand behind me, thinking about how stupid I was to have been hustled by my parents one more time. I had bought their stories as a child to make sense of the ridiculous way we lived, but how could I have kept on believing? How could I have missed that they scammed everyone they met—most of all their own children?

I concluded that there must be nothing in the federal files on which I'd pinned my hopes. Mom and Dad weren't being persecuted by the FBI for some dusty political reason. The talk about "bad lists" was either a lie or irrelevant. My parents were just a pair of con artists who settled in a place until they were close to being caught, then moved on to find their next victims. That explained just about everything: the dead-of-night departures, the hot business deals that never bore fruit, Dad's refusal to come get me in San Diego.

It occurred to me at that moment that the truth was overrated. In Mexico they know that truth is a burden. It's life that counts, not truth. Truth helps you live; if not, throw it away. Look at what happens when you find the truth.

I sat on the bench, paralyzed. My mind would not decide what to do next. *Decide!* I ordered it. It would not. My legs would not take me back to my hotel, so I stayed in the plaza as the cathedral bells in the blue-and-lemon towers rang the hours. Pigeons rose from the towers every hour, glided over the plaza, then returned. I sat, not deciding, not able to extract myself from the past. Parents took their children home from the plaza; then the balloon seller left; hours later, the couples were gone. I didn't move, except for a tremor now and then. I felt something deeper than fear; it was a feeling of no feeling at all.

In the morning I found myself in bed, at the hotel.

By that afternoon, Gerald Colca had assembled all the records from the lawsuits. The initial indications, he said, had been misleading. There were only two suits, both from 1951, both inconsequential. They reflected trifling disputes between Dad and a business partner, or perhaps an employee—the documents were unclear. The other man claimed he was owed $1,650, but the judge had dismissed both suits. Dad had not been found to be cheating anyone.

There was nothing there, but I took something from this episode nonetheless. For all this time, I'd been holding down the fear that Dad and Mom—that all of us—were somehow responsible for our trouble. When it had seemed that my father was a fraud, I'd reacted as a son who needed to believe that his parents were essentially good people but who feared in his heart that they were not.

I loved my parents, even if I had not solved our mystery nor been able to understand them and forgive them.

Through the rest of my fieldwork, and the writing of this book, I was never again ambushed by depression or anxiety. I expected it. But once I understood my ambivalence, the mission became less threatening. And it helped, too, that the truth seemed less dangerous as each layer of mystery was set aside.

THAT WAS THE most important revelation in Mexico. Carlos Oceguera knew a lot about what had happened in Dad's business but only what Dad had let him see about our family.

But there was something else to check out. Toying with the theory that the anti-Communist frenzy had somehow figured in what had been chasing us, I wondered if Mom and Dad had picked Guadalajara because it had been a kind of sanctuary for political exiles. Maybe, I thought, my parents would have felt safer, more talkative, with others like them. But after interviewing many longtime American expatriates, concentrating on those with leftist political views, I learned that Guadalajara had been a small backwater for political exiles. Mexico City had been the place to go. The Americans still living who said they had been in Guadalajara because they'd had political problems all knew one another, but none knew my parents.

Shortly after I left Mexico, Gerald Colca found out why we'd abandoned our home and our lives in Texas and moved back to the Villa de Santiago in 1958. He found the records of that three-car accident in Houston, when Mom had been driving and another driver had sued, and the subpoena ordering Mom to appear in court in June of that year. I flashed back to the black-and-white Chevy station wagon, packed with everything we could fit, and the sight of Prince, our collie, in the driveway, and the taste of panic in my mouth.

By early 2002, I'd nearly completed the family dossier. Mom's letter to Aunt Eleanor explained why we'd gone to Mexico the first time, in 1955: Dad had been arrested in Harlingen for the lack of a salesman's license. The second move to Mexico, three years later, stemmed from Mom's traffic accident and the ensuing lawsuit. Our return to the United States from Monterrey, in 1960, as Aunt Eleanor had confirmed, had been triggered by the inquisitive juvenile authorities in San Diego. Finally, Dad's letter to Aunt Mary corroborated my sister Mary's account of our parents' panicked reaction after she applied for college financial aid. Which, in turn, made the family flee San Jose like frightened refugees to Guadalajara in 1967. I'd learned how our parents' life together had swung into its last, steep descent after their daughter had filled out a financial aid form for college—because Mary had sought her piece of Dad's American dream.

I could trace each of these moves like someone deconstructing a chess game, but the essential question remained: Why had we run in the first place? With the facts we had in hand, I again took that question to the former police officers and federal agents. With two exceptions, none of them knew the others. Yet when they assessed the information I'd gathered, they all reached the same conclusion. Their analysis seemed plausible, though I resisted accepting it. The most likely explanation for my parents' initial run, they agreed, was simple paranoia. Perhaps, just perhaps, there had been something very small, way back in the late 1940s, but even so, it was long over with while we kept running. With no criminal records to be found, and nothing else to prove a government hunt for us, it seemed most likely that my parents had been driven by their own imaginations.

The dissenter was Sonny Barger, a founder of the Hells Angels Motorcycle Club, whom I'd known for thirty years. Sonny had seen a lot of federal investigations—as a target. He doubted that paranoia had started our flight. "Paranoia is what you get when they're chasing you," he advised. "The feds *make* you paranoid. You don't have to start out that way."

A friend, an ex-CIA operative whom I'll call Sandy, posed one more possibility: that Mom was a foreign intelligence agent who'd been discovered in Boston in 1946 and had gone underground. If this were true, Sandy thought, the FBI was unlikely to release any information they had on Mom. They'd simply say that it didn't exist.

Then Sandy said, "Of course, they would do the same thing if they had somehow thought she was an agent but had been wrong about it." *Right!* I thought. They'd keep the case classified just to avoid embarrassment. If the FBI had learned of Uncle Alfred's Communist Party membership, Sandy added, they would have wanted to talk with Mom, especially if they found out that she'd also been a pacifist. If she had gone to any meetings that the FBI had been monitoring, the agents would have been doubly interested. And if they'd been looking for Mom, or if they'd interviewed her before she disappeared, her flight would have confirmed to them that she was guilty of something—and the better she was at not being found, the more guilty she must have seemed.

In other words, Mom might have been damned not by anything she'd done but by hiding.

Then Sandy reminded me of something. When the FBI investigated foreign citizens, it often used the INS to help. The immigration agents could investigate openly while the FBI hid in the background.

Still, we were conjecturing, talking without all the facts.

Then two things happened, quickly. First, the FBI office in Boston reported that despite what they'd said before, after all the appeals from my lawyer, the bureau had found evidence of two files, somewhere deep in their archives: one on my mother and one on my father. They were looking for the files, they said.

Then, after three years of my lawyer's badgering and appeals, the INS found documents on a criminal case against my mother.

And they had discovered one more thing: a criminal case against me.

THIRTY-SIX

"There's something wrong in here."

It was in March 2002, when I was staying at my cousin Pat's, near Boston, that my attorney, Amy Atwood, called with the news from the INS. The missing files on Mom had been discovered in a government archive in Kansas City, Missouri. She had asked the agency to rush the declassification process, in which documents are reviewed to protect secrets, such as investigative techniques or the names of informants. Or, as I suspected, anything that might make the government look bad.

Two weeks later, Amy called to direct me to the JFK Federal Building in Boston, to a room on the fifth floor, where I'd find a particular INS person who knew about the files. The room had only a number, with no indication of what was inside. I knocked, and a young woman, a bit overweight, with glasses and an apprehensive look, cracked the door open. She was the one Amy had told me to ask for. She checked my ID and showed me a bulging manila envelope. But she had a nervous admonition. "Look at this very closely," she said. "There's something wrong in here."

I stared at her, hoping she'd say more.

"It's wrong," she said. "Don't ask me."

Had I been a real reporter at that moment, I would have smiled and charmed the woman. I would have seen that she had more to say but felt uneasy saying it there. I would have thanked her and asked, "By the way, when's your next coffee break?" And then I would have waited in the cafeteria until she appeared, until I could slide casually across from her and begin to chat. Until she told me what was wrong inside the manila envelope.

But I wasn't a real reporter then. I was an overjoyed mendicant, grateful that the government had at last given me something and yet deeply

afraid about what it might show. So I took the envelope and went to the
Souper Salad café across the street to read what was inside.

There were similar INS files from two cases, one on my mother and
the other on me. Together they totaled 169 pages, with each page num-
bered and 11 of them mysteriously missing.

Confirming Uncle Larry's story, the documents showed that my grandmother had reported my mother to the INS by telephone on April 28,
1947. The next day, they had interrogated Mom in their Boston office.
Her crime was that she'd entered the country by falsely saying she was
my father's wife.

The transcript showed that, without hesitation, Mom had admitted
entering the United States illegally twice, first on July 1, 1946, when we
arrived in New York on our way to Canada, and then in September
1946, when we went from Canada to Boston. They had her cold. My
parents had done the expedient thing. Postwar passage across the At-
lantic was easier for a returning soldier and his family than for a single
British national with a baby, and they were a couple, so they said they
were married. Legally, of course, my father was still married to Helen.

The transcript showed that Mom then told agents what they wanted
to hear: "My intentions now are to return to England as soon as I can secure the passage money, and I intend to take my son with me." The INS
gave her permission to stay in the United States temporarily but with no
set time limit—presumably, long enough to earn the money for a ticket
home. They were so indifferent that they didn't even bother taking her
fingerprints. They only gave her a batch of addressed postcards, to report
where she was living every three months.

It was a simple case for Immigration, it seemed. Simple and solved.

But I found another document in that overstuffed manila envelope
that opened a brand-new mystery. While the agents who interrogated my
mother didn't seem to know it, the INS already had been looking for
Mom for some time. On January 6, 1947—more than three months before my grandmother contacted them—they had interviewed my father.

My parents and I had been in the country less than four months at
that point. According to the transcript of my father's interrogation, the
INS inspectors questioned him about his service in the Canadian army,
asking if he'd taken an oath to the king of England. (He had not; his
army records show that, as an American, he'd sworn only to follow orders.) But soon it was clear that their real interest was in finding Mom.
Dad said that he didn't know where she was—that he thought she'd gone

to live in Canada but wasn't sure. That was it. They let him go. They didn't care about him.

But what had made them interested in my mother in the first place? I remembered Aunt Eleanor's story about the two FBI men accosting Aunt Mary and demanding that she tell them about Mom and me. It was, Eleanor said, "just before Christmas" in our first year in the States: Christmas 1946. The INS interrogated Dad less than a month later.

It seemed clear that the FBI and INS were investigating my parents at the same time. Which led me back to the original question: Why was the FBI interested in my mother? And why had the INS let her walk out the door three months after questioning my father? Did the two cases mesh only after Mom was allowed to leave? Were Mom's investigators doing a perfunctory job with some small-time violation, not realizing that other INS agents, not to mention the FBI, were tracking something bigger? I could only hope the answers would be in the FBI files, which were still to be released.

As I worked through the manila envelope, it became clear that something big had happened after they let Mom leave the INS office in April 1947. I supposed it was what the INS clerk was talking about when she said there was "something wrong" in the files. In September 1947, for a reason not noted in the file, the INS suddenly came after us—and kept coming after us for years. They applied for a warrant for Mom's arrest and for mine as well. The charges were the same for both of us. Specifically, for me, that I had violated "the Immigration Act of May 26, 1924, in that at the time of entry, [I] was an immigrant not in possession of a valid immigration visa and not exempted from the presentation thereof by said Act or regulations made thereunder." The documents accompanying my arrest warrant describe me as blond-haired, blue-eyed, and nineteen months old.

With the warrants, the INS began an extremely aggressive search for us up and down New England and into Canada. I found details of a decadelong investigation, one far more widespread and persistent than seemed reasonable given Mom's nearly petty violations. A dogged search, the reasons for which were not explained in the files. Immigration agents were sent to Canada to find us, which would seem to have violated Canadian sovereignty. They were told to arrest us and return us to the United States so that we could then be deported. In other words, they went into a foreign country to arrest two people whom the government wanted to send to a foreign country. Actually, I think the FBI wanted to get their hands on Mom for a while, then have the INS deport her. Over the years, field agents recommended that the case be dropped, but orders came down to continue.

In December 1947, my grandmother, still trying to save her son's soul, told the INS that she thought Dad and Mom and I might be in South China, Maine. The agents checked the area, asking residents if they'd seen any strangers matching our descriptions. A postal clerk, Lilla Winslow, remembered Dad's name on a letter. The rural mail carrier who delivered the letter, Chauncey Shorey, remembered us, too. He said he'd heard that about four weeks earlier, in the late afternoon, we had "left very hurriedly and appeared to be very nervous."

An INS investigator went to the isolated house where we'd been staying. He found snow covering the front and rear steps, meaning no one had been there for a while. He checked with all the neighbors and found one who said she'd heard we had gone to Canada. He learned of an outbreak of chicken pox among children in the area and contacted the local doctors to see if I'd been treated. Canvassing the town for leads, he found a mechanic who said he'd fixed the headlights on Dad's car to pass a Maine vehicle inspection. The INS checked car registrations for all of Maine, screening for all the John O'Connors. They checked out every one. None of them was Dad.

The INS sent agents to Toronto, Ottawa, and St. John in New Brunswick, Canada. They followed leads to Boston and to Turner, Auburn, East Vassalboro, Center Vassalboro, and Lewiston, Maine. They found out that Dad had been working at the R. J. Hinkley Company in Boston, but they got there too late. He was gone.

They discovered that a John J. O'Connor had been a patient at a veterans' hospital in Massachusetts and tracked him down. But the man turned out to be John Joseph O'Connor—not my father, John Jeremiah O'Connor.

They kept at it. They scoured motor vehicle, marriage license, and Social Security records in Massachusetts, and after a while they checked again. After receiving a four-month-old lead that we might have stopped at the Elm Hotel in Auburn, Maine, they sent an agent to search the registry at that hotel, then every other hotel in town. Nothing.

They came across a record of a 1947 car accident in Maine involving Dad, who hadn't stuck around to go to court. They checked so thoroughly that they learned we left South China, Maine, in such a rush that we still owed the milkman three dollars.

The INS's Boston office regularly nudged branch offices in New England about us. The district director in Boston told the officer in charge of Portland, Maine, that my family's case "should be given very serious consideration by your office." He sent lookout notices to border crossings in Maine, New Hampshire, Vermont, New York State, and the Port of New York.

They decided that my father was also an alien, "now residing illegally within the United States," who was "wanted for questioning relative to his immigration status." This, despite the fact that they knew both his parents were Americans and that he had a valid U.S. passport. The INS couldn't take away his citizenship, but calling him an illegal alien might have given the case more punch.

Obviously, something bigger than Mom's violations was driving the INS investigation. I kept on hoping that some logic would emerge with the FBI files. But then the Bureau notified me that their files on my parents could not be found. All that was left was a record in the FBI archives showing that the files had once existed but had since been destroyed. There was no indication of what information they'd held, just that they were gone. There was one telling clue, however. The FBI acknowledged that some of the missing records were from the INS, further evidence that the agencies had been working together.

The most workable leads were in the INS documents, in the names of the agents who'd been looking for us. Though many names had been blacked out, sixteen were still legible; maybe one would remember why Immigration had been so ferocious in their pursuit. But after a nearly three-year delay in getting the records, I could find only one agent who was still alive. He was Patrick Coomey, the former assistant district director for investigations in Boston in the mid-1950s.

I was too late. Coomey's grandson Patrick listened sympathetically to my story and responded with regret: "A year ago he was doing fine, but now he's not with us much. If you only could have come by last year."

I took my notes and the INS files to a friend of a friend, a man who'd spent much of his career investigating foreign intelligence agents. He said he was fairly certain of what he saw: The FBI wanted to find my mother because they'd played with the theory, early on, that she was a Communist. Then the unthinking logic of a bureaucracy took over. "Once that gets started," he said, "it's hard to stop. Especially if they don't find the subject."

THIRTY-SEVEN

FOLLOWING INSTRUCTIONS FROM SANDY, the former CIA operative, I walked up to the front door of a tract house in California in May 2002. There was a ten-year-old pickup in the driveway. The man who opened the door was in his early forties, with a genial face under tousled hair. He wore pinkish brown bib overalls and high, lace-up black work boots. He looked like a pleasant construction worker. But Sandy had told me the man might be able to get the files on my parents that the FBI said had been destroyed.

Beginning in the 1960s, Sandy told me, the FBI had ordered the destruction of files on many political cases to avoid embarrassment if the information became public, or to hide information agents had gotten illegally, by break-ins or wiretaps and room bugs set up without a judge's approval. But Sandy said that, contrary to the official policy, some FBI field offices had not destroyed all the files. Instead they had secretly given some of them to private right-wing organizations that were part of a clandestine network of extremist ideologues. He said the files were also used by private companies that investigated prospective corporate employees and groups that opposed the corporations' policies. Sandy did not know if transferring the files had been approved by top FBI officials or if it was done by rogue field offices. Officially the files were listed as "purged," but in fact they were still available to select agents and to the organizations that had received them.

Sandy knew the people who ran two of these private groups and promised to try to get them to see me as long as I agreed not to reveal who they were, or even much about them.

He had succeeded, partially. The man at the door was with an organization on the West Coast. The other group was in the Northeast, and Sandy was still trying to persuade someone there to meet me.

The man said, "I heard you were coming over. I went to put a jar of my son's urine in the refrigerator."

"Oh, right," I said affably. "What for?"

"Because that's where I got it from."

I changed the subject to the value of keeping good records. The man spoke quickly, shifting from topic to topic. I was glad of that, because I didn't want him to linger on something about which we might disagree. Though he completely trusted our mutual friend Sandy, he was still leery of talking to a reporter. The press and labor unions had almost ruined the country, after all. He said that he and his partners had hidden the FBI's West Coast files hours away, in a place where they could do countersurveillance on anyone approaching.

"Good thinking," I said.

I had brought a sheet of paper with biographical information on my parents, my sisters and me, and my parents' relatives, along with the names of two organizations. One was the Peace Pledge Union, the main British pacifist group with which my mother had been active. The other was the Community Church of Boston, where Mom had attended lectures or seminars in 1946. The man took my list and left for the secret place where the files were hidden.

Two days later, he had found nothing in their records that matched my list, except for one entry on me. It was associated with the New World Liberation Front, the 1970s group of insane leftist bombers with whom I had spoken as a reporter.

I had told the NWLF that I'd feel free to make public anything they told me—and to tell the FBI, which was desperate to find them. But there was one thing the bombers and I kept to ourselves: a code they used to prove that the person contacting me really was with the group. I told the NWLF I would inform the FBI that there was a code but not what the code was. Only the bombers, the FBI, and I knew the code existed. When that odd friend of Sandy's came back from wherever they were hiding the FBI files, he showed me his notes with the words "Newsman O'Connor has established an identifier code with subjects."

The man, and his group, were real. They had at least some of the "purged" files from the FBI. Which suggested that the second right-wing group Sandy knew also had legitimate FBI files. Because that group had files from FBI offices in the Northeast, it could well have information from the Boston office. But they were more difficult to deal with. It took months for Sandy to convince them to help. At the last minute, as I waited in a New York hotel room for the final call before our meeting, they refused to see me or even speak to me on the phone.

I thought the search was over, again. But four months after I struck out on the West Coast, Sandy convinced the second group to check my list of names against their records. They found something. There was nothing on my parents—not surprising, they said, since the FBI had kept "tens of thousands" of files on individuals in the Northeast, and many of those files really had been destroyed. But the group had two important leads. First, as they reported to Sandy, the FBI had had a deep interest in the Community Church of Boston from the early 1940s. And the files also showed that the FBI had infiltrated a man into church gatherings to report on people attending. His name was Herbert Philbrick, and he was the informant in late 1946, when my mother went there.

ON THE SURFACE, Herbert Philbrick seemed to be an average sort of ambitious young fellow back then, with a pretty wife and four daughters. He described himself as a man with deep Christian roots, a leader of youth programs in the Baptist Church.

But his FBI records showed someone else. After my attorney got the FBI to release Philbrick's file to me, I found a dry account of a man who'd helped wreck countless lives. The story began on March 14, 1942, when J. T. Madigan, the special agent in charge of the FBI's Boston office, called headquarters to report that a paid informant had been invited to join the Young Communist League. The special agent in charge—in FBI shorthand, the SAC—wanted clearance before telling the informant it was okay to join. Headquarters advised Madigan to be careful, to warn the informant that the Bureau wouldn't help him if he was found out. But Madigan was also to make it clear that the informant would be doing a great service to his country—and that he might get a pay raise.

Two months later, J. Edgar Hoover, who ran the FBI like a monarch from 1924 until his death, in 1972, sent Madigan a secret memo asking for details on the informant. Madigan replied that the man was Herbert Philbrick, born in Boston in 1915, married, who worked for a direct-mail marketing service called Holmes Direct. Madigan wrote, "This informant is under no circumstances to be contacted at home in view of the fact that his wife does not know of his connection with this Bureau."

Philbrick and my father were the same in many ways. They were born a few months apart into the same social class. Dad's father drove for the Railway Express Agency. Philbrick's father was a conductor on the Boston & Maine Railroad. Like Dad, Philbrick had curly black hair, an engaging smile, an earnest manner—and like Dad, he was a professional salesman. People liked him.

During the early 1940s, as Dad confided to his siblings that his marriage had gone sour and while Mom marched with the pacifists in Glasgow, Herbert Philbrick infiltrated groups in Boston, from school and church groups to political organizations. The agents directing him were impressed by how well he melted into groups that the Bureau was curious about. His mission was a political intelligence operation to find out what people thought. Philbrick kept mental notes and made diary entries almost daily. At least once a week, usually more often, he passed his reports to his FBI handlers.

Philbrick made his way through various gatherings—some put on by Communist Party fronts, others where the people he called "true liberals," good people, got together, as he later wrote in his book *I Led Three Lives: Citizen—"Communist"—Counterspy*. But he found Communists everywhere and went at them all like a human vacuum cleaner: "I made no effort to draw any inference from what I saw or heard," he acknowledged. Turn your back, and your Christmas list—or your child's reading assignment—could end up in his pocket. As Philbrick wrote, the job "of relaying such a mass of information was so great that I could not take the time to appraise it. I picked up everything I actually could . . . copies of directives turned out by mimeograph, sheets of discarded carbon paper, telephone numbers and addresses."

That was a time of increasing fear of foreign "Communist subversion." Already, in the 1930s, national politics had helped turn the issue into a weapon that conservatives used to batter President Roosevelt and the New Deal. Critics said that the administration was allowing the country to be subverted by left-wing extremists, even Communists, in government, and that labor unions and civic groups were also broadly infiltrated. Beginning in 1938, the House Committee on Un-American Activities had been holding widely publicized hearings to investigate subversive influences in government, unions, education, and Hollywood.

This was twelve years before Senator Joseph McCarthy would get the same kind of attention with the same kinds of investigations.

But it was not all cynical politics. By the time the United States entered World War II, the FBI knew that there were Soviet spy operations in Washington, at least. And the Bureau believed that a very few members of the Communist Party of the USA were helping the Soviet spies. The Party got money and instructions from Moscow.

Two things are true about the long-running anti-Communist crusade in America: (1) The Soviet Union was a threat. (2) The threat was wildly overblown by people who used fear to get power. This is where Herbert Philbrick came into play.

In Boston in 1943, the SAC was impressed with Philbrick's potential and asked permission to raise his pay; Hoover approved—a fine investment, as it turned out. Soon Philbrick joined the Communist Party. Although he never rose as high in the Party's ranks as he later claimed, he became one of the FBI's stellar informants. He was state treasurer for the Americans for Youth Democracy and helped start Boston Youth for Unity, billed as a group to fight anti-Semitism. He infiltrated local political campaigns and the Massachusetts Citizens Political Action Committee. Along the way, he reported on people who joined these groups. You might drop by a picnic he'd helped to organize, fall into a casual chat with him about politics or the Red Sox, and—bingo!—wind up with an FBI file.

Among the "secret communists" named by Philbrick were schoolteachers, ministers, members of the Advertising Club of Boston, retirees, a bookstore owner, university professors and students, secretaries, and members of Boston's elite, along with some of his neighbors in the suburb of Wakefield.

I BELIEVE PHILBRICK likely gave my mother's name to his FBI handlers in the fall of 1946. This is the sequence of events: On September 9, 1946, Mom made the last entry in her diary. We were in Canada. Two weeks later, we crossed the border on the way to Massachusetts, according to the INS records. We were put up in Malden, a suburb of Boston, at the home of friends of my father's, according to Aunt Eleanor. Social Security Administration records show that Mom applied for a Social Security card on October 10, giving her address as 119 Laurel Street, Malden.

Very shortly after we arrived there, Mom began attending political lectures and seminars at the Community Church, as she told Aunt Eleanor soon afterward. As it turned out, this was the same period in which the feds were paying extraordinarily close attention to the church. FBI records show that Hoover was pressuring the Boston office to confirm that church events were attracting Communists. According to Sandy's sources, the ones who claimed to have the "purged" relevant FBI files, the Bureau's undercover operative at the church was Herbert Philbrick. Indeed, Philbrick's own FBI files show that he attended a workshop at the church from September 20 to 23 and, according to the Boston SAC, "submitted a detailed report concerning the origin, program, faculty, organizers and courses given."

Over the last three months of 1946, Philbrick was filing informant reports on the church and other organizations nearly twice a week. (The FBI refused to release those sixty-year-old reports to me. They claimed, unconvincingly, that they couldn't edit out the identities of the people mentioned or the secret methods used in the investigations.) And whenever Philbrick infiltrated a meeting, by his own account, he grabbed every sign-up sheet, mailing list, home address, and telephone number he could. By coincidence, the name Jessie O'Connor would have drawn his notice, because a Jessie Lloyd O'Connor, slightly older than my mother, was a well-known pacifist and feminist in New England. And Philbrick had already told the FBI that a Justine O'Connor and a Francis O'Connor were members of the Communist Party.

After I got Philbrick's files, it took an additional three years to get the FBI's records on their investigation of the Community Church. First they said that there were no files, that the church appeared nowhere in their records. After more prodding and legal appeals, they found files on the church's minister (with references to the church throughout), but almost immediately they said those files were somehow lost. Then, in another unexplained mystery, the files reappeared in a shopping cart in a hallway of the Bureau's Boston office. They were sent from there to Washington for "final processing," in which the files are scanned into a computer and redacted. That step took two more years even to begin.

In the fall of 2005, the FBI began releasing the files, mailing them in nondescript manila envelopes to my brother Terry. He sent them on by courier service to our new home in Rome, where Tracy was (and remains) the *Los Angeles Times* bureau chief. The pages were often barely legible copies of typewritten documents, some suffering from rough storage for as long as six decades. By the spring of 2006, I had received a total of

2,236 pages on the investigation of the Community Church and its minister, the Reverend Donald Lothrop. For comparison, the FBI has released 2,397 pages of documents from its investigation of America's
most famous Mafia leader, Al Capone.

The FBI withheld a few pages of their files on the church and the minister and blacked out some names, but what was left told quite a story.
For me, it explains why the files had been so hard to get in the first place.

The records revealed that my mother's attendance at church events co-
incided with a serious dispute within the Bureau over whether the Community Church was a seedbed of subversion or simply had a left-of-center
minister who encouraged broad political discussions. The FBI first focused on Lothrop in June 1941. Over the next two years, they found
conflicting information about him. An undercover informant—Herbert
Philbrick, according to Sandy's right-wing friends—insisted that Lothrop
had been installed in the church by the Communist Party. But the Bureau
agents could not substantiate that claim, so in 1943 the SAC in Boston
notified Hoover that Lothrop was not involved in "Communist Party activities," and he closed the case. But Hoover rebuked him and ordered
the office to reopen the case, to look harder—it was the kind of order a
wise agent took seriously.

They watched closely for three more years. They followed Lothrop and
the people he met with, including a number of civic groups in which a few
of the hundreds of members were believed to be possible Communists.
The agents found that the list of speakers at Lothrop's services included
avowed leftists but also conservative members of the Massachusetts legislature, Congressman Adam Clayton Powell, as well as "an outstanding
Negro leader of the NAACP," and Frances Perkins, the U.S. secretary of
labor.

The agents heard from their undercover informant that on October 31,
1945, Lothrop cosponsored a dinner given by the Massachusetts Citizens Political Action Committee, a suspicious organization to the FBI.
But then they learned that the guest of honor was Eleanor Roosevelt, the
First Lady. It was confusing for the Bureau: What to think?

By 1946, after five years of investigating, the worst the FBI could say
about Lothrop was that he "has endorsed Communist authors," a reference to two books that he recommended in the weekly church bulletin.

On September 11, 1946, the month my parents and I arrived in
Boston, the Boston SAC began a telling exchange of memos with Hoover
about Lothrop and the Community Church. The field agents had found

so little linking the minister with the Communist Party, the SAC reported, that his office had closed the case again.

This was apparently not what Hoover wanted. Despite the lack of evidence, on December 5, 1946, he decreed in a memo to the Boston office that the minister was "very active in Communist Party affairs." He ordered Boston to continue investigating Lothrop and the church and to find something to prove he was right. He said he wanted "only such information of a legally admissible character which will tend to prove, directly or circumstantially, membership in or affiliation with the Communist Party."

Within three weeks of Hoover's orders to get cracking, his agents were at my Aunt Mary's office trying to badger her into telling them where Mom and I were. My family's stay in Malden was brief. After stopping at a friend's house on Laurel Street, we were suddenly paying for a room at the Bostonian Hotel. Then Mom got that job as a housekeeper and we moved to the one-room apartment over the garage at 3 Agassiz Park, in Jamaica Plain, to where Uncle Larry would follow Dad and discover Mom. Those two quick moves, I think, were prompted by FBI agents following what I believe was Philbrick's tip about my mother. They were trying to keep the boss, Hoover, happy by unearthing any possible proof of subversion at the Community Church. And Mom, who knew about the FBI visit to Aunt Mary, was trying to erase the trail between herself and the church. She might have succeeded, but in April, about four months after we had moved, my grandmother confronted Mom and turned us in to the INS.

From 1946 to 1949, I suspect that my parents played cat and mouse with the feds, never knowing how close the agents were. We lived in Maine, in Canada, in Marblehead, Massachusetts, and with Aunt Mary in Weymouth, near Boston. During that period, a police detective stopped Mary's son Billy on the street to ask him what he knew about a woman with a foreign accent who might be living in the neighborhood. A federal agent also stopped him to ask the same thing.

Dad generally stayed close to us when he wasn't off selling encyclopedias or Bibles. He wasn't making much money, and it seems that he soon stopped giving anything to Helen for his first two sons. In 1948 she filed a neglect-of-family charge, and a judge ordered Dad to pay two hundred dollars. He didn't pay, perhaps couldn't pay, and the county court issued a warrant for his arrest. Life was getting even more complicated.

Still, we stayed around, with Mom and Dad hoping that Helen would change her mind about the divorce and that he might reinstate himself in his mother's eyes—all the while hiding from the FBI, the INS, and with the county warrant, the local police.

Finally, in 1949, it must have simply become too much for my parents. The three of us left Boston, propelled by fear of federal agents and a big booster rocket of guilt.

We got only 230 miles away, to East Orange, New Jersey, before the money ran out. Dad sold asbestos siding, rain gutters, and even his own blood until we saved enough cash to get to Texas.

The records of Liberty County, Texas, show that Mrs. L. V. Hightower, the county clerk, issued a marriage license to my parents on September 27, 1949. They were married the same day by Judge R. E. Pitts. In the days before computerized records, they believed, apparently correctly, that they could do so with little fear of being caught, though Dad was still married to Helen.

Nine months later, as the Korean War was announced on our car radio, my family was stalled at that bridge to Laredo, looking over at the United States from Mexico, in an unforgettable panic.

THIRTY-EIGHT

WITH ALL THE TRAUMA of all the years on the run, why didn't my parents ever stop, clear their heads, save their money, get an attorney, and tackle the federal government head-on? Why didn't they just stiffen their backs and resolve the problem? Their crimes amounted to very little; they'd pretended to be married so that Mom and I could enter the United States at a time when British citizens generally had little trouble coming here anyway. From the standpoint of the Immigration Service, Mom's case and mine might have triggered some paperwork and perhaps a fine; we might have had to leave the country, have gone, say, to Canada or even England for a while, and then reenter legally. What's clear is that running made a small case much worse. According to the law of that time, foreign citizens had to notify the INS each year of where they lived. Mom didn't do that, of course, so her original violation looked worse and her crimes multiplied.

Then Dad was breaking the law by helping his wife. He was also violating federal law by not filing with the Internal Revenue Service. By a fugitive's logic, though, he was wise not to reveal where he was. The immigration agents were indeed checking to see if he'd filed tax returns. Still, had my parents only stopped running, a good attorney might have been able to work out some arrangement to get them straight with the IRS.

As I look back on it, it seems that my parents kept moving, in part, because they never stopped believing in their American dream, or maybe delusion: that Dad would achieve great success in business, and we'd be financially secure and reconciled with the O'Connors, and *then* we would take on the government.

But adding to all that was, for my parents, the essential, insurmountable problem that the mood of the country was against us. People who held unapproved political thoughts, who had been to the wrong meetings, who'd been labeled as Communists or pacifists and targeted by the FBI—these people did not expect fair treatment. My parents' pessimism was reinforced every day as they saw what was happening to others like them.

This is not a book about McCarthyism, or governmental abuses where fear is manipulated by officials who want more power. There are scores of those books, and today's newspapers have shocking current lessons. This is a book about a family. But we have to remember what America was like when my parents considered all their options and picked the one where they jumped in their car and drove like hell to get as far away as they could. As the country whirled into a frenzy of ideological cleansing, as neighbors suspected neighbors in their bowling leagues or on the job, as the FBI began to consider even Quakers who headed pacifist groups as treacherous subversives, it was not unreasonable for a bit player in British labor conflicts and in pacifism—a woman with a dodgy immigration record and a brother in the British Communist Party—to fear the worst, especially when she knew the FBI was looking for her. As she saw powerful people flattened, my mother believed that she had no chance to stand her ground and fight. She had to run, and my father felt he had no choice but to run with her.

In that national hysteria, Herbert Philbrick had a prominent role. His story shows how the government used a man it knew was dishonest but malleable to keep the anti-Communist craze aflame and make people like my parents feel they had to run to be safe.

In 1949, shortly before my family fled Boston in a panic, the U.S. government brought Philbrick out of his nine-year undercover assignment to testify as a surprise witness in the trial of eleven leaders of the Communist Party USA. The Justice Department claimed that the Party was organizing an insurrection and that its leaders should be jailed. Philbrick's testimony was crucial. But the trouble with Philbrick was that he was a liar, and an apparently willing tool of people such as J. Edgar Hoover, who used lies for political ends.

I don't know if Philbrick told the truth in his testimony against the American Communist Party. But I know he committed perjury on the stand. The prosecution presented him to the jury as an American hero simply trying to protect his country, one who never took a dime for his courage, a critical point for his credibility. On April 8, 1949, a defense attorney asked him: "You were a volunteer worker, of course?"

Philbrick said, "That's right."

"You received no remuneration outside of your actual expenses."

"No, sir."

I know this was perjury because I have Philbrick's FBI pay records dating back to 1941. In fact, he was still on the payroll while he was on the stand swearing that he'd never been paid. The FBI knew he was lying. But Hoover also knew that he had a likable, credible man who would lie for the Bureau. And Hoover was going to use him.

Philbrick was a devastating witness for the prosecution. According to a secret memo from a senior FBI official to Hoover shortly after the trial, "Philbrick was the first government witness who was able to provide current information of Party activity and created a sensation." Aside from decimating the Party leadership, who were sentenced to federal prison, the trial frightened millions of people. It seemed to prove that a sinister underground movement was plotting an armed revolution. As the country was still recovering from World War II, Americans feared a new attack. This time from Communists from without and secret Communists within. Anyone could be the enemy.

Fear escalated when Communists took control of China, and then the Soviet Union developed its own atomic bomb. Within a year of that, in the Korean War, Communist soldiers were suddenly killing American soldiers.

Capitalizing on the fear in America and impressed with Philbrick's trial testimony, Hoover approved a plan for him to meet Ogden Reid, Jr., the son of the owner of the *New York Herald Tribune,* at that time a prestigious newspaper with a broad circulation. Reid told the FBI he could probably double Philbrick's salary, by then, as the marketing director of a movie theater chain. Philbrick became Reid's adviser on the Communist threat and, according to Philbrick, the chief source for a regular column, "The Red Underground." He became a channel for McCarthyite propaganda. He was fed information by the FBI, and he passed it on to the newspaper. Of course, he had to make it look as if he were no longer an FBI operative. In a memo to the Bureau, Philbrick wrote, "I have let it be known in New York and at the Tribune office that: I have no connection with the F.B.I." Then, with a wink, he told the Bureau that he would "keep in touch as usual."

In 1951, while my family was in Texas, relying on our Cajun neighbor

~~Nannan to learn how to live near the bottom edge of poverty, a newspa-~~
per columnist in Boston started a campaign to have the state government
declare a "Herbert Philbrick Day." The columnist, Hal Clancy, wrote,
"Others have helped Uncle Sam fight the Reds, but they are not to be
compared with the quiet, bespectacled Philbrick who is now helping the
House Un-American Activities Committee to expose the comrades." The
state legislature passed a resolution asking the governor to proclaim a
day for Philbrick. He did, on November 27. A dinner was given for eight
hundred, including leading agents of the Boston FBI office.

That same year the FBI and Philbrick collaborated with writers from
the *Herald Tribune* on a series of articles about his days undercover, "I
Led Three Lives." It was promoted as a terrifying firsthand account of
how a naïve America was being assaulted by Communists. In reviewing
Philbrick's drafts, FBI agents reported to Hoover that the author had
grossly exaggerated some events, fabricated others, and falsely named
people (including the Reverend Donald Lothrop) as members of the
Communist Party. But unless the agents found something that might
harm the FBI's reputation, the lies were blessed by the Bureau and called
"literary license."

As the series ran, the *Herald Tribune*'s circulation jumped. The articles were syndicated in some seventy newspapers. With his cut from the
syndication rights alone, Philbrick bought a house in White Plains, New
York. In 1953, when Philbrick adapted the series for his book, the FBI
agents reviewing the draft found further distortions. But the book became a huge hit, and soon Philbrick was giving speeches around the
country, warning that Communists were everywhere and that Hoover
was the hero who could stop them. He campaigned with the same theme
on radio and television, in sworn testimony before Congress, and in a TV
series based on his book in 1954. In a secret review of the scripts, agents
found yet more gross exaggerations, but Hoover did not object.

By that point, Philbrick was known as one of America's leading authorities on Communist subversion. In April 1955, shortly before we ran
to Mexico the first time, the U.S. attorney general, Herbert Brownell,
told Hoover that the Justice Department was planning to use Philbrick in
several prosecutions. Was there any reason, Brownell wondered, to believe that Philbrick was less than absolutely reliable? No reason at all,
Hoover responded. The following year, Philbrick was consulted in nine
federal investigations of alleged Communist or leftist organizations and
one labor union.

Philbrick was still getting information from his contacts at the FBI. Maybe what he got was accurate, maybe it wasn't. Truth was not the point. The point, according to a secret Bureau memo setting out what kind of information to feed Philbrick, was to "harass or impede" people considered subversive. By the standards of the day, that was a great number of people.

It's clear that J. Edgar Hoover, the FBI, and my parents had something important in common: highly developed self-deceit. As facts undid what each of them wanted to believe, they refused to acknowledge the facts.

LONG AFTER JOSEPH MCCARTHY'S disgrace in 1954, the government continued to pursue people tarred with beliefs that it found objectionable. The pursuit was unforgiving and often unthinking. What was to happen to the Community Church of Boston is an example. For twenty-six years after the Boston FBI office concluded that the church wasn't affiliated with the Communist Party, the agents followed Hoover's orders to find something on Reverend Lothrop. They seeded the ground where the minister walked with informants to report what he said and where he went and who spoke at his church. They monitored his church meeting halls, where they found some speakers to be "highly controversial individuals" who were sometimes "critical of the United States Government, its policies and the FBI." Even though they also found that "Ministers of practically every known religion in the Judeo-Christian community speak at the church," their reports emphasized the worst.

The pretext was that they were looking for evidence of Communism, but, for members of the church, the real point was to intimidate. They say that into the 1960s FBI agents made a show of collecting the license plate numbers of cars parked near the church for Sunday services. Agents went to the owners' homes late in the evening to grill them about their political beliefs. The message was clear: *Keep your head down and your mouth shut. Stay afraid of us.*

This same message was flashed intensely across the country by state and congressional investigations of the left, which fed off information from the FBI and from the right-wing organizations that were the predecessors of the groups my friend Sandy contacted, which even today have the supposedly purged FBI files. Civic groups and churches shouted the message. It was reinforced over and over by businesses, universities, and governments at all levels, who harassed or fired those accused of having

~~dangerous ideas. It was repeated again by irresponsible journalists and,~~ once more, by what it meant to live in a country that had the Hollywood blacklist. Few in America—certainly not my parents—could have missed the point.

It wasn't until September 1972, four months after Hoover died, that the FBI decided conclusively that Lothrop was not a Communist. It closed its investigation of the Community Church for good—after thirty-one years. McCarthyism lasted much longer than McCarthy.

Undisputed evidence of the FBI's excesses emerged in 1975—too late to help my parents—with an investigation by a select committee of the U.S. Senate, chaired by Senator Frank Church.

From what the committee uncovered, it's not surprising that we weren't caught. The federal agents—those men all-important in our lives—had so many other targets that they simply forgot about us. We were too small-time. The INS lost their files on us, and the FBI threw theirs away.

Not knowing that we'd been forgotten, we kept on running.

The Church Committee said that during the Cold War, Americans had become so afraid of the Soviet Union that there was "a firm national consensus" to defend the country, no matter what. And that the FBI and other agencies thought they had the responsibility to do whatever they thought they had to do. The law didn't matter, and neither did the Constitution, because government agents felt that the public, terrified, was behind them. "Domestic intelligence activity was supported by that consensus," the Church Committee found, "although not specifically authorized by the Congress."

Feeling the same public mood as my parents did, and untethered from oversight, the FBI expanded its list of targets. At first it was "Communists," a very flexible category that the Bureau broadened to include people who couldn't be proven *not* to be Communists. Then the category "subversives" was added, though not defined. Before too long, agents were investigating people who it said were "rabble rousers" and also the leaders of what it called "Negro matters." The Church Committee found that, in a secret memo to Hoover, the Bureau declared the Reverend Martin Luther King, Jr., "the most dangerous Negro to the future in this Nation from the standpoint of communism, the Negro, and national security."

Among the committee's other findings were these: Investigations of Americans were massive and grew steadily wider from the 1930s to the 1970s. In 1972 alone (fifteen years after Senator Joseph McCarthy died), the FBI opened 65,000 new domestic intelligence files, adding to the half a million similar files FBI headquarters already had, without counting files held in the field offices. Even more groups and individuals were under investigation than the numbers imply because usually each file had information on more than one target.

People were frequently investigated for simply opposing a government policy or holding controversial views.

The army ran a surveillance program that monitored "virtually every group seeking peaceful change in the United States."

And at least 26,000 individuals were cataloged on an FBI list of persons to be rounded up in the event of a "national emergency."

As William Sullivan, who ran the FBI's Intelligence Division for a decade, told the committee, "Never once did I hear anybody, including myself, raise the question: 'Is this course of action which we have agreed upon lawful, is it legal, is it ethical or moral.' We never gave any thought to this line of reasoning, because we were just naturally pragmatic."

It went differently for the people my mother left behind in Great Britain, where there was more tolerance and less hysteria.

In Glasgow, David Gibson, who, with his wife, Sadie, had helped Mom out of Burnley and into pacifism, was elected to the city council in 1956. People who remember him today don't talk about his politics; rather they recall how he helped move thousands of families from Glasgow's slums into new government housing. My mother's kind of politics.

Mom's brother Alfred, the Communist Party organizer during the strikes in Burnley, taught history and English at Barden Lane school, near the home where he and my mother grew up. After he retired, he raised bees in his backyard. He never hid his political beliefs and never left the Party. It didn't matter in Burnley.

THIRTY-NINE

MY COUSIN MARY CALLED ME with news that what Aunt Eleanor had described as "a small problem" had turned out to be cancer. The surgery had failed, and Eleanor was about to die.

Over her last two days, in May 2001, Eleanor called her nieces to the hospital in groups and gave them instructions. This was the light blue suit she wanted to be buried in; this was how to close out her bills and distribute what was left. Be sure, she told them, to pay the parking fees for any of her visitors, and for any cell phone charges made to arrange for her funeral.

In those final hours, they told the old family stories. The lore that helped hold the family together. Aunt Eleanor corrected the errors she found in the others' versions—perhaps because her memory was still so good, perhaps because she was the custodian of the family honor and she knew exactly what she wanted people to remember . . . and to forget. When it was nearly over, she told them, "I'm going to miss you, but you're going to miss me more."

When my cousin Mary went to Eleanor's condominium to retrieve the blue suit, she found that even before her aunt had gone to the hospital, she had given away most of her clothes. She was staying in charge even after she was gone.

It was known without saying that Eleanor's wake would be at the Hurley Funeral Home, up the long hill from the house where she was raised. And that there would be a Mass the next day at St. Mary's, with burial at St. Mary's Cemetery next to Ma and Pa, and Uncle David, and my father.

Eleanor was lying in a burnished brown coffin in her blue suit and white blouse and good earrings, with a rosary in her clasped hands. People were coming to say goodbye, and she was there so they could say it in person. Some cried as they approached the blue kneeler in front of her coffin. Most cried after they said a prayer and stepped back. But they cried quietly, because the O'Connors didn't show it when they hurt.

On the other side of the room, another clan tradition continued. The tradition of carrying on, no matter what. After backing away from the coffin, people turned to talk and joke and trade Eleanor stories: how she got money from God knew where to pay the college tuition for a grand-niece, or how she worried about a marriage in trouble and how she fixed it. Soon there was so much chatter and laughter bouncing off the low ceiling of Hurley's that it seemed Eleanor might just call over to tell them to keep it down.

It was my first family funeral. I was still learning what it meant to be part of a clan. Unlike our family, which never shared a loss or a triumph outside the five of us, the Massachusetts O'Connors knew how to han-dle milestones and tragedies. Each event was felt by every member of the family, and there was always another one just ahead: a marriage or di-vorce, a birth or graduation, each felt by all. A strong, comforting wall encircled everyone, all together.

At the cemetery, Eleanor's coffin was poised on straps over the grave, with green Astroturf covering the freshly dug earth nearby. As the priest finished and a hundred or more members of the extended family pre-pared to leave, I saw a frail-looking woman standing a little bent be-tween Terry and Jack. She was slight, alert, and though in her late eighties and obviously sad, she was not withdrawn at all from the scene.

It's Helen, I thought.

How do you approach the woman your father abandoned? Normally you'd have the decency, the common charity, to spare her this meeting. But of all the people in the world I could find who might shed light on why my parents had run, the only one I had not spoken with was Helen. When I asked Terry if he'd introduce me, his eyes widened. But he walked over to his mother, and I could see her nod.

Helen was standing by the oak tree near Dad's grave, just a mile from where she and my father first moved after they were married, maybe three miles from the narrow second-floor apartment where she and her boys waited out the war for Dad to come back to them, as everyone knew he would.

I wondered if the oak's dappled shade was enough to protect that old face from the sun for a minute more, so that I might talk to her. I tried to

think of what to say. Would Helen ask me if I knew that my mother had
stolen her husband? Or if I realized how long she'd waited for her man
to come home? I imagined her eyes as the tears filled her lower lids, the
eyes of an old lady when she looks at the person from the life John
O'Connor had chosen over her and her children. Her husband was buried
in the shade of the same oak tree. Her children were at her side. Who the
hell was I to intrude?

There was no comfortable answer for that.

When I reached her, my mouth opened to mumble "How are you?"

"Fine," Helen said.

"It's nice to meet you," I said. "How are you?"

And she said, "Yes, it's nice to meet you, too." I was grateful that
Terry and Jack led her away at that point, because my brain had stopped
working.

However inept I was at that first meeting, what mattered was that
Helen and I had stood together before the whole clan. What happened
next was something I hadn't anticipated. The final veil of family secrecy
and shame began to lift. Later that day, Helen told Terry's wife, Rosemarie, "War makes people do terrible things. It made my husband leave
me. But you can't blame the children for what their parents do."

BY 1949, WHEN my parents and I left Boston, Helen and Dad's other
two sons had moved to Medford, the working-class suburb north of
Boston, to a small apartment owned by Helen's brother, Fred, and his
wife. My grandfather got Helen a clerical job in the accounting department of Railway Express.

Helen kept telling her sons that their father had not returned from the
war just yet. The truth was too shameful for her to think about. As it became obvious that Dad had abandoned his first family, she changed the
story to make it easier for her children. Their father, she said, "was killed
in the war."

This new myth brought some ethical complications. Terry and Jack
were crushed to hear that their father was gone from their lives forever. Meanwhile, all the people who knew John O'Connor was alive—
everyone closest to the boys—would have to sustain the deceit indefinitely.
It was an awful lie, but it seemed to everyone the most decent thing to
do. *It's best for the boys,* they all told themselves.

In 1950, when Terry registered at St. Agnes School, they asked him about his father's occupation. He told them his father was dead; he suspected it wasn't true by that point, but he said it anyway. Everyone he loved and upon whom he counted told him it was true. He knew he was supposed to believe it. But as he strained to reconcile what he intuited with what he'd been told, Terry became skeptical about his closest relatives. He says now, "The family was engaging, charming, bright, wonderful people. I love them. I don't know what life would have been like without them. But I couldn't trust them."

Just as I'd struggle to tell Mary that something seemed to be chasing us, Terry didn't know how to tell his brother, Jack, also four years younger, that he thought their mother and uncles and aunts were lying to them. You need to believe the people who love you, even when you know that you can't.

And just as Mary, and then Fiona, caught glimpses of our family's problem, Jack also began to think that his father wasn't dead. He watched men in suits and hats coming by to talk to his mother behind the closed door to the living room. He thought they might be policemen, except they always had cars that were nicer than the police cars he knew. Were they a special kind of police? Though his mother wouldn't talk about the men, Jack decided they must be looking for his father. He thought that when he grew up, he'd become a policeman so he could look for his father, too.

Jack and Terry were smart enough to sniff the air and smell the truth, but they never shared it with each other, just as for years my sisters and I had not shared our growing suspicions. That would have hurt too much.

For Terry and Jack, a lie they knew was a lie was also the way they could tell themselves not to be ashamed at being abandoned. In the 1950s, in working-class Catholic Boston, people believed that a man did not leave his sons and his wife unless there was something deeply wrong with them. In the crowded apartments on Medford's Orchard Street and at St. Agnes School, the only fatherless children were two or three kids whose dads had died in the war. Besides, Helen called herself a "war widow," and the boys wanted their mother to have the solace of that lie.

Helen rode the bus half an hour to her job at North Station, the same place where my grandmother had arrived from Tignish in 1905. The boys stayed in the apartment after school until she returned, well past nightfall in winter. When there were temporary layoffs at Railway Express, Helen cleaned houses to pay their bills. Before he was ten, Terry was selling newspapers to help. He'd be out the door at five in the morning, down to Medford Square to get his load of *Boston Globe*s, to hawk them to people who were off to better jobs than his mother would ever have.

Helen kept waiting for her husband to come back. She was in her thirties, slender and good-looking, with bright blond hair and blue eyes. She had so much spark that some called her sassy. But she considered herself still married, and she did not date. She did what a wife and mother was supposed to do when her family was smashed by a crisis. She pulled her sons to herself and made a home.

Remarkably, despite the anger she felt, anger from the soul of a woman cast aside, she did not turn it on the man who'd left her. She told the boys how completely happy she and their father had been before the war. To Dad's sisters, she'd blame the war for disrupting her marriage. But John would be back, she'd say. He would drive up in a car too fancy, with a smile a bit chastened and a story hard to believe, to their place on Orchard Street. Then it would be just like before.

In the summers, when school was out, the boys stayed with our aunts and uncles and grandparents so they wouldn't be alone while Helen worked. The family put its arms around Terry and Jack. They just didn't tell them the truth. Catherine, our grandmother, took them to Tignish and enchanted them with the old stories, the fables that taught the family's values and the values of that village. Nothing bad was ever said about their missing father. Catherine told her grandsons what she had once told her eldest son: *You are going to be someone, young man, because you are so bright and so good-looking and so charming. You are going to make us all proud, I'm sure.*

To the day of Eleanor's funeral, Helen and her sons had skirted the truth they found too painful to discuss. Then I went over to Helen to stammer out a greeting—for my own selfish reasons, I thought then. But in truth, there was more to it. I was doing what my father had never done. I'd gone back. I was telling Helen that it was not her fault she had been hurt so badly for so long, and that I was sorry. I was asking her to forgive if she could.

I had begun to forgive my parents. I understood more about why we had run and why they had lied about it. I was beginning to see why I had kept running, first from whatever was chasing my family and then from the family itself. Though the instinct to keep moving still nipped at me, much of its power was gone. Losing myself in a war was not so compelling.

My sons saw that. Their father was no longer mostly a voice on a scratchy long-distance phone call from somewhere new. Though I still lived overseas, it was a sedate life compared with the continuous frenzy in which I used to live. I don't think my sons were too angry that I was gone so much when they were children, gone even when I lived with them, because I was so driven as a reporter to uncover secrets. We saw one another once or twice a year, whenever I was in the States. Actually, my father, after abandoning his first sons, was around his second children more than I was with Sean and Gabriel. Still, I thought I was much closer to my sons. For one thing, a big one, I didn't keep secrets. Sean was helping manage a business office in San Francisco, and Gabriel was a producer for the NPR sports show *Only a Game*.

SEVERAL WEEKS AFTER I met Helen, Terry and Rosemarie took me to her apartment to sit with her awhile. I was sweating. Terry and Rosemarie were nervous. Jack was very nervous, and he wasn't even with us. But Helen was calm and gracious. She was short and slender, like Mom. Her eyes sparked stronger than they should have at the age of eighty-nine—they looked right at you and they paid attention. She was careful to be sure everyone was comfortable and in the right seats. "Dear," she said to me, "don't you want a cold glass of water? Get yourself one of those peppermint candies in that bowl."

Her home was a rough replica of my mother's last apartment, as if they'd been done by the same builder, down to the kitchen cabinets, varnished over what passed for a veneer of oak. It felt as though Mom could be in the apartment across the hall.

After we'd chatted for some time, Terry said, "Mike wants to know what you can tell us about that time after the war, you know, when . . ." Helen knew exactly. She looked at me fondly and said, "Sure, dear, we can talk about anything, but sometimes I forget things, you know."

We talked about the days before the war, when Dad was telling his brothers and sisters that his truck driver job and his marriage were strangling him—but not telling his wife; even now she didn't know. "We had a wonderful marriage," she said. "We had our family. It was a perfect marriage."

Although Dad joined the Canadian army to get away from his life with Helen, he didn't explain that to her. She followed him, she said, because that was what they both wanted. She lived near a training base in Fredericton, and then by other bases. "We went all across those plains toward the West. He was sent there, and I went right behind him," she told me.

I could not ask how their marriage ended. That was too much. But she said, unprompted, "I couldn't believe it. I couldn't believe it. I still can't, but it's so long ago now. I was heartbroken, it broke forever. You can't fix something that is so broken."

Of the two times when Dad saw Helen to press for a divorce, she said, "I asked about the boys, but he wouldn't say anything. He didn't say anything when I asked about what would happen to his sons."

How, I wondered, *could he do that? How?* She was talking about someone else, not the father I knew. In my memories of him, in all the searching for our history, I had not found a man who could simply throw away his children. But that evening he was there with us. My father. Terry's father. He was the same man.

Helen said she was not herself for a time after Dad deserted her and their sons. My grandmother stepped in. Helen remembered visits by detectives, for years, asking about Dad. "They went to see Ma, too. . . . If Ma knew more than I did, she didn't put it on my shoulders. It must have been killing her. Ma was always on my side and the boys'. She wanted to make the right thing happen again." Our conversation was wearing at her. There were pauses while she struggled.

Terry was hearing things his mother had never said before, not to him or to Jack. She said, "I always thought that Mary and Eleanor knew much more than they said. They were helping somehow. They never told me, because they didn't want to hurt my feelings."

She said, "I used to remember everything that happened. Not now." But while some details had escaped her, the emotions were still right here, on the surface, spilling out and biting hard. Then, to protect herself again, she pulled in those emotions so strongly that I could feel them whoosh out of the room. She was silent. As she raised a glass of water, her right arm trembled. Before I could change the subject to something we could all endure, she said, "You can't live in the past. I used to know everything that happened. I knew, but I have to forgive people and live for today. I just put those things away, because you have to look ahead."

Then she turned to her son and said, "You always knew you were loved, didn't you, Terry? You and Jack always knew that. It was just the three of us, but we were always together and we had love." Terry nodded. He knew.

By the time we left, Helen was bright again, snappy. She was sincere when she told me, "Come here to my house anytime. If you're around, you just come over and see me."

The next day she told Terry that she'd had a very nice surprise. She had met her other son, and she was glad she finally had, because it was about time.

A Note to the Reader

There are probably some mistakes in this book. Nothing critical, I'm sure. But it only stands to reason that a book that relies so much on people's memories probably gets something wrong. Memories are like that. Especially when they require excavating in deep caves of the mind, going past roadblocks intended to keep truths forgotten. And there is information here that comes from secondhand memories, when someone told me what another person said had happened, often from many years before.

There may be a difference between what a journalist writes and what a memoirist writes. After all, memoirs can be just what someone remembers. I am more comfortable with journalism. I want to believe that what I read is true.

Documents may give a reporter confidence because they are official or have inviting detail. But they can be a trap, too. You can never know what was left out that could give a different interpretation. And while you may know what documents are missing, even getting all the documents can be impossible. Documents disappear so as to cover up an unpleasant truth but also for mundane reasons. For instance, there is no record of our home on Mobile Street in Houston. Nothing, outside of a water bill from the 1950s that Mom kept in the cigar box. The official records were just lost, leaving only memories to confirm that the house existed.

Acknowledgments

Many people around the world helped me as I worked on this book. I'd like to thank a few who were particularly helpful.

Zev Chafets, Ray Bonner, and Jane Perlez believed I had a story to tell and yelled at me until I agreed. Will Robinson, the honorable journalist who was so encouraging from the outset on, died before he could see the book he had helped bring about.

Journalistic investigations are usually lonely things, but I had friends/ colleagues who were always with me, like a wind at my back. From the beginning to the last word, Tim Golden, Roger Cohen, and Michael Singer read and reread parts of the manuscript and advised me on the investigation from one surprise turn to another.

My attorney, Amy Atwood, took the search for what I needed from government archives so much to heart that she took the case with her when she changed law firms, so she could keep pushing. If I ever have something to hide, I hope she's not looking for it.

Thanks to James Kuykendall, formerly a senior agent of the DEA, who was the first former federal agent I went to for advice on how to investigate my family's secrets, and to Pat Webb, a former supervisory senior agent of the FBI, who also gave very helpful advice. Without naming them, I'd like to acknowledge the assistance of the other former agents who helped me with advice and sometimes with unauthorized searching of government files and who don't want to be identified.

Jeff Coplon helped me work and rework the manuscript.

Scott Moyers saw promise in this story and acquired it for Random House. Tim Bartlett, my editor, worked with emotion and precision. Dana Isaacson and Diana Fox aided Tim's efforts. Dana came up with the title for the book.

Esther Newberg, my agent, has been a constant source of support.

And thanks to my relatives, from both my parents' sides, who had barely heard of me until I appeared on their doorsteps asking questions about events they had thought—or perhaps, had wished—were too long past to think about, especially Uncle Tom, Uncle Larry, and Aunt Eleanor.

And of course, to Mary and Fiona, Terry and Jack. This is their book, too.

ABOUT THE AUTHOR

MIKE O'CONNOR reported on the Palestinian-Israeli conflict for NPR. He covered the wars in the former Yugoslavia and reported on Central America for NPR and *The New York Times*. He covered Latin America for CBS News and was a reporter for television stations in Los Angeles and San Francisco. He now lives in Italy with his wife, Tracy Wilkinson, who is the Rome Bureau Chief of the *Los Angeles Times*.